SOME SLAVES OF PRINCE WILLIAM COUNTY, VIRGINIA

PARTIAL WILL BOOKS 1734–1872

COMPILED BY

Sandra Barlau

HERITAGE BOOKS
2019

HERITAGE BOOKS
AN IMPRINT OF HERITAGE BOOKS, INC.

Books, CDs, and more—Worldwide

For our listing of thousands of titles see our website
at
www.HeritageBooks.com

Published 2019 by
HERITAGE BOOKS, INC.
Publishing Division
5810 Ruatan Street
Berwyn Heights, Md. 20740

Copyright © 2019 Sandra Barlau

Heritage Books by the author:

Some Slaves of Fauquier County, Virginia, Volume I: Will Books 1–10, 1759–1829

Some Slaves of Fauquier County, Virginia; Volume II: Will Books 11–20, 1829–1847

Some Slaves of Fauquier County, Virginia, Volume III: Will Books 21–31, 1847–1869

Some Slaves of Fauquier County, Virginia; Volume IV: Master Index, Will Books 1–31, 1759–1869

Some Slaves of Prince William County, Virginia, Partial Will Books, 1734–1872

Some Slaves of Rappahannock County, Virginia, Will Books A to D, 1833–1865 and Old Rappahannock County, Virginia, Will Books 1 and 2, 1664–1682

Some Slaves of Virginia, 1674–1894: Lost Records Localities Digital Collection of the Library of Virginia

Cover portrait: Mary Timbers Harrison

All rights reserved. No part of this book may be reproduced or transmitted in any form or by any means, electronic or mechanical, including photocopying, recording or by any information storage and retrieval system without written permission from the author, except for the inclusion of brief quotations in a review.

International Standard Book Numbers
Paperbound: 978-0-7884-5903-0

TABLE OF CONTENTS

PREFACE v

INTRODUCTION vii

ABBREVIATIONS ix

WILL BOOK C 1
   1734 - 1744 1

WILL BOOK G 11
   1778 - 1791 11

WILL BOOK H 29
   1792 - 1802 29

WILL BOOK I 45
   1803 - 1809 45

WILL BOOK K 57
   1809 - 1816 57

WILL BOOK L 77
   1816 - 1823 77

WILL BOOK M 93
   1823 - 1827 93

WILL BOOK N 109
   1827 - 1833 109

WILL BOOK O 121
   1833 - 1842 121

WILL BOOK P 137
   1842 - 1850 137

WILL BOOK Q 147
   1851 - 1858 147

WILL BOOK R 159
   1858 - 1872 159

ADDENDUM 167
INDEX 169

PREFACE

The idea for this book originated after I had compiled the Fauquier County Virginia Will Books 1-31 from 1759 to 1869. I wanted to find the mother of my 2nd gr-grandmother Mildred Timbers. I think I found her.

This time I am looking for an ancestor of my gr-grandmother Kitty Gaines. She and a descendent of Elvira Gaines, Lucy Gaines Grigsby, look enough alike to be sisters. The question now is – are they related and if so, how?

Mathew Whiting of Prince William gifted slaves Tom and Juno to Molly Brown in 1783. Molly willed Juno and her daughters Lucy and Kitty to her seven nieces and nephews in 1796. A coincidence? I decided to take a break from researching each niece and nephew and explore Prince William County. Even if Juno is not the most distant ancestor between Lucy and Kitty it would be interesting research.

INTRODUCTION

Will Books are a good source in the search for slaves only if the owner named the slave(s). Many times a Will lists property without specifying if it includes slaves. For example: "I will and bequeath to my (wife, son, daughter, etc.) all my estate both real and personal of every sort." or "...the property I have already given to my (wife, son, daughter, etc.)..." The documents often do not include the slave's name, sometimes only girl, runaway, boy, etc.

Each chapter is one Will Book. The documents include Administrator's Estate, Executor and Guardian Accounts, Wills, Inventory and Appraisals. Each slave owner is listed first followed by the page number, date and type of document. The list of slaves follows below. The new owner is listed if known. Surnames of the owner's children are indexed only if noted in the document. The slaves who were emancipated, freed or manumitted are listed in the index under Emancipated. Servants are also indexed.

Not included in this summary is a slave's monetary value, if the slave was sold, hired by the estate, hired out or who hired the slave. The original text should be read to determine which occurred. Sometimes the estate or guardian account listed people paying money to the estate but not why the remittances were paid.

Some first names were standardized in order to make your index search easier. When you go to the original Will Books be aware that different spellings were used. Be creative in looking for first names: Seaser (Cesar), Ausker (Oscar), Fillis (Phillis), etc. Sometimes the written nn could be rr and many times S resembles L. Some of the entries have only a few letters separated with a blank space such as Marj__i_.

<u>It would be a good idea to peruse the entire index.</u> You may recognize a name under another spelling. The same name can also appear more than once on a page under different owners.

It is important to note the slave's age since the value of a slave increases or decreases with age and ability. It can also be used as a tracking tool. The ages are approximate.

Some of the microfilmed pages are very faint. The quality of the films varies and some microfilm copies were difficult to read. There were many guesses as to the written names and I take full responsibility for any errors in transcription.

The A, B, D, E, and F Will Books are missing. There does not appear to be a Will Book J. Will Book I ends at 1809 and Will Book K starts at 1809.

The Will Books read for this volume are on microfilm held by the Family History Library at Salt Lake City. They are available on-line through Family History Centers.

The Addendum contains Wills and Deeds from the Lost Records Localities Digital Collection of the Library of Virginia, 1674 – 1894: http://www.virginiamemory.com/collections/lost

I hope this book helps you to locate a slave or an owner. Good luck in your search.

ABBREVIATIONS

adm acct – Administrator's Account

exec acct – Executor Account

gdn acct – Guardian Account

inv & appr – Inventory & Appraisal

div – Division (of slaves, land, property)

comm acct – Committee Account

WILL BOOK C
1734 - 1744

Pages 1 – 6 missing

Charles BROADWATER..........................pg 8, 21 Aug 1734, inv & appr

    man Toby, Luce & 2 children, men Harry, Adam, old woman Nan, ___y, woman Ammuzuow, girls Abigail, Dorcas, Nan, boys Hugh, Daniel, girls Lucy, Bess, mulatto girl, mulatto boy

John TILLETT .... pg 12, 19 Sept 1734, inv & appr

    man servant

Thomas SIMSON..pg 16, 13 Oct 1734, will

    2 negros to wife Jane Simson, to be divided among children at her death

Michael ASHFORD..pg 28, 20 Oct 1734, will

    Dick to son George

Ann ASHFORD ....pg 32, 25 Nov 1734, will

    boy Sam to daughter Ann; man Peter, woman Mary to daughters Mary & Constance

Capt. Charles BROADWATER ....
.... pg 33, 20 Mar 1734, inv & appr, 3rd part of the estate

    man Toby, Sue & 2 children, woman Nan, girls Bess, Nan, Dorcas

Mark HARDIN..pg 36, _th Mar 1734, will

    Sambo to son Mary HARDIN & at her death to son Mark HARDIN

William BEAN ....pg 40, Mar 1734, inv & appr

    old Mose, old Bell

John FISHBACK................................... pg 42, 21 May 1735, inv & appr

    servant woman to serve 5 more years

Phillip NOWLAND.................................pg 48, 18 June 1735, estate acct

   to Bryan CONNER for Freedom Dues

George MASON........................ pg 49, 21 May 1735, inv & appr

   man Pocus, boy Job, servant man James, girls Lucy, Jenny, boy Stephen, man London, woman Ann Wilson, servant man John Webb, servant men Morgan Carpenter, Windsor, Matt, boy Jack

John FARROW.....................................pg 60, 8 Aug 1735, inv & appr

   3 negro men

William GREGG..pg 62, _July 1735, inv & appr

   servant Mary Phillips

Thomas SIMSON......................................pg 63, 15 Oct 1735, inv & appr

   2 negro men, 1 man servant, 1 woman servant

Thomas HARRIS ....pg 64, 3 Nov 1734, will

   servant woman, orphan boy Thomas Mantier to wife Ani

William LINDEN................................. pg 72, 21 Apr 1736, inv & appr

   men Robin, Will, women Julia, Phillis, Sue, girl Kate, boys Boy, Jacob, girl Sarah, boy Jimmy, men Harry, Will, old wench Grace

Daniel FRENCH .... pg 81, 21Apr 1736, inv & appr

   men Mingo, Pompey, Tom, women Ivy, Nan, Judy, girl Nan, boys Jack, Will, Tom, Harry

Charles BROADWATER...................................... pg 86, 1734, inv & appr

   negroes

George ELDRIDGE .... pg 88, 19 May1736, inv & appr

   boy Will, woman Sue, boy Sambo, woman Binah, men Cummey, Dick

John WALKER ....pg 107, 5 Nov 1736, will

   I set at liberty ___ Campbell he not demanding freedom...

Joseph CHAPMAN................................ pg 121, 24 May 1737, inv & appr

   2 male servants

Thomas OSBORN................................ pg 131, 9 May 1737, inv & appr

   servant boy John Cooper, man Will, woman Jenny & child, men Jack, Joe, Bangar, girls Judy, Lucy, man George, servant Charles, man Daniel

John ASHMORE................................pg 138, 25 Nov 1737, inv & appr

   man Whitehaven, Jane & her child; boy, child

Thomas TRIPLETT............................. pg 140, 24 June 1737, inv & appr

   woman Pat

Matthew ORGAN ....pg 147, 28 Mar 1738, estate acct

   Hagan an orphan under my care

Robert ALEXANDER.......................... pg 150, 17 May 1738, estate appr

   man Stue, woman Nan, girl Sue, boy Sam, woman Peg, boy Joe, child Nan, woman, servant David Kelly

   Peg, Joe, Nan, servant David Kelly to widow; woman Sue to John ALEXANDER

John EDGE... pg 153, 16 July 1737, will

   lad Harry, woman Ginny to Rachael SPILLER, wife of William SPILLER & at her death to Elizabeth MAGUIRE

John EDGE...pg 155, 11 July 1738, inv & appr

   lad Harry, woman, child Ned

John DAVIS ....pg 156, 21 July 1738, inv & appr

   man

Joseph BUCHANAN .... pg 170, 28 May 1739, inv & appr

   Phillis, Jenny, Gabril, Jack

Edward SUTO .... pg 176, 30 Apr 1779, will

    man Cupid to wife Elizabeth SUTO & at her death to daughter Margaret SUTO; Sarah & to daughter Margaret; child Jamie son of Sarah to daughter Mary SUTO

Catherine PADDERSON .... pg 180, 28 May 1739, will

    man Robin to son Elixander GOING; male Jerkey to daughter Susannah GOING

Jonathon NEALE .... pg 182, 28 May 1739, inv & appr

    woman & 2 children, man Matthe; lad George, boys Frank 5 & Will 10, girl Hanner

Jon QUEEN .... pg 183, 23 July 1739, inv & appr

    1 woman, 1 boy

Edward SUTO .... pg 184, 18 July 1739, inv & appr

    man Cubit, woman Sarah, boy Jamey

Catherine PADDERSON .... pg 188, 17 Aug 1739, inv & appr

    2 negroes

Thomas OSBORNE .... pg 190, 1737 - 1738, estate acct

negroes

Thomas OSBORN .... pg 194, 24 Sept 1739, estate acct

    men James, Daniel, girls Judy, Lucy allotted to Mrs. OSBORN; man Will, woman & child, men Jack, Joe, Banjar, effects left at Bull Run to 2nd widow? his care of Mrs. Jon KINCHELOE

the orphans of Wansford ARRINGTON pg 200, 25 Nov 1738, estate acct Will

Richard BULLOCK .... pg 220, 21 Feb 1738/9, will

    men John, Robin to daughter Rachel BULLOCK; Harry, Toney to daughter Sarah BULLOCK; Monmouth, Will, Cardnecher to son Richard BULLOCK

Vallantino BARTON ....pg 222, 25 Feb 1739, inv & appr

 servants Edward Magoo, Richard Willard

Charles BROADWATER .... pg 228, 7 Aug 1739, estate acct

 boy sold to Hugh WEST; hire of man; Harry

Richard BULLOCK .... pg 231, 26 May 1740, inv & appr

 Tom, John, Robin, Harrie, Toney, Monmouth, boy Will, woman Carne

Mary, Ann, & Margaret OSBORN, orphans ....
.... pg 235, 25 Apr 1740, inv & appr

 men Jack, Will, Joe, Bangar, woman Jinny, 2 children Jerry 3, Hannah 1 ½

David DODSON .... pg 250, 7 Apr 1740, will

 all negroes to wife Amey DODSON; man Peter to brother Thomas DODSON; woman Dina to brother George DODSON; if Dina has another child it will go with those young negroes to brothers Greenham, Abraham, Joshua, & Elijah DODSON who will draw lots

John GOSLING .... pg 255, 27 Mar 1739, will

 man Jack to son Simon GOSLING; man Caesar to daughter Mary COLVERT

David DODSON ....pg 259, 22 Sept 1740, inv & appr

 man Peter, woman Dinah, boys Adam, Tom, girl Sue

Joseph GUESS .... pg 261, 24 Mar 1739, inv & appr

 woman Hagar, boy Burgus, man Caesar

Thomas HUDNALL .... pg 265, 15 Dec 1738, will

 negro girl Lusey (Lucy?) to wife Winney HUDNALL which I had with her; fellow George to wife until she marries or dies then to son William HUDNALL, wench Winney & boy Jack to William HUDNALL

Scarlet HANCOCK .... pg 272, no date, will

 Cloe, Bess, Cato, Bristoll to wife Anne during her natural life then to son John & daughter Anne HANCOCK; Titus, Sharper, Sarah, Giles to daughter Anne HANCOCK; Nero, Galba, Poll, Jacob to son John HANCOCK; Dick to be sold

George MASON .... pg 275, 1735-1740, estate acct

London, Windsor, Matt, Porus, Nan, Wilson, Jack, Stephen, Joe, Lucy, Jenny, Clio

John DUNCON .... pg 299, 27 Apr 1741, inv & appr

servant man

Samuel BRONAUGH .... pg 309, 15 Apr 1741, will

all my negros to sons Francis BRONAUGH & Thomas BRONAUGH

Richard DRAKEFORD .... pg 317, 25 May 1741, inv & appr

servant woman Margaret Poor, servant man Bryant Alliston

Giles EASTER .... pg 319, 25 July 1741, inv & appr

young man

John JENKINS .... pg 321, 27 July 1741, inv & appr

servant woman

Scarlet HANCOCK .... pg 325, 25 Aug 1741, inv & appr

men Bristol, Titus, Harper, women Cloe, Kate, girl Sarah, girl Poll, 2 boys; Galba, Jacob, woman Bess

Thomas HUDNALL .... pg 327, 28 Sept 1741, inv & appr

2 girls to wife

Francis AWBREY .... pg 341, 14 Dec 1741, will

woman Bess, boy Cuss, man servant Jacob Wilson to wife; Scotch hands William Trashor, John Davidson, boy Fa__ory to son Howard; old Cuss, Mingo to son Richard; fellows Jack, Henry to son Henry; fellow Ned & his daughter little Bess to son George; great Bess, boy Cuss to son Samuel; Winney to daughter Sarah; 2 negroes to be bought from sale of land; Butcher, George to son Thomas

Richard BULLOCK .... pg 346, 24 Mar 1741, estate acct

boy; midwife for laying a negro woman

Daniel TEBBS..pg 358, 27 Oct 1740, will

    Abram to son James TEBBS; great Jack to son William TEBBS; Tapsalow to son George TEBBS; little Jack to son Tusbee; woman Sarah to daughter Charlote TEBBS; Jack, Abram to wife Charolet for her natural life then to the above named sons; Frank to son James TEBBS after the death of his mother

Daniel TEBBS..pg 361, 26 July1742, inv & appr

    Tepson, Jack, Abraham, Sarah's boy Tom, Frank, little Jack

William LOUIS.................................. pg 365, 17 Apr 1742, inv & appr

    man

Col. George MASON................................pg 367, 1739-1741, estate acct

    for maintaining negroes

Francis WRIGHT.....................................pg 376, Mar 1742, will

    negro stock to wife Ann WRIGHT & at her death amoung my children

Francis WRIGHT.................................pg 378, 16 Oct 1742, inv & appr

    white servant man, negros: men Robin, Ned, girl Peg, young woman Cate, young Nimrod, Cate, boy Cubbo, woman Sarah, young child Co___ey, young maid Betty

Rodham NEALE ....pg 380, 7 Aug 1742, will

    man Baker, woman Sue to brother Christopher NEALE; man Cupid, woman Lucy, my little orphan girl Ann Digen to wife Lidia NEALE

Edward BALL..pg 387, 28 Feb 1742, inv & appr

    Betty & her child, Sue, fellow Harry

John OBERALL.......................................pg 392, 16 Sept 1742, will

    Caesar, boy Judah, girl to son John OBERALL

Rodham NEALE ....pg 398, 28 __ 1743, inv & appr

    women Sue, Lucy, men Sepio, Baker

John OBERALL .... pg 401, 28 Mar 1743, inv & appr

   servant man, servant boy, boy, girl

John GREGG .... pg 413, May11743, inv & appr

   men Newton, Belfast, boy Peter, woman Doll, girls Sarah, Moll, women Judy, Eve, Lettice, white servant man Andrew Garner, white servant boy Alex Grant

Marmaduke LAWSON .... pg 417, May 1743, inv & appr

   servant man Richard Fox, servant boy James Cuthull

Samuel BRONAUGH .... pg 431, no date, estate acct

   man

William LINTON .... pg 432, 20 Sept 1743, estate acct

   man Harry to Nathaniel CHAPMAN; old man Will, old woman Grace to John TURLEY

Abram FARROW .... pg 443, 18 Mar 1741, will

   Boatswain to son Isaac FARROW; Susan to wife Sibell FARROW; Sylvester to daughter Lidia, Tom, Phillip to son Abram; Gowen to son John, Judy to daughter Elizabeth

Abraham FARROW .... pg 455, 6 Mar 1744, inv & appr

   man, girl

Edward FEAGAN .... pg 461, 26 Mar 1744, inv & appr

   servant boy William Smith, servant man Edward _oarzison; servant boy Peter Grant; woman Sue, girl Judy, women Sary, Bess, boy Dublin, men Limbrick, Kildare, child Peter, boy Bob, girl Jenny, women Kate, Nan

Thomas T. DEAHERS .... pg 476, 10 Feb 1743/4, will

   orphan boy John Edwards to John WRIGHT

John MARR .... pg 482, 8 May 1744, will

   boy Peter, orphan boy James Sims to wife Elizabeth MARR; boy Tom to John BRADFORD Jr.; girl Cate to John MARR son of Daniel MARR; woman Isabel Sims to son Christopher MARR

John PAGE .... pg 485, 10 Nov 1743, will

   negroes to be sold after wife Elizabeth PAGE's decease

Francis LACON .... pg 487, 30 Apr 1744, will

   boys Joseph, Jimmy to Rachel SPILLER wife of William SPILLER, Jr; woman Peg, girl Tender, boy Ben to wife Jane LACON

Thomas DACONS .... pg 494, 17 Apr 1744, inv & appr

   servant boy

Jons WILLIAMS, Jr. .... pg 497, 23 Apr 1744, inv & appr

   man, servant woman

John MARR .... pg 498, 28 May 1844, inv & appr

   3 negroes, servant man, 1 servant woman, 1 orphan boy, 2 single girls

Abraham FARROW .... pg 503, 25 June 1744, inv & appr

   boys Tom, Gowen, old servant man

Edward FEAGAN ....pg 504, 25 June 1744, add inv & appr

   Harry 1 ½ yrs, woman Maria

Francis LACON .... pg 513, 20 May 1744, inv & appr

   woman & child, 6 boys

Simon GESHING .... pg 514, 18 July 1744, inv & appr

   man _aik

WILL BOOK G
1778-1791

(pages are numbered 1 – 9 then 8, 9, 10, etc)

Thomas NEWMAN .... pg 1, 4 May 1778, inv & appr

   men Guy, Bob, Silvia & child Nelly, Daphne & child Judy

Reuben CALVERT .... pg 7, 28 May 1778, inv & appr

   Moll & child, Jim, Phil, Ben

Charles THORNTON .... pg 8, 4 May 1778, inv & appr

   Dick, Jenny, Cate, James, Daphne

Henry WILSON Sr. .... pg 9, 1 May 1778, will

   man George to wife Sarah WILSON which I had by her; boy Bob to son Rupert WILSON; man Tom to son Henry WILSON; woman Juda to daughter Elizabeth WIGGINTON; girl Phillis to daughter Agatha SMITH; boy Caesar to son Jeremiah WILSON; the child which now sucks Judah to Mary HOLISFIELD

Richard JARVIS .... pg 9, 6 July 1778, inv & appr

   woman

Thomas FALKNER .... pg 10, 6 July 1778, estate acct

   negroes

Mary CANNON .... pg 11, 3 Aug 1778, inv & appr

   Moreah, Hagar, Jesse

Samuel JONAS .... pg 11, 6 Aug 1777, inv & appr

   Sambad, Harry, Hester, Rachel, James, David, Betty

John CULLINS .... pg 17, 12 May 1778, inv & appr

   man Harry

Christopher CURTIS .... pg 20, 15 Oct 1778, inv & appr

   boy Sandy

Joshua OWENS..........pg 20, 6 Oct 1777, inv & appr

woman Grace, girl Agga, boys Garrard, George, James, Juba

Henry WILSON..........pg 23, 11 July 1778, inv & appr

Tom, Judy, boys Jack, Caesar, girl Phillis, boy Bob, child Sarah

George FOSTER..........pg 26, 5 Oct 1778, inv & appr

one child?

William? Thomas RENOE..........pg 33, 2 Feb 1779, inv & appr

mulatto girl, negro girl, man Ben, woman Jude

Henry HAMPTON..........pg 36, 4 May 1778, inv & appr

George, Abraham, Daniel, Charles, Amy, Winney, Charlotte & child, Fanny, Let, Milly, Elijah, Adam, Jonney, Molly, Jesse, Francis

Thomas HOGAN..........pg 39, 19 Jan 1776, will

slaves to be divided among children: Thomas HOGAN, Elizabeth HOGAN, Sarah HOGAN, Al__n HOGAN, William HOGAN, Charlotte HOGAN

Simon LUTTRELL..........pg 41, 6 Apr 1779, will

Sarah, Juda, George to wife Jean, after her death to sons Robert & Simon; fellow Adam, wench Juda, girl Aggy; to son Robert LUTTRELL; wench Amy, wench Lucy, boy George to Simon LUTTRELL; girl Nell to be valued and cash to be divided between sons Robert & Simon

Robert DALE..........pg 44, 7 Feb 1778, will

girl Esther to son Robert DALE son of Reuben DALE; boy Henry to Abraham DALE; 8 negroes Sam, Juda, Athena & their increase

Richard FOOTE..........pg 44, 28 Aug 1778, will

girl of her choice to each daughter Catherine & Elizabeth FOOTE at her marriage or comes of age

Zephariah CROOK..........pg 53, 2 Aug 1779, inv & appr

woman & child

Zephariah CROOK..........................pg 54, 2 Jan – 3 May 1779, estate acct

    negro

Robert DALE .... pg 55, 2 Aug 1779, estate acct

    Sam, Minor, Harry, Easther, Jack, George

Thomas HOGAN...pg 57, 1 Mar 1779, inv & appr

    Dan, Peg, Jimmy, Lett, Nan, Seilla (Cilla?), Dick, Hannah, Frank, Winney, Amy

Nancy OWENS ....pg 61, 1 Jan 1778 – 2 Aug 1779, orphans acct

    Juba

Thomas FALKNER.....pg 62, 16 Jan 1779, estate settlement, in Chancery

    one half of negroes to the heirs of Mary HARRIS alias CALVERT & Sally CORTNEY; 4 negroes Gabriel, Fanny, Polly, Dennis & the other half divided between the twelve children of Mary ELLIOTT

William MELTON Jr. .... pg 63, Sept 1777, inv & appr

    Harry Jack, Nate, male child 1 year old

George FARROW ....pg 65, 1 Mar 1779, inv & appr

    girl Rachel

Francis TENNELL .... pg 66, 11 Apr 1777, will

    Moses to son Joseph TENNELL; Tapley to son John TENNELL, Gowen to son Francis TENNELL; James to son Benjamin TENNELL; Elijah to daughter Elizabeth GERRARD; Imy to daughter Charity; Jemmy to daughter Jemima TENNELL; Mary to daughter Mary TENNELL; Thomley, Thom, Nan to wife Margaret TENNELL & after her death money arising from negroes...be divided between my grown surviving children

Cuthburt HARRISON ....pg 70, 20 Oct 1778, will

    wench Lucy to sister Seth HARRISON

Andrew LEITCH.. pg 75, 2 June 1777, inv & appr

    wench Dinah, fellow Harry, Hagar & her child

Thomas DAGG .... pg 80, 8 Dec 1778, inv & appr

 young Dick, Dick

Cuthburt HARRISON .... pg 81, 1 May 1780, inv & appr

 Bob, Will, Buck, Samuel, Bess & child, Moll, Jane, Lott, Lucy, Hannah, Stephen, old wench Lucy, white servant boy

William WATKINS .... pg 86, 6 July 1778, inv & appr

 boy Dennis

Richard FOOTE .... pg 93, 6 Nov 1778, estate div

 David, Moses, Peter, Will, Bob, Sarah to widow now Mrs. Margaret FITZHUGH

Richard FOOTE .... pg 94, 6 Nov 1780, inv & appr

 Moses, Ned, Charles, Ben, Butcher, Ned, Peter, David, Will, Jesse, Harry, Bob, Kelley?, Rose, Sarah, Rachel & child, Talitha?, Sarah, Jack, Nance

Joshua BOTTS .... pg 104, 7 Nov 1780, will

 boy Bob to son Thomas BOTTS; Nell, Rodham, Aaron, Mary to wife Frances BOTTS

George THOMAS .... pg 107, 27 Feb 1781, inv & appr

 lad Ben, Dick, boy John, Jude

Francis TENNELL .... pg 111, 2 July 178_, inv & appr

 Tom, Samboy, Nan & child, Jenne, James, Moses, Elijah, Gowin, Mary, Amy

Henry PEYTON .... pg 119, 22 May 1781, will

 Dorcas & her children Celia & Frederick to daughter Mary MASSON; Sarah, Nathan, Charlotte, Joshua to son John PEYTON; Frank, Jim, Rachel, Phoebe to daughter Frances PEYTON; Sinah, Harry, Ralph to daughter Betty MARTIN; Seth, Betty, Lewis, Tate to son Thomas PEYTON; Lee, Anthony, Phil, Dennis, Rawley, Rose, Patience, Davie to wife Margaret PEYTON

Richard SPRIGG .... pg 122, 11 July 1781, inv & appr

   white woman servant, negro woman 40 years old, negro boys 14 & 7

Joshua BOTTS .... pg 126, 3 Sept 1781, inv & appr

   Nell, Aaron, Rhodum, Moll, Bob

William RAWLINGS .... pg 128, 5 Nov 1781, inv & appr

   Peter, Jude, Patrick

Timothy SEALE .... pg 130, 10 Aug 1781, will

   man Sambo, boy George, woman Jenny to wife Anne SEALE, woman Jenny to son John SEALE after wife's decease; man Abraham, woman Letty, girl Rose to son John SEALE; boys Moses, Ben to son Anthony SEALE; Judah & her child Hagar to daughter Betty BROWN

Henry PEYTON .... pg 132, 28 Aug 1781, inv & appr

   Lee?, Anthony, Phil, Rose, Frank, Sarah, Lettice, Davie, Ralph, Jim, Dennis, Rawleigh, Joshua, Phebe, Rachel, Betty, Nathan, Sinah, Dorcas, Clia, Frederick; Patience, Harry, Lewis, Charlotte of Sall

George FARROW .... pg 139, Sept 1781, estate acct

   negro

Francis JACKSON .... pg 142, 10 Dec 1781, will

   boy Jesse to George MASON; woman Bridget, men Moses, Daniel, to daughter Janney FIELDER; young man & young woman to Jane MARLOW

Francis JACKSON .... pg 146, Feb 1782, inv & appr

   boy Jesse, Daniel, Bridget, Moses

Elizabeth WHALEY .... pg 150, 14 Feb 1782, dower

   Tom, Sharlotte, Grace & child

Anthony SEALE .... pg 151, 5 Nov 1781, inv & appr

   men Sambo, Abraham, George, boys Moses, Benjamin, woman Judah, man Jenny, girls Rose, Hagar, woman Letty

Jabez DOWNMAN .... pg 156, _ Nov 1774, inv & appr

> Harry, Charles, Sharper, James, Lewis, Peter, Humphrey, Will, Titus, Charles, Mall & her child Nan, Sarah, Bett, Sue & her child Lucinda, Cate, Lydia & her child Celia, Chiriss?

William LINDRUM .... pg 162, 24 July 1779, will

> slaves to wife Sarah

William LINDRUM .... pg 167, 5 Aug 1783, inv & appr

> Dick, Dinah, Eve, Mima & child Anne, Robin, Winney, Hannah, Ben, Candis

William WHITLEDGE .... pg 170, 7 May 1782, will

> Henry, Rodger to son William WHITLEDGE; Lucy, Jim to daughter Liby GRANT; Ben, Moll to daughter Frances PERSELL; Suck (female) to grandson Baldwin COPPEDGE; Jane, Tate to granddaughter Frances COPPEDGE

John REEVE .... pg 173, 5 Apr1782, will

> wench Mona, girl Moll, boy Daniel to Daniel OBRIAN; girl Sharlot to Thomas BIRD; girl Lucy to William MATTHEWS

John REEVE .... pg 176, 27 Aug 1782, inv & appr

> Maria & child, Molly 14 years, girls Charlotte, Lucy, boy Daniel

James SCOTT .... pg 179, 2 Aug 1782, will

> Seth, Ben, June, Nell, Joe to son William & after the death of his mother Elgin, George, Suck, Milley, Sarah; Caesar, Manuel, Stephen, Charlotte, Simon, Daniel, Bett & her 2 daughters Daphne & Nance to grandson Alexander after the death of his grandmother; slaves belonging to Col. Thomas BLACKBURN...now...the rest of my slaves to my wife Sarah

.... pg 182, 22 Aug 1782, codicil

> ...slaves left to my wife except the girl Marinda...& bequeathed after her death or marriage to son William & grandson Alexander son of Robert be sold...

James BROWN .... pg 186, 10 May 1782, will

    girl Bender, boy Ben to wife Elizabeth BROWN; Bender to daughter Betsy BROWN after her mother's decease; Ben to son Robert BROWN after his mother's decease; Dinah, Seppio, Sam, Judith, Harry to be divided between sons James BROWN, Lewburton BROWN, Robert BROWN

Frances BOTTS .... pg189, 5 Nov 1782, dower

    1/3 of slaves set aside

John MURRAY .... pg 189, 18 Oct 1782, will

    wench Sall & her child Betty to wife Elizabeth MURRAY; men Tony, Sharper to brother Hugh MURRAY then Tony to Solomon EWELL after the term for which he was hired

James BROWN .... pg 193, 11 Dec 1782, inv & appr

    woman Dinah, man Sipyou? Tipyon?, girl Bender, boys Harry, Ben

George GREEN .... pg 194, 23 Dec 1782, inv & appr

    woman

William TACKETT .... pg 197, 30 June 1872, will

    girl Pat to son Lewis TACKETT when he turns 18, Afro boy Joseph Buchanan to son Lewis TACKETT at my death; woman Mary to granddaughter Mildred RENOE

James SCOTT .... pg 199, 25 Nar 1783, inv & appr

    Nanny, Beck, Charlotte, Joe, Daniel, Moll, Cloe, Stephen, Betty & her child Maria, Daphney, Ben, Caesar

John BURROUGHS .... pg 202, 8 Apr 1783, inv & appr

    men Jacob, Sam, woman Moll, Nell & child Francis, boy Abraham, girl Jane, woman Phillis

John DELGRIN .... pg 205, 7 Feb 1783, will

    wench Charity to son James DELGRIN; Charity's increase to go to John DELGRIN, William DELGRIN, daughter Elizabeth CASH, & Maryann DELGRIN; girl Rachel to son George DELGRIN; Peg to daughter Salley DELGRIN

John MURRAY .... pg 208, 4 Apr 1783, inv & appr

    Bristow, Sharper, Tony, Bob, Sall, Ailse, Jan, Daniel, Dick, Minny

Dr. James NISBETT .... pg 214, 6 May 1783, inv & appr

    Bob, Jack, Will, Sam, Joe, Jem, Phillis, Mary, Lizzy, Lett, Jesse, George

Dr. James NISBETT .... pg 223, 2 June 1783, inv & appr

    Bob 52 years, Jack 27, Will 25, Sam 23, Joe 20, Jane 10, Phillis with her child 8 days old, Mary 12, Lizzy 8, Lett 6, Jesse 5, George 2

.... pg 227, 20 June 1783, estate div

    Lot 1: man Bob, girl Mary, to children of Susanna NISBETT wife of John JOHNSON; Lot 2: man Jack to George NISBETT; Lot 3: man Will to Anne NISBETT; Lot 4: man Sam, girl Lett to William LUNTON; Lot 5: man Joe to James NISBETT; Lot 6: man James to Samuel BAGLEY; Lot 7: Phillis with her child 8 days old, boy George to Mary NISBETT; Lot 8: girl Lizzy, boy Jesse to Margaret NISBETT

Evan WILLIAMS .... pg 234, 7 July 1783, inv & appr

    Hannah, Abraham, Joe, Nell, Mary

Thomas SMOOT .... pg 238, 20 May 1783, will

    negroes to wife Elizabeth & after her marriage or death to sons Henry, George Mattox, James Mattox SMOOT & the child my wife is now pregnant with; at the marriage or death of my wife there should be one for each of my children except Mary BALLENGER...sons Notly, William Mattox, & Thomas St. HENLY have first choice

Thomas SMOOT .... pg 241, 10 July 1783, inv & appr

    man Jerry, woman Judith, girls Hannah, Pat

William WHITLEDGE .... pg 244, 5 Aug 1782, inv & appr

    man Harry, boy Tom, women Sue, Nell

Joshua BETTS .... pg 246, 4 Aug 1783, inv & appr

    Nell, Aaron, Bob

John DELGARN ....pg 251, 6 Oct 17__, inv & appr

    wench & child, girl

William TACKETT........................... pg 253, 12 Apr 1783, inv & appr

    wench & child

Traverse DOWNMAN ....pg 257, Nov 1783, inv & appr

    Jesse, Abraham, Roger, Frank, Winney, Phillis, Tom, Agathy, child little Winney, Barbary, Jenny, Manuel

Anne HARRISON..pg 261, 13 Sept 1783, will

    negroes to sister Seth HARRISON by brother Cuthburt HARRISON, also Luke, Esther; Peg to sister Frances SHORT; Spencer to nephew Thomas HARRISON; Henney to Frances Barn HARRISON

James SCOTT ....pg 264, 19Feb 1784, inv & appr

    Sarah, Milly & child, Suck & child, Maranda, Letty, Simon, Ned, Daphney, Manuel, Jack, Jinna

William BIRD .... pg 270, 6 May 1782, inv & appr

    Jack, William, Bach, Delmount, Stafford, Elijah, Charles, Harry, Chloe, O_endo, Priss, Lewis, _am, Sally, Thomas

William TENNISON............................. pg 275, 12 Dec 1783, inv & appr

    fellow Daniel, wench Agatha

Fanny SHUTE... pg 281, 6 Jan 1783, will

    Cate, Henry to sister Peggy MADDEN; Sam to niece Fanny NEWMAN

Travers DOWNMAN ..... pg 283, 23 Aug 1773 – 20 Mar 1784, estate acct

    James, Abram, Manuel, Jess

John ASHMORE...pg 286, 2 Feb 1778, will

    fellow Harry to brother William ASHMORE

Sarah SCOTT .... pg 287, 10 Jan 1783, will

    girl Marinda to Sarah BROWN daughter to William & Catherine BROWN

Lydia Musgrove ISMONGROVE .... pg 290, 4 June 1784, will

    woman Pat & her child Amy to daughter Ann Guy ISMONGROVE

Reginald GRAHAM .... pg 294, Sep 18 1782 – 1 Oct 1784, estate acct

    sundry slaves claimed & detained by William GRAHAM; Betty & child, Daniel 9, George 6, Davy 4, Peggy 2, girl Kate, boys Jim, Francis Atwell, wench Beck Harmon Utterback, boy Jerry Utterback, fellow G. Graham

Reginald GRAHAM .... pg 298, 5 Oct 1784, inv & appr

    boy Will, Buck, James, Levi, Kate, Moses

Reginald GRAHAM .... pg 299, 3 June 1782, inv & appr

    Betty & child, Daniel 9, George 6, Davy 4, Peggy 2

Foushee TEBBS .... pg 302, 30 Mar 1783, will

    Bowson, Mary to daughter Margaret MOOR; rest of slaves to be sold

Elizabeth BROWN .... pg 303, 9 Dec 1783, will

    girl Esther to son Anthony BUCKNER; woman Juda to daughter Ann CORSWILL; girl Hagar to daughter Clary BYRNE

Giles CARTER .... pg 303, Feb 1785, will

    Jude, James, Ben to son William CARTER; little Aggy, Winney, Jack to son Samuel CARTER; Jane, Mille, Mo to son David CARTER; George, big Aggy, Diner, Sucky to son Robert CARTER; Sarah, Jesse to daughter Sarah CARTER

Thomas CHAPMAN .... pg 307, 11 Mar 1785, will

    4 slaves of her choice to wife Susanna CHAPMAN; 2 slaves to Elizabeth OVERALL; girl Betty daughter of Nelly to daughter Jenny C__n CHAPMAN

Rev. Isaac CAMPBELL .... pg 314, 17 Mar 1785, inv & appr

    Henry, Glasgow, Africa, Peter, Cate, Cornbon, Centofy, Nan, Sal

William PURCELL .... pg 315, 24 Oct 1783, will

    man James, now in possession of Samuel JACKSON, to son John

George BIGBEE .... pg 317, 10 Aug 1778, inv & appr

    servant boy Barny Dan

Joseph PETTY ....pg 322, 5 Feb 1785, will

    Sue & 2 of her children Lizza & Charles to be disposed

Thomas DAGG .... pg 326, 16 Dec 1779 – 15 Feb 1782, estate acct

    carpenter Dick, young Dick, old Dick

William PERCELL ....pg 329, 8 Feb 1786, inv & appr

    Bett & child, Lelah, boy Fortune, James, old Dick; old Buck at George PERCELL's, woman Eve at Samuel JACKSON's

Joseph TYLER .... pg 331, date unreadable, inv & appr

    women Winney, Sarah, Lucy, Milly, girl Charlotte, boy John, girls Sylvia, Darkins (Dorkus?), boy Shadrack

William PERCELL .... pg 333, inventory

    Too faint to read.

Samuel JACKSON .... pg 334, 29 Jan 1785, will

    man Jacob, girl named _anerlso, man named Seaser (Caesar?) to son Francis JACKSON; man Peter, girl Hanna, to son George JACKSON; man David, boy Daniel to son John JACKSON; woman Esther, girl Cate, man Billy, man James, girl Janey to son Samuel JACKSON; girl Milly, woman Sue, boy Shadrack to daughter Naney RECH?; men Abraham, Dick, woman Saray to be sold

Valentine PEYTON .... pg 336, 20 Dec 1785, will

    girl Lett to daughter Prudence PEYTON; Harry, Barnaby, Sol, Sall, Aaron, Cloe, John, Charlotte, Fanny to be divided between children Craven, Prudence, John, & Robert PEYTON

John HASKINS Jr. ....pg 338, 10 Oct 1785, will

> fellow Dick in her possession to daughter Rachael JORDAN, to be sold when children come of age; fellow Harry to daughter Rachael JORDAN; fellow Cable to grandson James SEUR?

Samuel JACKSON .... pg 340, 4 Apr 1786, inv & appr

> men Barnes, Jacob, Abraham, woman Suck

Thomas GREEN ....pg 344, 3 Feb 1786, inv & appr

> Primus, Dinah, Cate, James, Davy, Ned

John HASKINS ....pg 345, 4 Sept 1786, inv & appr

> Harry, Dick, Cable

John BURROUGHS..pg 350, 4 Sept 1786, will

> all of my estate to my wife Mary BURROUGHS and after her decease wench Elenor to daughter Matthus BURROUGHS; man Samuel to son Joseph BURROUGHS; boy Abraham to son Benjamin BURROUGHS; lad Jacob to son Clement BURROUGHS

Richard RIXEY ....pg 354, 5 Sept 1786, inv & appr

> 2 servants, 6 negroes; Samuel, Mimah, Mary, Geofrey, Lucinda, Lucy

Capt. Thomas W. EWELL .... pg 355, 5 Apr – 3 May 1784, estate acct

> hire of negroes

Capt. Valentine PEYTON ....pg 357, 5Feb 1787, inv & appr

> Barnaby, Harry, Sarah, Sibyll, Fanny, Sarah, Ki__y, Arch, Letty, Chloe, John, Charlotte, David

Elizabeth RIXEY.. pg 359, 3 Oct 1786, dower

> Mary, Lavinah

Richard GRUBBS .... pg 361, 4 Apr 1787, inv & appr

> woman Winney, boy Adam

Joseph PETTY .... pg 365, 4 June 1787, inv & appr

> Peter, Susanna, James, Siner, Lemuel, ___ & child Adam, Sib, Princz, Ben, Elizabeth, Charles

Lawrence BUTLER .... pg 367, 3 Sept 1787, inv & appr

> fellow Pack, wench Peg

John BURROUGHS .... pg 368, 4 Sept 1786, will

> all of my estate to my wife Mary BURROUGHS and after her decease wench Elenor to daughter Matthus BURROUGHS; man Samuel to son Joseph BURROUGHS; boy Abraham to son Benjaman BURROUGHS; lad Jacob to son Clement BURROUGHS

John GRAHAM .... pg 369, 1 Dec 1783, will

> executor may purchase a negro girl for my daughter Pane GRAHAM; servant man Peter Daniel Macin to son William GRAHAM, about 5 years to serve

Henry LEE .... pg 373, 10 Aug 1787, will

> Alice, Beck, Rachel, Dick, Cath, Hom, Lemuel, Kate daughter of Beck, carpenter Dick, Winney, Jesse, all Winney's children, Daniel, Tom, old Winney to wife; Bill, Bett & her child in possession of son Charles heretofore given to him which are to be his forever? or to son Henry?; Phillis, Sol, Sinah, Betty daughter of Franky to daughter Marjary LYON?; Charlotte, Nancy to daughter Lucy; Alice daughter of Margery, Milly daughter of Penny, Darkey daughter of Dinah to daughter Nancy

Samuel LOVE .... pg 377, 23 Apr 1785, will

> women Vanessa, women Frank, Lidia and Frank's daughters Pat, Cate to son Augustine LOVE

John DISKIN .... pg 383, 4 Dec 1787, acct of sale

> Harry to Benjamin BRICK; Tom, Judy to James TEBBS; Tom to William BROWN; Ben to Anthony SEALE

Henry LEE .... pg 391, 19 Dec 1787, inv & appr

> Solomon, Guonby, Ben, Stephen, Henry, Maskill, Amy, Annie, Joe, Moses, ___, Phillis, Manuel, Robin, H__, Milly & child, Moll, Nancy,

black Moll, Fanny, Nanny, ___, Sam, Abel, Tom D__, Tom, Dacy, Dick, Nat, Jesse, Cate & child, Rachel & child, Henny & child, Sarah, Bill, Betsy, Beck, Rachel, Suckey, Frank, Alice, Fanny, old Frank, Judy, Dick, Lott, Daphney, Phil, Charlotte, Daniel, Sinah, Filice, Cato

John CALVERT .... pg 395, June 1788, inv & appr

Ben, Daniel, Catherine, George, Spencer, Keziah

William LANDMAN .... pg 401, 3 Dec 1787, estate div

Ben, Jemima, Ann, Dinah, young Dinah, Daphney to Alexander CLEVELAND husband of widow of William LANDMAN; Candice, Hannah, Bob to Archebald NILSON husband of daughter Mary Ann LANDMAN; __nny, Eve, Harriet, young Jamima to Peter TA_TE husband of daughter Elizabeth LANDMAN

John SEAL .... pg 402, Sept 1788, inv & appr

Jenny, Rese

William LEACH .... pg 403, 3 May 1787, will

all negroes to wife then to grandson William Haney LEACH

John DUDLEY .... pg 404, __, will

man Bob, woman Suckey to wife Mary DUDLEY

William LEACH .... pg 409, 5 Jan 1789, inv & appr

man, woman

George GREEN .... pg 410, 17 Dec 1788, will

all negroes to be divided between my sons Thomas, Jesse, James, my daughters Mary, Patty, Margaret, Nancy, Amy GREEN & grandchildren the son & daughter of son George GREEN dec'd

David FORBES .... pg 413, 22 Dec 1788, will

all slaves to wife Margaret FORBES & at her death to be divided among all the children

James TRIPLETT .... pg 414, 1 June 1789, inv & appr

men Joseph, Adam, George, Peter, woman Milly

Thomas ATWELL .... pg 416, 16 Apr 1777, will

> James, Harry, Joe, Jenn, Cooper?, Sarah, Winney, & __ (wife of James) to wife Ann ATWELL at her decease to be divided between children Charles, Margaret, William, Thomas, & Hugh; Simon, Gabriel, Sall to son Charles ATWELL; Dick, Alice to son William ATWELL; Kent, Hannah to son Thomas ATWELL; Frank, Susan, Jack son of Sarah to son Hugh ATWELL; Phillis, Dinah, Judith, George son of Sarah to daughter Mary ATWELL; Amy & her children Jenn, Nancy, & Robin to daughter Ann ATWELL; Clara & her children Beck & Abraham to daughter Margaret ATWELL

George LANPKINS .... pg 422, 6 July 1789, inv & appr

> Joan, Winney, Ruth & child, Stephen

George GREEN .... pg 424, 15 May 1789, inv & appr

> wench Winney, Hannah, Sarah, Mill & child Lewis, Cate, Nell, Alce & child Tom, fellows Frank, Joe, Jack, Abram, Ben, Harry, boys Moses, Tom, girls Poll, Fran, Ann Rachel, Henny

Giles CARTER........................... pg 427, 7 Mar 1785, inv & appr

> man George, boy James, woman __ile, wenches Agga, Fanny, Sarah, girls Agga, Winn, Milla, boy Jesse, Diner, Mary, boy Jack, girl Suck, boy Ben, woman Tab

Valentine PEYTON............... pg 430, Dec 1785 – 3 Aug 1789, estate acct

> negroes; to Mrs. FANON for delivering 2 negro women of children; Sarah as yet unsold

John CHICK ....pg 434, 15 Nov 1786, will

> women Mary, Esther to wife Ann CHICK & at her death or marriage divided between daughters Celia & Susannah CHICK

Lynaugh HELM .... pg 438, 2 May 1789, will

> slaves to wife Hester; girl Penny to daughter Elizabeth HELM; gift of slaves to daughter Celia; gift of slaves to son Thomas

Thomas ATWELL................................ pg 441, 5 Apr 1790, inv & appr

> men Simon, Kent, boys Zach, Abraham, man Frank, Winney & child Dennis, woman Nan, girls Alce, Dall, Nell, Cloe, woman Clary, men

James, Harry, woman Sarah, boys Ralph, Peter, girls Jane, Lucy, boy Richard

Foushee GEBBS .... pg 453, 5 July 1790, inv & appr

Jannis?, Moses, Ben, Violet, young Harry, Bill, Sall, Charles, Bett, Leotha, Hagar, Mill, Samuel, Sandy, Zach, Harry Sr., Minum, Lewis, Jude

Joseph TYLER .... pg 457, 8 June 1790, estate acct

Winney, Sarah, Lucy, Milly, Charlotte, John, Lydia, Sylvia, Dorcus, Shadrack

George GREEN .... pg 460, 17 Aug 1790, estate acct

woman

John RANDOLPH .... pg, 462, 11 Sept 1789, will

woman Lucy to wife Ann RANDOLPH; negroes to be sold at decease of wife

Robert YOUNG .... pg 467, 16 Oct 1790, inv & appr

woman Jenny, boy Sandy, girl Patience

Nathaniel WICKLIFF .... pg 473, 3 Jan 1791, inv & appr

man Daniel

Burr HARRISON .... pg 474, 5 Feb 1789, will

Poll & her child Sall, girl Rachel daughter of Amy, boy Will to daughter Ann Catharine HARRISON; boy Sauney to son Matthew HARRISON; big Jerry to son Cuthbert HARRISON; man Frank, boy Gabriel a child of Amy to son Thomas HARRISON; fellow Tom, wench Rachel, Ruth's child Suck, child Sharlett to daughter Mary Ann HARRISON

William CARR .... pg 479, 23 Jan 1790, will

negroes to wife; Hannah & her children to daughter Betsey TEBBS; Aga & all her children Jack & ___ to son William CARR after the death of my wife; Lucy and all her children Tim, Harry, & Nancy to son John CARR after the death of my wife; if any are for sale they are to be immediately liberated

.... codical

    man Abner may be set free

Joseph TYLER .... pg 486, 2 Mar 1791, estate div

    Sal, Jenny, Lucy the oldest, Suck, Beck, Sylvia, Mary to Elizabeth TYLER his wife; Mellory, Lucy the youngest, John, Dorcas, Elizabeth to son Benjamin TYLER his son; Winney, Matthew, Charlotte, Shadrach, Nancy to Samuel TILDER who married Nancy TYLER

John RANDOLPH .... pg 487, 5 Oct 1790, inv & appr

    Lucy

Joshua BARKER .... pg 490, 30 Apr 1791, inv & appr

    Will, girl Maria, boys James, Edmond, Lucy, boy Daniel, girl Hester

Thomas CHAPMAN .... pg 498, 25 Apr 1785, inv & appr

    Jesse, Manuel, Thomas, Trunion, Thomas, Nelly, Jem, young Nelly, Betty, Charles, Polly, Nelly's young child little Jesse, Sal, Doratha, Daniel, Fanny

John LOWE .... pg 502, 14 Feb 1791, will

    fellow Ned to son Edward LOWE

Richard FOOTE .... pg 504, 24Sept 1770 – 12 Apr 1780, estate acct

    delivery of negro woman; negroes; Charles

WILL BOOK H
1792- 1802

John LOWE..pg 2, 22 Oct 1791, inv & appr

    fellow Ned

John TYLOR... pg7, 14 Jan 1792, inv & appr

    men Cesar, Ben, Jesse, Richard, James, Will, Grace & child Winney, women Poll, Nelly, Frank, Nell

Charles LOVE... pg 26, 7 May 1792, inv & appr

    woman, boy

William BRYANT .... pg 27, 3 Apr 1792, inv & appr

    man Peter

John Lee WRIGHT .... pg 28, 2 July 1792, inv & appr

    man Solomon, wench Pat, girl Cebra, wench & child, girl Hethaliah, boy Simon, Jane, Susannah, boy Jesse

Thomas MONTGOMERIE .... pg 33, 8 Apr 1792, will

    girl Kate daughter of Grace to Jean CONNER who has lived with me; ...estate to purchase 3 fellows for son Thomas likewise; Grace & her children Bill and Mary, my negro girl little Fanny, my boys Davie & Daniel the last three children to Fanny my house keeper; Fanny to be free on my death & I leave her her daughter & my girl Polly; servant John to be set free on my death

John SHUTE .... pg 37, 13 July 1792, inv & appr

    men George, Harry, women Cate, Judah, girl Celia

John Lee WRIGHT ....pg 40, 17__ - 1 Dec 1784, estate acct

    Solomon, Sebra to Enoch RENOE; Jane & child to John WHITLEDGE; girl Jane to John WOOD; Suke to John YOUNG

William RANDOLPH ....pg 42, 2 Aug 1792, will

    all negroes to wife Ellender RANDOLPH

Peter SMITH .... pg 43, 17 Apr 1792, will

   wench Nan to wife Elizabeth SMITH to be sold after her decease

William RANDOLPH .... pg 44, 25 Oct 1792, inv & appr

   woman Mary, girl Darcus

Strother SUTTLE .... pg 45, 22 Aug 1792, will

   men Nace, Jack to son William SUTTLE, Jack to be free if he lives longest; girls Libby, Alley to grandson Henry Hampton SUTTLE; girl Dinah to daughter Ann RENOE

Col. Burr HARRISON .... pg 47, 7 Jan 1793, inv & appr

   wenches Ruth, Anny, girls Rachel, Sharlett, Sall, boys Gabriel, Davy, girl Suck, Doll with child, wench Rachel, old fellow Tom, old women Poll, Ginny, fellow Charles, boy Jury, fellow May, old fellow Frank

Joseph BUTLER .... pg 50, 22 Sept 1788, will

   after wife Anne BUTLER's decease or marriage: man Jack & negroes already deeded to dec'd son Laurance BUTLER's children Sarah Anne, Joseph, Jacob COLVERT, Mary COLVERT; Lydia, Charlotte, Preston to daughter Anne BUTLER; Hanner, Silve, Ruth, Sam to daughter Mary CARTER; Will, Phill, Daniel, Eliah, Cate, young Jude, old Jude to be disposed at wife's decease or as she deems proper

John JORDON .... pg 53, 16 Jan 1893, inv & appr

   Phillis & child, boy Anthony, girl Charity, boy Jacob

Richard FOOTE .... pg 55, 16 Sept 1791 – 2 Apr 1793, estate acct

   hired negroes, Charles, Celia hired out to J.F. ALEXANDER

John DUDLEY .... pg 61, 9 Dec 1788, inv & appr

   Bob, Suck

John RANDOLPH .... pg 62, 1 Mar 1793, estate acct

   Luce

(Wm?) Joseph BUTLER .... pg 63, 8 Jan 1793, inv & appr

    men Preston, William, Elijah, Phillip, women Catherine, Liddy, Hannah & child, girls Silvy, Ruth, boys Samuel, Thomas, Daniel, woman Judy, girl Sharlotte

Strother LUTTLE .... pg 66, 7 Jan 1793, inv & appr

    Mingo, Hannah, Jack, Mary & young child, Kate, Mary, Daniel, Syl, Elinor, Dinah

Benjamin THOMAS .... pg 67, 7 May 1793, will

    boy Tom to wife Mary Lucas

Frances BALLENDINE .... pg 68, 2 Jan 1793, will

    slaves except the lot heretofore given to Frances Ballendine MUSCHETT daughter of _ James MUSCHETT to the said Thomas LEE Sr. & Daniel Carroll BRENT in trust for nephew Thomas William BALLENDINE

William RANDOLPH .... pg 69, 2 Sept 1793, estate acct

    woman Mary, girl Darcus

Thomas MONTGOMERIE .... pg 74, 8 Oct 1793, inv & appr

    girl Fanny, boys David, Daniel, girl Kate child of Grace, girl Polly, Grace & her 2 children Bill & Mary, man Moses

Benjamin THOMAS .... pg 80, 5 Aug 1793, inv & appr

    Randall, Rachel, Sarah, Daniel, Henry, Tom

William FAIRFAX .... pg 82, 4 Oct 1793, will

    Ge__t, Linney, Fanny, Sibba to wife Elizabeth FAIRFAX, at her marriage or decease to daughters Ann WARDER, Benedecter FAIRFAX, Catherine GAINES, Elizabeth PELL, Eada CALVERT & Sarah FAIRFAX

Dr. David FORBES .... pg 87, 7 Nov 1793, inv & appr

    Phillis & child Phillis, Suckey, boys Jesse, Manuel, girls Lucinda, Nancy

John FARROW .... pg 89, 2 Oct 1778, will

   fellows Charles, Chatham to wife Elizabeth FARROW

David JAMESON .... pg 90, 5 Mar 1788, will

   Tom, Abraham, Milly, Hannah to wife Patty JAMESON; Bob to daughter Jane SMITH; girl Nancy to daughter Mary GREGORY; boy Peter to daughter Sarah JAMESON; girl Sinah to daughter Elizabeth RALLS

John FARROW .... pg 95, 3 Dec 1793, inv & appr

   man Chatham, woman & child Sarah, boys Lewis, William

David JAMESON .... pg 99, 6 Jan 1794, inv & appr

   Bob, Peter, Milly, Hanner, Joseph, Abraham, Sinah, Daniel, Nancy

John CALVERT .... pg 102, 21 Aug 1788, acct of sales

   1/3 of hired slaves to widow: Daniel, Constance; slaves sold – Daniel to John JACKSON; Spencer to John DAVIS; Kesiah to Francis CALVERT; George to John REDMAN; Constance to John CALVERT

Jean MATTOX .... pg 113, 18 Dec 1793, will

   Sarah & her children Ellender & Tom to daughter Margaret TRIPLETT; Sarah's youngest child Joe to John COCKE son of William COCKE

William POWELL .... pg 114, 5 May 1794, inv & appr

   Will, Peter, Dinah

Alexander BROWN .... pg 115, 21 May 1794, inv & appr

   John, Michael, Beck, old woman Sarah

William FAIRFAX .... pg 118, 3 Dec 1793, inv & appr

   man Gerard, woman Sawney?, girl Fanny, girl child Sibba

William TYLER .... pg 122, 6 Oct 1794, inv & appr

   men Catesby, Harry

William SCOTT .... pg 126, 3 Jan 1792, will

> Sall, Peter to wife, at her death to be divided among daughter Lettie's children; Kate, Ralph, Dinah, Fanny to the children of my daughter Letitia COLQUHOUN

Francis McCORMICK .... pg 127, 2 Dec 1794, inv & appr

> man Lud, woman Nancy

Cuthbert BULLITT .... pg 130, 3 Oct 1791, inv & appr

> London, Matt, Joe, Jim, boys Bob, Abraham, Jim, Solomon, Letty & child, Cloe & child, girls Jilly, Hannah, Nancy, Lydda, Nanny, lad Will at John SINGER's; Peter, Bristoe, Anthony, Jenkins, Flora, Phillis, Judah, Hannah, Cate, Mimey, Winney, girl Jude at James WOODs; Rose, child Charlotte, Charles, boys Jesse, Ned, Billy, Tom, Ben, George sold

Cuthbert BULLETT .... pg 141, 25 Nov 1791 - 18 June 1795, estate acct

> negroes, runaway slave, 2 children sold

Robert HEDGES .... pg 156, 12 Oct 1793, inv & appr

> woman & child

Catherine MARTIN................................ pg 157, 6 Oct 1795, inv & appr

> woman Esther, girl Jane

Thomas OLIVER ....pg 165, 25 Feb 1796, will

> girl Betsy to Nancy NOEL

William HERNDON .... pg 169, 24 Nov 1795, will

> woman Phoeby, boy Bartlett after wife's death to daughter Ann COLLING; 1 boy & boy Bartlett, woman Phoebe before lent to daughter Ann COLLING, woman Lucy to son George HERNDON; woman Amy to daughter Peggy HERNDON; girl Phillis to daughter Betty Taylor HERNDON; man __, Charlie to son John HERNDON; man Tom Bolaz to son James White HERNDON; girl Darcus to daughter Fanney HERNDON; boy George to son Jeremiah HENDON; woman Rose, boys Joseph, Gabriel to daughter Rachael HERNDON all after death of wife Frances HERNDON

William HERNDON .... pg 174, 5 Apr 1796, inv & appr

> Phoebe, Tom Boling, Tom Charles, Bartlett, Phillis, Lucy, Darcus, Gabriel, Rose, Grace, George, Joe, Charles, Amy, Jane

Howson HOOE .... pg 178, 8 Apr 1796, will

> Ben, Hincheloe (Kincheloe?), Lucy to son John HOOE; Moses, Milly, Frank, Charley to son Dade HOOE, to be free if sold; Venus, Amos, Patt, Bill, Nancy, Tom, Harry, Kessey to daughter Frances HOOE

Vincent DYE .... pg 180, 5 Sept 1796, sales

> man to William DYE

Richard GRAHAM .... pg 181, 15 June 1791, will

> Fanny & her children to daughter Catharine; Stephen, boy Will to son Richard GRAHAM; sons George & John GRAHAM have all the negroes at the death of their mother; rest of negroes to be divided among all my 4 children

Thomas CHAPMAN .... pg 186, 8 Oct 1793, division

> Tom, Jesse to Thomas THORNTON and Jane Carr his wife; ...a part of each child left in the hands of James G___ & Susannah his wife...

Richard GRAHAM .... pg 189, 5 Dec 1796, inv & appr

> men Sam, Manuel, Peter

Elizabeth BRAZIER... pg 194, 29 June 1795, will

> man Ben, left to me by my mother Mary FOWKE, to daughter Sarah Harrison CANNON

Benjamin THOMAS ....pg 195, July 1793 – 5 June 1797, estate acct

> fellow Randall, woman Rachel, boys Daniel, Harry, girl Sarah sold

Lynaugh HELM .... pg 197, 1 Jan 1790, inv & appr

> old James, Daniel, Moses, Ben, Bob, Harry, Ephraim, John, young James, Moll, Suck, Nance, Sinah, Cate, Jenny

Thomas NORMAN ....pg 198, 6 Feb 1797, inv & appr

> woman Cattron, Ailse & child Sharlott, boy Ealy, girl Sukey

Henry WHITING .... pg 207, 2 May 1797, inv & appr

> Oliver, Will, Gloster, John, George, Robin, Richard, Coxon, Amos, Nelson, Michael, Tom, Will, Jude, Charity, Hester, Sall, Phillis, Nelly, Moll & child
>
> The above negroes being under mortgage to Sir John PEYTON we cannot say whether they be the property of Henry WHITING dce'd.

William SCOTT .... pg 209, 3 Jul 1797, inv & appr

> woman

Henry WHITING .... pg 212, 2 May 1775 – 7 June 1776, estate acct

> negroes all being mortgaged are not entered as being liable for Henry WHITING's debts

Scarlet MADDEN .... pg 221, 5 Sept 1797, inv & appr

> men Ben, William, Sall & 2 children

Francis RENOE Sr. .... pg 224, 18 Oct 1794, will

> boy Frederick to son Enoch RENOE; fellow Dick, boy Ben to son Francis; fellow Page to daughter Lidie MOSE; wench & child, Celia, Rachel, boy Lige to son George; boys Page, Simon to son Baylis; wench Poll to daughter Nancy WHITLEDGE; wench Winney to daughter Fanny TACKETT; Rachel, Ben to daughter Milley JAMISON; women Nell, Carshaba to daughter Dolley RENOE; woman Sib, wench Delph to daughter Jane RENOE; women Sue, Violet to daughter Susana CROSBY; Bob, James to be sold or hired

William MADDOX .... pg 229, 30 Sept 1798, inv & appr

> (late of Maryland) Sarah, Elenor her daughter, Thomas, Cesh, Mary

Cuthbert BULLITT .... pg 231, 3 Oct 1797, inv & appr

> Davy, Roger, yellow Janey, Jack, black Janey, Kate, Aggy, Anny, Polly, London, Nelly, James

M.H. Math MANKIN .... pg 237, 4 Sept 1797, inv & appr

> wench & child, girl

Vincent DYE .... pg 239, 4 Apr 1796, inv & appr

 man Tom

Snowden HORTON .... pg 245, 18 Dec 1797, inv & appr

 Sam, Adam, Harry, Jack, Ben, little Sam, Nan, Milly, Hannah, Moll & child Judy, Hester, Fan, Mary, Rose, little Milly, Pheby

William DAVIS .... pg 256, 6 Feb 1798, inv & appr

 man, woman, girl

Zacharia LEWIS .... pg 261, 9 Apr 1796, will

 negroes now in the possession of daughters Ann BLACKWELL & Hannah BRENT & my grandsons Lewis & Presley MOOREHEAD; girl Charlotte to granddaughter Mary Lewis ATWELL; boy David to grandson George William Brent BLACKWELL

William PERCELL .... pg 268, 8 May 1798, estate acct

 girl sold to KINCHELOE; girl Winney to widow Sarah PERCELL; Bett abt 35 years, Winney 15, Dennis 8, Eve 6, Willis 2 (sold or for dower?)

Benjamin GREGORY .... pg 289, 30 June 1798, will

 girl Nancy to wife Mary GREGORY

Thomas FAULKNER .... pg 290, 1780 - 1797, estate acct

 child Poll, Fanny, Gabriel, boy Dennis, Charles (Courtney?)

Frances BALLENDINE .... pg 296, 2 Dec 1797, inv & appr

 Hannah, Moses, Fanny, Bee?, Hannah, Anna, Rachel, Belinda, Jenny, Billy, Esther, Daphine, Sally, Maria, Harry, Ned, Milly, Robin, Polly, Joshua

Thomas BALLENDINE .... pg 298, 25 July 1797, adm acct

 Prue with child, Allison, Sandy her children, woman Winney, Lucy child of Prue

Zachariah LEWIS................................ pg 299, 7 May 1798, inv & appr

    George, Winney, old Dick, James, young Dick, Tom, Charles, Peter, Stephen, Joe, Bett, Jude & child Williamson, Catoc, Abner, Aaron, Willis; Manuel, Harry, Isaac, Vine in the possession of David BLACKWELL

Thomas OLIVER .... pg 304, 2 May 1796, inv & appr

    woman Elce, girls Fanny, Betsy, boy Joe

Sarah MASON ....pg 320, 28 Dec 1798, div dower slaves

    formerly Sarah DADE wife of Caduallader DADE dec'd between Townshend DADE & the orphans of Francis DADE dec'd, brother to _. TOWNSHEND

    No. 1 – Phillip, Samuel, James, Nathan, Rachel, Letty, Vergin & 2 children Thornton & Minta; No. 2 – Daniel, Sall, Benjamin, Jenny, Betty, Susan, Frank & 3 children Mildred, Even, & Susan

    No 2 to Townshend DADE; No 1 to orphans of Frances DADE

James JOHNSON................................pg 321, 4 Feb 1799, inv & appr

    old fellow

Benjamin GREGORY ....pg 329, 1 Oct 1798, inv & appr

    girl

Mary DADE ....pg 331, 24 Feb 1799, will

    negroes now in his possession to son Langhorne DADE; wench Winney to Laurence ASHTON of King George Co; fellow David to grandson Horatio Dade ASHTON; Cloe & all her children to daughter Sarah DADE except boy Edmond, girl Heathy, young wench Mima & all her children; Jenny & her son Ellzey and the other slaves which he now has in his possession to son Townshend DADE; _acher, Jack, Dick to son Townshend DADE; fellow Ben to son-in-law James GWATKIN whom he purchased of my son Charles; boys Edmond, Nelson to son Charles Stuart DADE; girl Heathy to daughter Mary Stuart ALEXANDER; girl Lucinda to granddaughter Margaret GWATKIN; the second daughter of the slave Jenny to Sarah Ashton DADE daughter of my son Langhorne; boy George to daughter Sarah DADE

John GRANT .... pg 335, 28 July 1798, will
    Lucy, Phillip, John, James, Diner to sister Mary Whitledge GRANT

Mathew SANDERS .... pg 339, 3 Dec 1798, inv & appr
    Reuben, Jim, Grace

John KINCHELOE ....pg 341, 4 Feb 1799, inv & appr
    men Nace James, small boy Hepney, Bosin, woman Sarah, man York

William MADDUX .... pg 364, 7 Nov 1799, estate acct
    woman Sarah, girl Elender, boy Thomas, John, girl Mary

Moses WICKLIFFE .... pg 366, 2 Dec 1799, inv & appr
    man Ben, wench & 3 children, old wench Nell

Rev. Spencer GRAYSON .... pg 368, 14 June 1799, inv & appr
    Tom, Iris Cook, Dorcas, Jess, Bob, Joe, Clara, Alice, Henry, Betty, Molly

Zachariah LEWIS .... pg 372, 26 Oct 1799, negro appr
    Caroline, Sam, Minnea, Nathan

Vincent DYE .... pg 373, May 1796 – 4 Nov 1799, estate acct
    William DYE for 1 negro

Thomas MONTGOMERIE ....
.... pg 381, 15 Oct 1792 - 30 Apr 1798, estate acct
    servants Somersett, Charles

Simon LUTTRELL ....pg 402, 2 Sept 1799, inv & appr
    Charles, Daniel, Sal & child, Amy & child Lebey, Delfery, Nancy, George, Agathy, Milly, Hanney, Judy, Sarah, Betty

William PERCELL .... pg 406, 5 May 1800, inv & appr
    Bet & child Harry, young woman Winney, boy Dennis, girl Eave, boy Willis

James FOSTER .... pg 408, 20 July 1800, will

    Benjamin THOMAS…& the negroes he gave me…

Francis RENOE .... pg 419, 2 Mar 1801, inv & appr

    men Bob, James, woman Cate, man Page, young women Sib, Bash, Delphy, Violet, Nell, man Seymor, small girl Lucy, small boy Aaron, child Charlotte, boy Ben, girl Rebekah, boy Thornton

John CORNWELL .... pg 425, 2 Mar 1801, inv & appr

    man Isaac, woman Sarah

William HORTON .... 427, 7 Apr 1800, inv & appr

    men Charles, Henry Dade, Benjamin, Henry, Jeremiah, women Nancy, Sally, Elizabeth, Sarah, Phoebe, Jane, boy Shadrach, girl Judah, boys Ralph, Daniel

Valentine PEYTON .... pg 429, 20 Dec 1786, acct of sales

    Daniel to Burr PEYTON; Barnaby, Sil & child to Richard DOWNTON; Aaron to Francis CORNHILL; Chloe to Peyton HARRISON; John to William NORMAN; Charlotte to James NORRIS; Riz to Zaphemiah POSEY; Sal & child to John BROWN

Thomas ATWELL .... pg 432, 30 Nov 1795, acct of sales

    James, women Nan, Sarah, man Harry, girls Sall, Alse, Luce, boy Richard to Ann ATWELL; boy Peter to William DITTWILL; man Frank to William CARR; boy Dennis to John THOMOY; girl Chloe to Robert THURMAN; man Simon to Charles ATWELL; girl Jenny to Thomas ATWELL

John HAMMILL .... pg 437, 3 Sept 1800, inv & appr

    men James, Will, Abraham, lads Sandy, Moses, Nelson, Willis, Lewis, Daniel, woman Fanny, child Selah, old woman Nancy, woman Beck

Helen BUTLER .... pg 439, 7 Sept 1795 – 3 July 1798, estate acct

    Will

Elizabeth HOOMES .... pg 445, 1 Sept 1800, inv & appr

    Phillis & child Ealan, Nan & child George, Benjamin, Daniel, Bet, Sharlot, Washington

Thomas BIRD .... pg 446, 30 May 1801, inv & appr

    Caty, Milly, Mason, Cate, Charles, Hannah, Charles, Tom, Sally, Suckey, Jack, Elija, Stafford, Tom, Delman, Daniel, Harry, Ann, Joe, Jesse, Hannah, Lewis, Chloe, Caty, Hector, Lucinda, Rachel, Boyton, America, Americus, Mimy, William, Gusty, Betsy, Ailacy, Gilbert, Charlotte, Darkey, Alex, Maria, Bender, Dianh, Frank, Ester, Milly, Jenny, Peggy, Fanny, George, Ben, Dolly, Kizzey, Cloe, Lemuel?, Lucy, Beck, Daphine, Luke, Mary, Hannah, Phillis, Tom, Harry

Landon CARTER .... pg 450, 19 Jan 1798, will

    all slaves to sons Wormly, John Fantleroy, Moore Fantleroy, & Charles Landon CARTER; Betty, Sukey, Charlotte, Caty, Mimah, Jenny, Judah, Vincent, Hill, Joe, old Will to daughters Elizabeth, Margaret, & Judith; Peter & Sukey his wife with all their children, & also girl Jenny to daughter Elizabeth CARTER; George & Charlotte his wife with all their children & a girl Judah to daughter Margaret CARTER; Mimah, Matty, Kitt to daughter Judith CARTER; woman Lucy to daughter Mary BRUCE; boy Merideth son of Will, woman Katy & her child to grandson Landon BRUCE; boy Na__ace son of Will to grandson John BRUCE; girl Becky daughter of Sukey to granddaughter Eliza BRUCE; girl Betty daughter of Sukey to granddaughter Judith BRUCE; girl Sephia daughter of Lucy to granddaughter Eleanara BRUCE; old Will & his wife Betty and his daughter Suckey before loaned to daughters in Item 5 while they remain single to be at liberty to choose a master among my 4 sons

John ESHEW .... pg 461, 30 July 1801, inv & appr

    man Harry, girl Jenny

Thomas BIRD .... pg 465, 15 June 1801, acct of sales

    Hannah, Sally, Suckey, Charles __, Jack, Lyah, Stafford, Tom, Delmond, Daniel, Harry, Ann, Joseph, Jesse, Cloe, Cate, Lucinda, Cate, Milly, Mason, Cate, Charles, Hector to Margaret BIRD; America, Americus, Mimy, William, Gusty, Betey, Alicy, Gilbert, Charlotte, Darkey, Alick, Meriah, Bender, Dinah, James, Kempe, Frank to Rachel BOSON; Milly, Ginny, Peggy, Fanny, George, Ben, Polly, Lucey to Margaret Bert EASTER; Cuzzy, Clowe, Beck, Daphne, Suck, Mary, Hannah, Phillis, Tom, Harry to Margaret BIRD

James FOSTER ....pg 469, 3 Nov 1800, inv & appr

   men Frank, Charles, boy Nace, girl Phebe, boys Ben, York, woman Kate

Landon CARTER .... pg 477, 7 Dec 1801, inv & appr

   Archy, Joe, Paul, Vincent, Griffin, Hill, Martin, Katy, Mary, Joe son of Archy, Parlow son of Sukey, Janny & child Clara, Winney of Martha, Paul son of Billy, _aussa of Billy, Judy, Nichols, Dennis, Harry, George, little Katy, Maria & child, Betsy of Billy, Sally, Merideth, Sally, Esther, Robert, Abigail, Sarah, Bill, Martha, Nancy, Phillis, John, Harriet, Sally, Silvia, Tennison, Nancy, Pat, Tasker, Sukey, Gabriel, Barshaba, Tolly, __hy, Esther, Harry, Arthur, Talbot, Phil, Billy, __tty, Mimah, Philander, Caroline, Charlotte & child Jack, Betsy, Penny, Sammy, Peter, Judith, Daniel, Joe, Moses, Polly, Peggy, Beck, Judith, Sukey, Harshall, Alfred, Carlos, George, Beck & child Sarah, Simon, Edmond, Jose, Abigail, Ralph, Billy, Whitley, Peggy, Dolly & child Jonathan, Judy, Willoughby, Saunders, Lavinia, Hannah & child Martha, Nancy, George, Amy, Buliegh & child Nancy, Liddy & child Eleanor, Harry, Julia, Hannah, Joe, Betty & child Rando, Anny & child Luisa, Stephen, Kitt, Jack, Gowin, Patty, Ellzey, Ephrain, Sam, Levi, Unis, Dinah, Tom, Judy, granny Sukey, granny Sarah, Harry, Martha, Mary, (___), Jesse, Ben, Sam, Tom, Simon, Agcy, Miles, George (___), Phil, Peter, Fanny & child Sally, Sarah & child Ben, Jammy, Nancy, Jack, Nancy, Greasten, Beck, Liddy, Joyce, Natt

Peter SMITH .... pg 482, 13 Dec 1792, inv & appr

   Nanny & 2 children

Richard GRAY ....pg 493, 20 Nov 1798, will

   man Adam, boy Anthony, girl Janney to son William GRAY; woman Sarah, boy Daniel to son James GRAY; any further children of Sarah to be divided between Richard & James GRAY

Ann ATWELL................................... pg 494, 5 June 1802, will

   Harry, Richard, Sarah, Sall & daughter Ann to daughter Nancy SMITH; girl Alice daughter of Dinah to son Hugh ATWELL; man Joe which my husband gave me in lieu of Dinah to daughter Mary LINTEN; child Douglas son of Luce to grandson Thomas ATWELL; woman Luce to granddaughter Margaret SMITH; girl Nell to grandson Hugh SMITH; girl Mary to granddaughter Margaret ATWELL daughter of Hugh ATWELL; old James & Nan to choose one of my children they will live with

Ann ATWELL .... pg 510, 6 Dec 1802, inv & appr

   James, Nan, Harry, Richard, Sarah, Sall, Luce, Alse, Ann & child, Nell & child, Mary & child, Douglas

Elizabeth NAILER .... pg 521, 7 Mar 1803, inv & appr

   woman Susan, girls Becky, Nell

Jacob PALVERT .... pg 522, 25 Jan 1803, will

   Jacob to be emancipated

Isaac DAVIS .... pg 523, 8 Mar 1803, inv & appr

   woman Lett

George CALVERT .... pg 524, 5 Apr 1803, inv & appr

   2 women, 3 children

William HERNDON .... pg 524, 14 Aug 1802, inv & appr

   man Tom

William HORTON .... pg 526, 1Apr 1800 – 17 Mar 1802, estate acct

   negroes

Peter COTTRELL .... pg 528, 18 July 1803, will

   man Jacob, woman Kate to wife Frances COTTRELL; girl Hannah to daughter Nancy COTTRELL; boy Ben to daughter Sarah DANIEL; woman Nan to son Jeremiah COTTRELL; woman Kate after his mother's death to son Jesse COTTRELL; boy Harry, girl Fanny to son Moses COTTRELL; man Jacob to be divided bewtween sons Jesse & Moses after wife's decease; girl Maria to daughter Peggy RIED if she chooses or Kate's next child

Richard GRAY .... pg 531, 23 Apr 1803; inv & appr

   Adam, Sarah & child, Fanny, Jenny, Daniel

Issac DAVIS .... pg 533, 7 Mar 1803, inv & appr

   3 women, 3 girls

Cuthbert BULLITT............pg 542, 2 July 1795 – 4 May 1801, estate acct sale of Abraham to George LANE; negroes sold

Peter COCKRELL...............................pg 548, 5 Sept 1803, inv & appr men Luboy, Jacob, women Nanny, Cate, boy Henry, girls Maria, Fanny, Hannah, boy Benjamin, girl Mariah

WILL BOOK I
1803-1809

Thomas WRIGHT .... pg 1, 3 Oct 1803, inv & appr

    woman & child, girl

Francis RENOE .... pg 2, 1797 – 3 Aug 1803, estate acct

    woman Cate, man Robert to Jeremiah MOORE; James to George RENOE

Elizabeth HOOMES .... pg 4, 1800 – 11 June 1803, estate acct

    Phillis, Ben, Daniel, Adam

Maryann HARRISON .... pg 8, 4 Nov 1803, will

    boy David to granddaughter Maryann HEREFORD; use of other slaves for 3 years to daughter Maryann DADE, if she does not survive slaves, except David, to be sold

Willoughby TEBBS .... pg 9, 6 Dec 1803, inv & appr

    man Moses, girls Alle, Letty, women Sall, Hagar

Moses JEFFRIES .... pg 12, 13 Aug 1784, will

    fellows Harry, Jess, Ned, Jeffery, wenches Jane, Sall to wife Rachael JEFFRIES, after her death to Rachael BURROUGHS, Charlotte GRIGSBY, & Robert HEDGES son of Robert HEDGES Sr.

Sophia C.M. BULLITT .... pg 14, 27 May 1803, will

    boy Fredrick; David, Antony, Joan & her son Frederick to be emancipated after 1 year servitude; my proportion of my negro Jenny's hire to Mary BARNES

Clement WOODARD .... pg 17, 13 June 1803, inv & appr

    woman Jude, boy Philip, girl Hannah

Maryann TAYLOR .... pg 18, 26 Dec 1803, inv & appr

    Daniel, Billy, Jesse, Mary, young Daniel, child Edward

Isaac FARROW .... pg 19, 2 Dec 1803, will

> woman Patience, David, Jane, Sarah, Charles to daughter Libby RENOE; boy Lawson to grandson William RENOE; woman Lucy, Frank, Jesse, Samuel, Jacob to son John FARROW; girl Alse to grandson Isaac FARROW; Nell, Robert, David, Tom, Mason to daughter Mary JACKSON; boy Robert to Mary's son John Farrow JACKSON; boy Lawson to granddaughter Nancy STROTHER; boy Lewis to granddaughter Susannah BOTTS; girl Agg to granddaughter Libby DAVIS; girl Patience to granddaughter Elizabeth CARNEY

Aaron WICKLIFF .... pg 30, 28 Dec 1785, inv & appr

> Dick, Beck

John HAMMITT .... pg 33, 3 Sept 1804, acct of sales

> man James, old man Abraham to Ann HAMMITT; man Bill to William GAINES; girl Beck to Bailey POWELL

Isaac FARROW .... pg 38, 7 Feb 1804, inv & appr

> James, Seaman, Thomas, woman Betty, boy Haden

William FITZHUGH .... pg 41, 2 July 1804, inv & appr

> men Benjamin, George, woman Mary, lad Braxton, men Randolph, Mingo, girl Peggy, boy Barnett, Lucy & child Rosanna, women Fanny, Daphney, boy Reuben, child Nelly daughter of Fanny, Lucy's children Sidney, Frank, & Beverly, Roberson son of Mary

John SMITH .... pg 43, 15 Dec 1804, will

> boy Chessor to wife Elizabeth SMITH
>
> (pages 49- 52 missing)

Obed COLVERT .... pg 53, 20 Sept 1804, will

> (first part of will missing)
>
> residue of estate except Frank to be sold…assist executors…then to be free

John SMITH .... pg 55, 1 Apr 1805, inv & appr

> lad

Jabez FRYAR.. pg 57, 17 Jan 1805, inv & appr
    man Lewis

John BRIDWELL................................. pg 61, 11 May 1805, inv & appr
    men James, William, woman Lynda

William COPIN.................................pg 64, 6 Aug 1805, inv & appr
    Frank about 51 years

Thomas LEE Sr. .... pg 72, 15 Jan 1805, will
    woman Sarah

John HAMMITT ....pg 74, 23 Oct 1800 – 10 Sept 1805, estate acct
    negroes to William GAINS; Beck to Bailey POWELL; James, Abraham to Ann HAMMETT; Sandy, Moses, Nelson

Jesse EWELL .... pg 111, 4 Apr 1805, will
    Sarah & her daughter Sophia to daughter Emma

Joseph BRAWNER .... pg 115, 30 Apr 1806, inv & appr
    boy Ben, girl Jane

John CHESLEY .... pg 118, 20 May 1806, inv & appr
    Will 55 years, Sam 40, Frederick 27, Peter 20, Chloe 60, Lucy 58, Nan 55, Page 36, Margery 30, Poll 29, Anikey 35, Shadrach 13, Jacob 8, Sam Button 6, Daniel Lloyd 4, Titus 2, Henry 2, Fanny 12, Sook 10, Anna 9, Celia 8, Letty 6, Fender 8, Nell 4, Eliza 4 weeks, Gilbert 2

Gavin ADAMS.................................. pg 121, 5 May 1806, inv & appr
    woman Esther

Thomas MASON...............................pg 123, 8 Oct 1800, inv & appr
    Cyrus 65 years, Jacob 40, Tom 24, James 22, mulatto Jack 30, Frank 36, Jack 32, Will 26, Jeremiah 18, Charles 16, James Clark 14, Joe Clark 12, lame Will 12, Jenny Roley 30, Polly 25, Lucy 35, Molly 18, Daphne 28, Alice 45, Milly 15, Pompey 10, Ancilla 6, Nancy 3, Bill 3, Sam Montjoy 4, Sam 6, Bob 5, Milly 10, Lucy 7, Anne 3, Henry 1, Dinah 6 months, Winney 6 months

John PATTERSON ....pg 142, 17 Nov 1804, inv & appr
 man Osten
....pg 143, 1 July 1805, estate acct
 negroes

Major Richard Scott BLACKBURN ....
.... pg 147, 2 Mar 1805 – 19 Mar 1806, estate acct
 woman sold at public sale

Edward CARTER ....pg 148, 24 Feb 1797, will
 ½ the slaves if unborn child is a son; negroes to be sold
....pg 150, 13 Apr 1799, codicil
 1/3 part of all negros to new son

Jesse EWELL ....pg 152, 1 Sept 1806, inv & appr
 man Tom, boys Sandy, Addison, young men Daniel, Denis, small boy Armistead, old men Jim, George, woman Frank, small girls Syller, Harriet, woman Prue, small girls Elenor, Sophia, Cordelia, young woman & child, girl Lucy

Gavin ADAMS ....pg 154, 1 Sept 1806, inv & appr
 woman to Susanah ADAMS

Col. Henry PEYTON ....pg 158, 2 Nov 1781 – 26 Feb 1789, estate acct
 3 negroes to be sold at Manchester

Thomas LEE ....pg 164, 28 Aug 1806, inv & appr
 girl Molly, men Charles, Jupiter, Phil, Caesar, Newman, Abram, Jupiter, Tom, Jacob, George, Jupiter, _on__, Dick, boys Aaron, Sam, John, Jim, Edmund, Joshua, Sandy, _Domingo, Isaac, Brooks, Armistead Albert, woman & child Esther, Sukey & child Rosetta, Sall & child Sukey, old woman Jenny, young yellow Hannah, young black Hannah, Patty, Letitia, child Sophia, child Eddie, child Harriet, men Dick, Adam, Howard, boy Toby, woman Sarah

Peter COCKRELL............pg 169, 11 Aug 1803 – 4 Oct 1806, estate acct

    Nancy COCKRELL, Samuel & Sarah DANIEL their part of Maria; boy delivered Samuel DANIEL

James ANDERSON........................pg 171, 12 Mar 1806, will

    fellow Joe to son James ANDERSON

William CARR............pg 172, 19 Mar 1792 - 28 Nov 1806, estate acct

    Lucy & Aggy & their children, (pg 202), Hannah (pg 204), Winney's children (pg 205), child Joe buried (pg 207), Fame & 2 children (pg 217)

John PERCELL.....................pg 315, 2 Dec 1806, inv & appr

    men Bob, Jilson, boys Davy, Jeffery, woman Winney, girl Alce, girl Lett, boy Jess, woman Hanner, 3 children, Frank, Mariah, Mill & child Esther, girl Mary, boy Harry, Jane & child Jane, boy Alfred, girl Ann

William W. BROWN.......................pg 319, 8 Jan 1807, will

    Sarah, Stefany to daughter Mary Anne TEBBS; 14 slaves to be divided among my 3 children sons John & Thomas BROWN, & daughter Lydda BURN wife of Uriah BURN

Edward CARTER......................pg 321, 8 Sept 1806, inv & appr

    John Wall, Jane, Ambrose, Jack, Eliza, Charity, Billy Wall, Cela, Nat, Jemmy, Peggy, Wilson, Sam, Archy, Anthony, Judy, Ned, Daniel, Bob, Harry Canab, Fanny, Dick Canab, Dolly, John Canab, Nat, Judy, Celia, Milly, Jacob, Nancy superannuated, Mary, Catesby, Absalom, Polly, Abram, Manuel, Patience, Dinah, Jemmy, Wilson, Sylva, Sarah, Lemont, Lilah, Annanica, Tom, Simon, Dick, Willoughby, Charles, Anthony, Manuel, Mary, Mary Wall, Leanna, Charlotte, Clarissa, Joshua, Charity, Jesse, Joe, Edmund, Hampton, John, Jack, Nancy, Abberilla, Letty, Betty, Phillis, old Judy, Lucy, Peggy, Ellen, Sam, Charlotte, Chloe, Dick, Sam Bolling, Billy Birch, Burton, Tyll, Robin, Dinah, Nelly, Rachel, Betty, Hannah, Tabby, Esther, Amos, Phillis, Adam, Aggy, David, Beck, Mimah & young child Solomon, Delsy, Amos, Delilah, Mingo, Huly, Lige, Tom, Jesse, Nancy, Lucy, Caty, Melinda, Sally, Ruthe, Sukey, Nance, Abram, Rachel, Baker, Harry, Maria, Randolph, James, Joe, Sarah, Isaac, Mimah, Winney, Joe, Nancy, Betsy, young child Eleanor

James ANDERSON ....pg 325, 2 Feb 1807, inv & appr

Peter, William, Manewell, Bob, Easter, Phebe, Adam, Sutte, Winney, Susan

Henry Dade HOOE ....pg327, 31 July 1806, will

slaves that wife Jane points out to be sold

William DOWNMAN .... pg 329, 25 Jan 1807, will

girl Molly youngest child of Nanz to cousin Margaret HANCOCK; girl Harriet to Frances MUSCHETT daughter of James MUSCHETT; man George & Roses his wife and their child to Fleming BATES for 2 years at that time secure to them their liberty; Bob & Willis to Enoch WARD

William BROWN ....pg 330, 4 Mar 1807, inv & appr

fellows Elijah, James, John, Bill, boys Buckner, John, woman Hannah and children Strother & Patience, girl Hester, small girl Sally, girl Sophia, small boy Peter, woman & child Ligge

John BRIDWELL....................................pg 335, 4 Apr 1807, estate acct

man William to John BRIDWELL of John; man James to William SINGER

James GRINSTEAD .... pg 338, 23 Jan 1807, will

Lib, Samuel, Lucy to wife Elizabeth GRINSTEAD, to be sold at her death; girl Violet to son John GRINSTEAD; girl Hagar to son Leonard GRINSTEAD; girl Henna to daughter Jane BARKER; boy Tom to daughter Elizabeth KEES; girl Sophia to daughter Susanna SPILMAN; girl Sharlot to son William GRINSTEAD; Fanny, Cornelius to daughter Lynna GRINSTEAD; Jesse, Mariah, Lewis, Hanner, Davy, Jarrett and any increase to be sold

Henry D. HOOE... pg 340, 4 May 1807, inv & appr

men Peter, Henry, girls Martha, Sidney, Milly & child Betty, girls Cate, Ann, woman Milly, Hanner & child Daniel, Pat & child John, men Nace, John, boy Edmund

Richard GARNER................................pg 343, 14 Mar 1807, inv & appr

woman Diner, boy Gerrard, girl Mary, woman Milly

James GWATKIN .... pg 343, no date, will

   man Jesse son of Hagar to brother Charles GWATHIN; choice of one of Hagar's daughters to niece Elizabeth GWATHIN; girl Lucinda given to daughter Margaret by her grandmother

David JAMESON .... pg 345, 9 May – 6 July 1807, estate acct

   Bob, Nancy, Peter, Sinah – legacies delivered

James GRINSTEAD .... pg 347, 25 June 1807, inv & appr

   Jess, Mariah, Sabrina, Hanner, Samuel, Davy, Lewis, Lucy, boy Jerret

Isaac DAVIS .... pg 348, 13 Jan 1803 – 1 Jan 1807, estate acct

   hire of slaves

John GIBSON .... pg 352, 10 Dec 1806, will

   exceutors to make choice out of my Slave Estate of 7 young working hands…4 to be men, the rest women…

.... pg 355, 25 July 1807, codicil

   Rachel and her son William to be emancipated

Michael LYNN .... pg 360, 27 Apr 1805, will

   woman Nell to daughter Elizabeth ARNELL; Sam to be divided between my 2 sons Moses LYNN & John LYNN

Lee CONWAY .... pg 361, 9 Aug – 23 June 1806, estate acct

   negro sold by auction

James GREEN .... pg 363, 5 Oct 1807, inv & appr

   Sara, Daniel, Gilson, William, Cease, Ben

John GIBSON .... pg 365, 12 Nov 1807, inv & appr

   At Staly Run:

   Will, Moses, Phil, Daniel, Jesse, John, Ned, Cyrus, Willoughby, George, Cloe & children Stepney, Easter, Cumford, Edmund, Matilda; Liddy & child Barney, Aaron, Darcus & child Charlotte, Nanny, Winson, Agnes & child Cila, Charles, Minny & child Harrison, Hannah, Nelly & children Easter, Harriet, Henry, Sucky, Lizy, Mary & child Isabell, Delia, Harry

John GIBSON ....pg 367, 30 Nov 1807, inv & appr

Fairfax County:

men Leny, Sampson, Jenny & child, Fanny & 3 children, Henny & 4 children, Lucy, Lucy, Winna, Ben, Juber, Hanner & 2 children, Clary & child, Penny, Charles, Alsey

Col. Thomas BLACKBURN .... pg 369, 15 June 1807, will

Jim, Hannah to grandson Bushrod W. BLACKBURN

Francis POWELL .... pg 371, 8 Dec 1801, inv & appr

girl

Col. Thomas BLACKBURN .... pg 372, 4 Jan 1808, inv & appr

Gabriel, Moses, Nancy & one of her children sold; John, Pompey, Peter, Judy Cook, Sam, Nell & 2 children, Allen, Nancy & 3 children, Gabriel, Hester & child, Moses, Roger

Col. Thomas BLACKBURN .... pg 375, 27 Jan 1808, inv & appr

Rachel 55 years, Anthony 60, Hannah 15, Betty 9, Jim 15, Rachel 7

Charles H. MUSCHETT ....pg 376, 19 Feb 1808, inv & appr

John, old John & wife, Moses, Mary, Charles, Anne, Elizabeth, Dick, Jenny, Polly, Tacey

SIDE NOTE: John & wife, Moses, Polly, Dick, Elizabeth, Jenny, Charles were held in trust by Charles H. MUSCHETT dec'd for the late Elizbeth H. MUSCHETT & at her death to descend to Edward MUSCHETT

William GRAYSON .... pg 379, 28 Jan 1808, inv & appr

Bob, Baccus, Betty, Spencer, old Irish?

Matthew HARRISON .... pg 382, 12 Dec 1807, inv & appr

Prince William:

Ruth 45 years, boy Moses, George 60, George 23, Joan 6, John 4, Lewis 8, Sal 20, Lucy 35, Mariel 2, Lizza 25, Kate 12

Matthew HARRISON .... pg 387, 22 Dec 1807, inv & appr

  Loudoun:

  Jacob, Jenny, Alfred, Abraham, Ara, Henry

  Rap Goose Creek Plantation:

  Mary, Betty, Matthew, Sarah Ann, Aaron, Anna, Nathan, Margaret, Susan, Andrew, Sharlot, Luke, Jack, Frank, Will, Susan, Rachel

Peter SMITH .... pg 389, Dec 1892 - 11 Jan 1808, estate acct

  ...after negroes belonging to P. SMITH's estate, negro belonging to the estate, sale of Lucy, boy

William CROSBY .... pg 390, 5 Apr 1808, inv & appr

  Peter, Enoch, Daniel, Harry, Sarah, Serena sold; man Haden; woman Nanny sold

Jeremiah DOWELL .... pg 392, 4 Jan 1808, inv & appr

  2 women, 1 girl, 3 boys

George KITCHEN .... pg 395, 29 Feb 1808, estate acct

  boys Shadrack, Lewis to William WHITE; wench & child to David RENNOW (RENOE?); Dick taken by Mathews to John OVERALL? & sold

Frances DICKINSON .... pg 397, Dec 1807, inv & appr

  man Joe

Edward CARTER .... pg 401, 18 Nov 1803, codicil to will

  5 males & 5 females to daughter (not named, born a few days ago)

Townshend DADE .... pg 410, 3 Nov 1808, will

  slaves can be sold to pay debts; Matilda & child Thompson, girl Araminta to daughter Elizabeth; Heziah, Juliana to daughter Verlinda I. WASHINGTON; girl Maria to daughter Ann; boy to son Langhorn

Phillip DAWES .... pg 415, 21 Dec 1808, will

  Caty, Frank, Robert to wife

Richard GARNER .... pg 416, 2 Jan 1809, inv & appr

>woman & 2 children, old woman

Richard GARNER .... pg 417, 16 June 1806, estate acct

>negroes

Townshend DADE .... pg 418, 3 Dec 1808, inv & appr

>Phil, Harry, Davey, Brooks, George, Daniel, Ben, Tom, woman Sophia, boy George, Sarah, Molly & child Martha, Keziah, child Tom, Frances, George son of Frances, Solomon, Jacob, Frances, child Lucinda, Mary, Jane youngest child of Frank, Matile & young child, boy Davy, Sally, Hester, girl Sophia, Winney, Sucky, Bonaparte, Franklin, old Janney, Araminta, Maria, Betty, Evelina, Johnston, Townshend

Jane HUTCHINSON .... pg 422, 5 Jan 1809, will

>man Nelson to be sold

Henry Dade HOOE .... pg 423, 10 Jan 1809, sale acct

>boy Edmund to William SMITH; man Peter to Enoch JEMMISON; Pat & her 2 children Kate & John to Francis JOHNSTON; man John to Nathaniel TRIPLETT; Hannah & child, girl Sidney to Benjamin GEORGE; man Nace to John MADDOX; man Henry to Gerrand ALEXANDER; Milly & 2 children to Enoch JEMMISON; old woman to Aaron GRIGSBY; girl Ann to William SHAW

James WHITE .... pg 425, 27 Oct 1801, will

>Daphney to be free at my death

.... pg 426, 1 Feb 1803, codicil to will

>Daphney be a slave & equally divided with other personal property

Thomas Pratt HOOE .... pg 427, 30 Dec 1808, will

>man Moses to father Bernard HOOE Sr.; James, Manuel now hired out may be sold, also 5 negroes hired out which belonged to wife Susan before she was married

David LEE .... pg 432, 17 Mar 1809, will

>negroes to be sold at death of wife Margaret LEE

Obed CALVERTZ .... pg 433, 23 May 1809, inv & appr

 young woman & child

Mary HOOE .... pg 435, 29 May 1809, inv & appr

 men Burdett, John Cole, Ausburn, boy Gustavus, man Ben Coal, girls Cate, Charlotte, boy Jesse, girls __m, Dinah, Lavina, boy Charles, girls Esther, Sarah, Cecy, Mary, boys Emanuel, Henson, girls Jane, Celia

John GRANT .... pg 438, 1798- 1804, estate acct

 negroes

Susanna THARP .... pg 442, 12 June 1809, will

 men Jacob, Jesse, Richard to children John STEWART & Nancy CHICK

Mary WALLACE .... pg 443, 2 Apr 1809, will

 Nancy Taylor & daughters Jane, Elisa, Ann, & Hannah be emancipated; James Wilson to be freed provided he serve the present year for which he is hired; boy Charles Mitchell to sister Mrs. Martha JAMES; little girl Betsy Mitchell to niece Mary Wallace MACRAE; Nancy Taylor's 2 eldest daughters Jane & Elisa to serve 4 years bondage to sister M. Euphan WASHINGTON and then be free

Henry D. HOOE .... pg 445, May 1807 – 25 Nov 1808, estate acct

 girl Martha sold;…after the negroes was (sic) sold

John Thornton FITZHUGH .... pg 446, 5 Jan 1809, will

 George HELM's part with the slaves…slaves given to them to sons John & George HELM & daughter Frances TEBB; Lewis to daughter Frances TEBB; to John his choice of a negro from mother's dower; rest of slaves to sons Lina HELM, Francis Thornton & Phillip; all the dower slaves to be equally divided among my children

John PERCELL .... pg 449, 1807 – 6 Mar 1808, estate acct

 residue of slaves to be sold

WILL BOOK K
1809-1816

Mark THARP .... pg 1, 19 Aug 1809, inv & appr

    old woman Cate, men Jesse, Jacob, Dick

James EWELL .... pg 3, 19 July 1809, will

    all negroes I possess & hold in consequence of my marriage to wife – Williamson, Henna, Sandy, Harriet, Dick, Rose, Cordelia, George, Edmund and at her death to son James BALL; all negroes on the plantation Greenville to son James BALL; man little George & all negroes on the land he now lives to son Charles; Immanuel, Moses, Patt, Aaron & all negroes on the land he now lives to son Solomon; Rose & negroes on the land he now lives to son Jesse; negroes mentioned in deed of trust to Solomon & Jesse EWELL in her behalf to daughter Marianne COMPTON; woman Lavina to granddaughter Maryann Mariah HEATH; girl Kitty to granddaughter Marianne WEEMS; little Hagar & her children Mimah & Agathy to son Jesse; boy Steven to grandson James Ewell HEATH

David LEE .... pg 6, 7 Aug 1809, inv & appr

    Joe, Bob, Anthony, Jenoral, George, Jesse, Roger, Charles, Hannah, Husley, Jamima, Henny, Susanna, Lucy, Esther, Nancy, Patience, Linney

Ignatius M. WHEELER .... pg 8, 10 Nov 1809, inv & appr

    Thomas, Verlinda, Joseph, Hanny, Carline, Ned

John MURRAY .... pg 10, 1 Jan 1810, inv & appr

    Daniel, Dick, Fanny

Bernard HOOE Jr. .... pg 14, 3 Oct 1809, will

    2 male slaves & 2 female slaves above the age of 16 to eldest son Bernard, 2nd son Richard, & 3rd son John; a female slave between age of 12 & 20 to each daughter; Lewis, Matilda & their children Daniel & Grace, big Judy, Dinah, Jesse, Moses Cate, Mary the younger, David to wife

Levi Scott .... pg 21, 3 Apr 1810, will

    woman Charity, Milly, Harriet to wife Ann SCOTT; girl Eliza, boy Henry to daughter Henrietta Price SCOTT; girl Mary to son Richard Price SCOTT; boy Stephen to son Levi SCOTT

Phillip DAWE .... pg 23, 6 Feb 1809, inv & appr

    man Frank, Caty, Robert to widow; Lizzy, Jenny, Nell, Lewis, Harriet 2 weeks old, born in June 1810

Francis TENNILL .... pg 26, 30 Apr 1810, estate sale

    Tom to Garner FORTUNE; Milly & child, Bill, Harry, Nancy, Eljah children of Milly to George TENNILL

Levi SCOTT .... pg 27, 3 July 1810, inv & appr

    women Milly, Charity, lad Stephen, girls Harriet, Eliza, Mary, boy Henry (pg 34)

James FAGANS .... pg 39, 10 June 1810, will

    boys Cornelius, Bill to sister Jenny FAGANS; woman Milly to sister Margaret FAGANS

James GWATKIN .... pg 41, Dec 1810, inv & appr

    John 49 years, Frank 49, Maria 48, Siller 48, Hagar 45, Moses 30, Juliet 26, Ramos 24, Lewis 23, Ned 21, Hester 19, Alce 18, Jeffery 18, Reuben 16, Caleb 14, Tom 13, Lotty 10, Amy 10, Charlotte 10 Ally 8, William 4, Charles 4, Jane 2, Thornton 1, Latitia 1, Frederick 1

Edward CARTER .... pg 43, 12 Apr 1806 – 5 Sept 1810, estate acct

    negros; Joe, Harry, sale of E. CARTER's 8 negroes (to WOLFORD?); boy Catesby to Mrs. THOMPSON, gift from her relation Edward BARTER; slaves sold 10 Jan 1810: Tom & wife Patty & children; Lucy & children to J. CARTER; Mary Wall & child, one handed Mary, Charity, Baker to B. BROOKE; girl Dilsey to Richard B. ALEXANDER (Sept 1810)

Elizabeth NAILER .... pg 66, 16 Dec 1802 – 6 Feb 1810, estate acct

    Suck, Nell, Beck

Jacob ADAMS .... pg 67, 5 Nov 1810, inv & appr

    woman, girl

Major Townshend DADE .... pg 72, 4 – 6 Jan 1809, hire of slaves

    Ben, Winney, Suckey, Franklin, Davy, Nate?, George Washington, Sarah, Brooks, Molly & child, Matilda & child, Franky & 2 children, Sophia, George, Daniel & family, Sophia, Hester, Betty & children, Maria, Harry, Davy, Keziah, Tom
.... pg 72, 29 Dec 1809, sale of slaves

    Sarah, Brooks to John H. WASHINGTON; Suckey to William A.G. DADE; Winney to Benson LYNN; Molly & child to Michael KEOGH; Betty & child, Johnston, Evelina to William STARKE; Sally to Benjamin GEORGE
.... pg 76, 1 Jan 1811, sale of slaves

    Ben to William A.G. DADE; Lucinda to David JAMESON; Polly to Benson LYNN; Bonaparte to Presly GILL

Moses DAVIS .... pg 76, 3 Jan 1807, will

    all slaves to wife Libbey DAVIS

Matthew WHITING .... pg 77, 6 Feb 1806, will

    ½ negroes to wife; Ciller & her children, Eliza & her children, Fanny the granddaughter of Peg may fall into the division & set apart for my wife; ½ slaves to Matthew Whiting BROOKE Jr. son of W. Edmund BROOKE, Jack, Jerry, Peg to fall into his division

William CARTER .... pg 81, 14 Oct 1810 – 29 Jan 1811, estate acct

    negroes

Moses DAVIS .... pg 82, 4 Feb 1811, inv & appr

    Dennis 28 years, Sharper 38, Susan 24, Easter 28, Adam 7, Maggy 5, boy Sandy 3, Mary 3, Peggy 3 months

William CARTER .... pg 84, 14 Nov 1810, inv & appr

    woman Betty, man James, woman Meriah, man George, boys Henry, Samuel, girl Leviney, Alexander, Alpherd (Alfred?), William, Thomas

Thomas LINCOCKS .... pg 89, 7 Jan 1811, inv & appr

> man Dick, lad Harry, men John, Jim, women Rose, Cate, Esther, boys Lewis, Bill, George, girls Charlotte, Clary, boys Jeffry, Sam, Nelson, girl Ceal, boy Mark, girl Sinah

John T. FITZHUGH .... pg 91, 15 Jan 1810, inv & appr

> woman Nelly, girl Ann, boy Craven, woman Winney, girls Lucy, Suckey, Leney, woman Delilah, boy Emanuel, woman Virgin, boy Daniel, girls Alice, Jenny, woman Isabella, girl Matilda, woman Juda, girls Lizy, Tabithy, Suckey, boys John, Jacob, woman Charlotte, girl Verlinda, boys Charles, Osmond, girl Delphia, woman Winney, girls Betty, Peggy, Daphne, boy Billy, girls Hannah, Nelly, woman Hannah, men Dennis, Davy, Will, Arthur, Reuben, Frederick, Ben, Adam, Frank, Moses, Tom, Willis, Jack, Henry, Lewis

Benjamin ADIE .... pg 96, 4 Mar 1811, inv & appr

> Harry, Tom, Charles, Jiles, Sam, Reuben, Job, Sally, Mathew, Rose, Patience, Lyda, Lyna Nelly

William BUTLER .... pg 97, 9 Apr 1811, inv & appr

> woman & 2 children

Elizabeth WHITING .... pg 99, 29 Apr 1811, will

> girls Sarah, Celer granddaughters of my woman Pegg to niece Cecelia G. BROOKE wife of Matthew W. BROOKE of Page Land, then Sarah to her niece Cecelia Beverly WHITING and Celer to Ann daughter of Lewis B. WHITING; girl Eliza daughter of Peg & all her future increase except Letty Felicia Corbin to niece Eliza Francis CARTER; girl Fanny daughter of Peg to niece Elizabeth ALEXANDER wife of Gerard ALEXANDER; a girl each to nieces Levinia BROWN, Sarah SCOTT, & Maria WHITING; husband in his lifetime verbally gave to my dear little Edmonia BROOKE the little girl Letty Felicia Corbin granddaughter of Pegg, said girl shall belong to her; the above named negoes that are specially bequeathed are all descended from Peg; boy Zachary son of Pegg, Zachary's wife Lizza & her child Fenton Mercer, boy Jerry, little boy Richard grandson of Peg to nephew Matthew Whiting BROOKE; the slaves not before given away to be divided among nieces Martha Lavinia BROWN & all the granddaughters of my sister BROWN & may be sold

Benjamin GEORGE ....pg 102, 1 Jan 1811, will

> lad Lewis, woman Lysha to wife Hannah GEORGE; girl Mary to daughter Frances GEORGE

Townshend DADE estate ....pg 103, 1808 - 1811, exec acct

> negroes

Baily STORK & Eliza his wife vs John H. WASHINGTON exec ....7 Mar 1811, in Chancery

> ordered to settle acct

Major T. DADE.............pg 105, 12 Nov 1808 – 25 July 1811, estate acct

> negroes; release of George; Phil; crying sale of Franky & her 2 children; Tom; sale of negroes; sale of Franky & her 2 children to James FERGUSON

................................pg 111, 1810, acct of hires

> Washington, George, Lucy, Davy, Matt, Franklin, Sophia, G. Blackston, Fanny, Hester, Ben, Tom, Phil, Keziah, Sophia, Davy, Harry, Daniel & family

Thomas HARRISON......................pg 112, 31 Aug 1810, will

> boy Sandy son of Cinthy to son Philip; young woman Maria of Ciller, girl Sharlott of Lucy to daughter Betsey; young woman Celia of Lucy, girl Fanny of Lucy, to daughter Sally; woman Cinthy to wife Sarah HARRISON; other slaves to work the land

Capt. Bernard HOOE, Jr.....................pg 118, 7 May 1810, inv & appr

> Han's Farm:
>
> Charles, Tom, big Mary & child, Janny, Lucy, Eliza, Matilda, Manuel, Abraham, Rachel, Robin
>
> Bushy Ridge Farm:
>
> Teny, Daniel, Beck, Mary, Dudley, Malinda, James, Will, Harry, Kitty, Winney

Locust Grove:

Jesse, Matilda, Annecha, Warner, Lewis, Bacchus, Judah & child, Peggy, Mariah, Rose, David, Hannah, Shadrach, Dinah, Lucy, Alse, little Mary & child, Moses, Cate

Cancer Farm:

Edenborough, Abraham, Patience & child, Nancy, Selah, Grace, Presley, Beverly, Betty, Beck, Daniel, Tom, Samuel; Berkeley to have 6 years 6 months to serve

heirs of Thomas FAULKNER .... pg 122, 1799 – 27 June 1810, estate acct

Gabriel; 14 negroes hired; Gabriel Sr., Dennis, Charles, Fanny, Gabriel Jr.; sale of Gabriel; valuation of Dennis, Charles, Gabriel Jr., Fanny, Harry

John McMILLIAN, Jr. .... pg 126, 18 Oct 1811, will

Betty daughter to Rachel, Maria daugher to Mary, Alfred son to Winney to Sarah KEICH

Jesse BARRON .... pg 128, 4 Mar 1811, inv & appr

James 30 years, Cyrus 25, Dick 12, Cloe 60, Mary 50, Amy 20, Lucy 15, Dolly 17

John LANSDOWN Jr. .... pg 132, 31 Dec 1811, will

4 negroes to daughter Elizaeth DICKERSON wife of Edward DICKERSON

Thomas HARRISON .... pg 133, 3 Mar 1811, codicil to will

boy Henry to be sold; girls Mariah, Ann, Sharlott to daughter Elizabeth; girl Cecelia to daughter Sarah

Isaac FARROWS .... pg 133, 9 – 10 Mar 1804, acct of sales

boy Haden, Thomas, James, Betty

Rev. Thomas HARRISON .... pg 138, 3 Feb 1812, inv & appr

Stephen 35 years, Frank 25, Rodger 40, Matthew 24, Ben 20, Henry 12, Stafford 10, Matilda 17, Cecelia 15, Janney 12, Anne 10, Charlotte

10, Fanny 10, Lucy 42 & her child, Cinthya 42, boy Sandy, Maria 15, old woman Moll

William SHAW .... pg 141, 13 Jan 1812, inv & appr

Bob & Sarah his wife, James & wife Betty, woman Pru, Lucy & child, William, Joe, Phil, Matilda, Robin & wife Juda, Lott & child, Ben, boys James, James

James DALTON .... pg144, 21 July 1811, will

man Ben to granddaughter Katy CASH oldest daughter of my daughter Elizabeth LEE

Henry HAMPTON .... pg 144, 11 Nov 1811, inv & appr

woman Kitty

John LANSDOWN .... pg 146, 6 Mar 1812, inv & appr

woman Jane, boy Joseph, woman Rachel, small boy David

Matthew WHITING .... pg 147, 19 Nov 1811, inv & appr

Joe, Peg, Dick, Edmund, Zachariah, Matt, Eliza, Fanny, Letty Felicia Corbin, Richard, John Oliphant, Gustavus, Lavinia, Sarah, Nancy Williams, Lucy, Nancy, Hannah, Harriet, Charlotte, Henry, Lizza, Charles Fenton Mercer, Jack, Jerry, Bob, Sam, old Joe, Dolly, Dodson, old Phill, young Phil, Dinah, Beck, Grace, Milly, Godfrey, Willis, Mary, Milly, Jesse, Michael Sr., Michael Jr., George, Mongo

Elizabeth WHITING .... pg 149, 19 Nov 1812, inv & appr

Eliza, Letty Felicia Corbin, John Oliphant, Gustavus, Lavinia, Sarah, Nancy Williams, Richard, Fanny, Zachary, Lizza, Fenton Mercer, Milly, George, Godfrey, Sam, Matt, Milly, Jesse

Edward CARTER .... pg 150, 1 Oct 1810 - 31 Mar 1812, estate acct

Simon sold 1 Jan 1812

Gilbert J. MOXLEY .... pg 151, 2 Dec 1811, inv & appr

Dick, Daniel, Len, Nancy, Letty, James, George, Andrew, Polly, Judy

Capt. John M. WILLIAM .... pg 152, no date, inv & appr

> Ben, Charles, Bob Norman, Harry, Davy, Pompey, Bob Newton, Stephen, Fanny & her child Armistead, Sophia, Fanny & her child Ben, Eda, Gusta, Henny, Flora, Lucy, old big Hannah, Molly Ramsay, Nancy, old little Hannah, old Hagar, old Frederick, Rachel & child John, Harriet, Eliza, Lewis, Bernard, Cato, Janney; girls Betty, Maria, boy Alfred to Sally KEECH

William ROBINSON .... pg 158, 1 July 1812, inv & appr

> woman Lucy (pg 163)

John LANSDOWN .... pg 170, 3 Nov 1812, debts due

> woman

James FEAGAN .... pg 185, 29 Sept 1810, inv & appr

> man Thaddeus, woman Milly, boys Neale, Billy

Sarah FEAGAN .... pg 186, 29 Sept 1810, inv & appr

> Daphney & child Guy, boys Charles, Amos, man Guy

James GRAHAM .... pg 188, 7 Dec 1812, inv & appr

> Adam 50 years, Frederick 35, Isaac 22, Margret 25, Dainey 8, Mima 5, Harry 4

John MACRAE .... pg 191, 14 Nov 1812, inv & appr

> Charles, Billy, Sam, Abraham, George, Nace, Dennis, James, Ned, Jack F., Jack H., Jack M., Thomas, William W., William R., Fanny's son, Washington, Richard, Sandy, Argyle, Daniel, Addison, Jesse, Amy, Suckey, Matilda, Letitia, Maria, Polly, Fanny, Grace, Courtney, Rachel K., Judah, Mary Ann, Rachel Dix, Kitty, Esther, Nancy, Ann, Grace's daughter, Polly's daughter, Lucy C.'s daughter, Amy

Maryann THORNTON .... pg 203, 3 Mar 1813, will

> girl Ann to orphaned granddaughter Susan CHAPMAN; Tom, Mary Ann to youngest daughter Sarah CHAPMAN

Jesse BARRON .... pg 205, 24 June 1811 - 22 Mar 1813, estate acct

> negroes, Cyrus

James WHITE Sr..............pg 211, 8 Dec 1812 – 7 June 1813, estate acct
.... pg 214, 4 Sept 1809, acct of sales

   old woman to John GILL Jr.; man George to William H. TEBBS; man Harry to John CAMPBELL

John LANSDOWN........................ pg 218, 1812 – June 1813, estate acct

   negroes

William DOWNMAN.......................... pg 224, 16 Apr 1807, inv & appr

   men Osburn, John, women Lydia, Grassy, Nan, Lavina & child, George his wife & child for 18 months, girl Winney, boys Lewis, Billy, Daniel, woman Celia, man Bob, woman Kate & child, girls Hannah, Sally, boy Galba, man Conway
.... pg 230, 5 June 1809, slave sale

   Conway to George COLERT; Winney to G. HUBER; Celia to B. RICHMOND

Sarah CHALMERS.......................... pg 233, 10 May 1813, will

   Willoughby, Bet, Harriet, Milly, Edmond to Elizabeth Battaile STROTHER; Anthony, Ralph to Ann HOLLIDAY; Mary, boy Dick to Sarah DAVIS; bond for purchase of girl Lissy to sister Carolina GREGORY; Caesar, Johnston, Lucy, Jacob, Suckey to Jane EWELL wife of Alfred EWELL

Thomas LEACHMAN .... pg 236, 23 Aug 1799 - , estate acct

   woman's services for Agga in child bed, child Mitchell

(pages 237 & 238; 240 & 241 missing between Thomas LEACHMAN & William CARR)

William CARR the younger..................... pg 238, 7 Jan 1802, estate acct

   negroes; Jim, Jesse sold

James WHITE Jr. ....pg 247, 1809 - Dec 1812, inv & appr

   hire of Lewis, Bob, Jack, Winney
....pg 248

   certain negroes sold

....pg 249, 30 Dec 1811, sale of negroes

    Jack to Carr BAILEY; Winney & child Alford to Anderson KEBBLE

James WIATT .... pg 249, 5 Oct 1813, inv & appr

    old Harry, Daphney & child, Fender & child, Esther, Dick, Henry, Windsor

Levi SCOTT .... pg 254, 15 Feb 1813, estate acct

    Charity, Milly, Harriet to Ann SCOTT; Mary to Richard Price SCOTT; Stephen to Levi SCOTT; Eliza, Henry to Henrietta Price SCOTT

John WILLIAMS .... pg 258, 6 Dec 1813, inv & appr

    Mary & child Esther, Agga, Cat, Jess, Gowin, Henry, old Kent & Clara his wife

John GIBSON .... pg 267, 8 Sept 1807, inv & appr

    Peter, Ned, Anthony, Moses, Amy

Elizabeth WHITING .... pg 268, 5 July 1811- 20 June 1812, estate acct

    sale of negroes; ...M.W. BROOKE for the slaves allotted to him...; George, Sam to E. BROOKE; Godfrey to J. BOOTMAN; Milly to William RODGERS; old Milly to her husband; Jesse to Phil ALEXANDER; Jerry to John LOVE; Matt to William HAMPTON

James WIATT .... pg 273, 15 Nov 1813, inv & appr

    man Tom

James WIATT .... pg 274, 1 Jan 1814, hire of negroes

    men Windsor, Tom, Harry, girls Esther, Fender, girl & 3 children, boy

Posey D. GRANT .... pg 275, 7 Feb 184, inv & appr

    woman Maria

John R. WRIGHT .... pg 278, 8 Feb 1814, inv & appr

    man Jesse, women Charity, Maria, boy Sandy, girl Mary

William HORTON .... pg 280, 2 Oct 1809, estate acct

>boarding 7 negro children for: 3 years, 9 months, 1 year 9 months, 18 months, 2 years, 4 years; hires of negroes; Nathaniel HORTON's dividend of negroes: man Jered, woman Judah, child Lucy, old woman Nan; James HORTON's dividend: man Henry Dade, woman Phebe, girl Delila; Cravon HORTON's dividend: man Jack, woman Jinny, boy Dennis; Darcus HORTON's dividend: man Ben boy Shadrach, woman Sal; Snowden HORTON's dividend: man Henry, boy Ralph, girl Milly; William HORTON's dividend: man Charles, woman Lizzy, boy James

Athaliah ROBERTSON .... pg 283, 3 Dec 1812, will

> man Daniel to daughter Lucy ROBERTSON; woman Suckey to daughter Elenor ROBERTSON

James DALTON .... pg 284, 1812 - 1814, estate acct

> Ben

William ALEXANDER .... pg 286, 10 Sept 1813, will

> Seymour, Sawney, Nero, Dick, Jess, Will of Juno, Polly, big Lucy, Hester, Sidney, Sukey, George, Mary, twins of Polly to son Laurence Gibbons ALEXANDER; Letty, Nancy, Kitty, Lewis, William to granddaughter Jane Alexander SLAUGHTER; Letty for use of wife Sigesmunda Mary ALEXANDER; (female) Frank

Benjamin COOPER .... pg 288, 4 Apr 1814, inv & appr

> man Sanford, boy Mason, woman Phoebe, Pat & child, men Sam, Moses, boy Watt, girl Liza, boy James, boy Burr, small girls Kitty, Lucy

Francis MONTGOMERY .... pg 298, 27 July 1814, will

(There must be some pages missing as the following will seems to start without a first page. Lots of repetition, difficult to follow.)

> Jesse to nephew James LEWIS; woman Lettice & her unborn child, girl Rachel to niece Catey LEWIS; man John to nephew Searles LEWIS; Charles, Jenny to nephew Francis Montgomery LEWIS; man David to niece Susanna LEWIS; man Nace to niece Nancy LEWIS; woman Winney to niece Betsy OBANNON & her husband Joseph OBANNON & lend to her 2/3 of the children that girl Mime may have;

the other 1/3 of Mime's children to be divided to niece Anna LEWIS' heirs; boy Archy to niece Sally LEWIS; boy Dennis to niece Harriot LEWIS; girl Siller to niece Louisa LEWIS & man Jesse after death of her parents; boy Travis to nephew Henry LEWIS; man Daniel to James LEWIS; man Harry to Frances COLLENS; servant Milly Starks to be set free but any children to remain in the estate; same for Sally Starks, Patty Starks, & Mary Ann Starks; Tom to be bound out at age of 15 and freed at 21; man Bill, all Lidda's children, to nephew William M. LEWIS; man Luck, woman Lucy & all children of Hanner & Milly to Francis M. LEWIS; at age 40 Hanner to live with her children that have been freed

Elizabeth TYLOR ....pg 306, 5 Nov 1814, inv & appr

men Edmond, Anderson, boys Joshua, Andrew, Alfred, Armistead, Bradley, William, Talliaferro, John, woman Jenny, Silvy & youngest child, girls Harriet, Amy, Silvy, Delila

Stephen K. KING ....pg 307, 4 Sept 1814, will

(first page or more missing)

man Nelson & wife Darky, Charlotte to wife Pricilla; man Phil to son John; man Nelson to son Benjamin; girl Lucy, boy Noah to daughter Theodosia; woman Delph & her daughter Mary to son Ephraim; girl Sophia to son Alfred; woman Anna to daughter Catharine; boy Grayson to son Stephen; boy Jess to daughter Precilla; Melinda to be divided between 2 last named children

Richard TOMLIN .... pg 315, 10 May 1814, inv & appr

Charles, Phil, Dolly, Alfred, John

Thomas HARRISON ..... pg 329, 28 June 1811 - 31 Dec 1814, estate acct

hire of negro belonging to Mrs. STARKE; negroes, Matilda (her child died), Betsy & Sally slaves?, Ben, Benjamin sold, Matthew

Townshend DADE ....pg 339, 8 Aug 1811 - 29 Oct 1814, estate acct

negroes, Matilda, Fanny, Harry, old Jenny, Davy, Sophia & her infant, Phil

.... pg 34_, 31 Dec 1810 for 1811, hires of negroes

Sophia, Kegeah, George Blackstone, Esther, Phil, Franklin, Harry, Davy, Nat, George Turtle, Daniel & family, Tom

.... pg 349, 28 Dec 1811 for 1812, hires of negroes

Sophia, Kegeah & child, George, Matilda & child, George Blackstone, Daniel & Family, Davy, Nat, Franklin, Esther, Harry, Tom, Phil

.... pg 349, 31 Dec 1812 for 1813, hires of negroes

Harry, Davy, Nat, George Blackstone, Tom, George Turtle, Esther, Daniel, Keziah, Matilda, Sophia, Phil

Francis MONTGOMERY .... pg 352, 7 Nov 1814, inv & appr

men Elijah, Charles, Harry, Jack, Daniel, Bill, Dave, Jess, Nace, boys Arch, Dennis, Travis, girls Winney, Jane, Siller, woman Luce, woman & 2 children Rachael & Sarah

Mary NEALE .... pg 357, 13 Aug 1813, will

Ben, Job, John, Bob, Charles, Lewis, Westwood, Washington, Ben, Nancy, Polly, Melinda to only son Lewis M. SMITH; Daniel was sold; Dick, Cary, Cate, Peter, Suck to only daughter Nancy wife of William PROSSER; boy Aaron to granddaughter Mary Nelson NEALE; girl Fanny to grandson Richard H. NEALE; boy Madison to grandson William P.L. NEALE; girl Dinah to granddaughter Elizabeth J. PROSSER

Richard ALLEN .... pg 358, 9 Feb 1815, inv & appr

man Sipeo

George RAINIE .... pg 361, 11 July 1813, will

boy Jesse to son Samuel Symour RAINIE at his mother's decease

Thomas BARRETT .... pg 363, 6 Mar 1815, inv & appr

Jim 5 years 7 months, Nuly & children Mary 3 & Easter, old woman 65

William ALEXANDER .... pg 365, 6 Mar 1815, inv & appr

Harry, Sall, Sally, Nat, Sook, David, Frank, Nelson, Fanny, Matilda, Mahala, Lucinda, Nelson, Jim, Joshua, Frank, Joshua, Jonathan, Eliza, Thomson, Jacob, John, Let, Linus, Jacob, Peter, Charles, Dishman, Kitty, Aaron, Alce; Jane A. SLAUGHTER's legacy: Letty, Nancy, Kitty, Lewis, William, Austin

William DAVIS..pg 366, 10 Feb 1815, will

    man Aaron to son-in-law Derby BYRNE; Moses, Joseph, Eve to be sold

Stephen KING ....pg 368, 25 Mar 1815, inv & appr

    women Delfy, Darky, Charlotte, girl Luce, men Phil, Nelson, boys Jess, Grayson, Noah, girls Mary, Sophia, Malinda, Levina

James LUTTLE ....pg 369, 6 Mar 1815, inv & appr

    boy Ellis

Ann DEALY ....pg 371, 7 Oct 1814 – Mar 1815, estate acct

    woman, girl to George FLORENCE

Richard COLE........................... pg 376, 4 Apr 1815, inv & appr

    William, John, Benjamin, Sylvia, Moses, Lettice

Jesse EVENS............................pg 384, 21 Sept 1814, inv & appr

    man James, woman Mary, girls Matilda, Linnney, boy Charles, girls Sarah, Ann; girl Polly put into __ by Francis JACKSON

John KEYS.................................pg 386, 1 Aug 1815, inv & appr

    girl Sal

Samuel JACKSON ....pg 388, 28 Feb 1815, will

    man Moses to be sold; London, Robin, David, woman Sila to wife Mary JACKSON; boy Mason to son George Washington JACKSON; boy Joshua to son John Farrow JACKSON; girl Matilda to daughter Sarah STROTHER; boy Jacob to daughter Libby DAVIS; boy Phillip to daughter Susanna LANGFIT; girl Hester to daughter Jane JACKSON; girl Charlotte to daughter Elizabeth JACKSON

George N. BROWN .... pg 396, 2 Jan 1815, inv & appr

    men Lewis, Tom, Daniel, George, Edmond, Anthony, Jerry, woman Hanny, Luce & child, girls Fan, Esther, Jenny

William WYATT .... pg 399, 24 Dec 1813, will

    Dick, John, Harry, Hannah to wife Elizabeth; Milly to daughter Mahala; Patience to daughter Melissa

William DUVALL .... pg 403, 16 Jan 1815, will

    boy Joshua to son William Henry DUVALL; boy William to daughter Nancy; girl Charlotte to daughter Sarah Elenor DUVALL; Mary, Ben, Valmore, Tom, Emeline to son John Pearce DUVALL

Joseph PETTY .... pg 404, 4 July 1814, inv & appr

    woman, child, younger child

.... pg 407, 6 Jan 1815, slave sale

    woman Sib, Louisa to Henly MADDOX; girls Jane, Louisa to Henry R. PAYNE

William WYATT .... pg 407, 6 Mar 1815, inv & appr

    Dick, John, Harry, Daniel, Hannah, Milly, Patience, Melindy

Richard BRENT .... pg 411, 6 Dec 1813, will

    Peter, of whom I purchased from Mrs. GRAHAM, to brother Daniel Carroll BRENT of Stafford Co; if Peter is disposed to leave Virginia I bestow his freedom; no deed yet from Mrs. Jane GRAHAM who has her life estate in Peter

Ann LINTON .... pg 413, 16 Aug 1810, will

    boy Lunnon to nephew William A. LINTON; boy Tom to nephew John T. LINTON; old Winney, old Tom to brother John LINTON; Nelly to be sold to her husband who is free; rest of slaves to be divided into 3 equal parts – 1/3 to sister Mrs. PEYTON, 1/3 to brother John, 1/3 to be divided equally between 3 nephews John, Thomas, & William A. LINTON the sons of my late brother William; Hannah & her 4 children to my sister Mrs. Sybilla PEYTON; 2 boys or a fellow to be purchased & delivered to said sister; Sam to brother John LINTON; Jesse, Betty & her daughter to nephew William A. LINTON

Charles O'NEIL .... pg 416, 6 June 1815, inv & appr

    Isaac, Polly, Harriet

Richard TOMLIN................................ pg 423, 9 May 1814, adm acct

   negro

Stephen HOWISON .... pg 427, 9 May 1815, inv & appr

   man Joe, Matilda & child, woman Amia, boys Enock, Bernard, John, George, Shaderack, Jesse, girls Sarah, Isabel, Fanny

Thomas GRAHAM ....pg 441, 7 Aug 1815, inv & appr

   man 55 years old

George RAMEY..................................pg 441, 7 Aug 1815, inv & appr

   man 70 years, boy 7

Samuel JACKSON............................... pg 445, 12 May 1815, inv & appr

   men London, Moses, Bob, Davy, Seally & her child Julya, Nell, girl Cisily, boys Jeffry, Jack, Mason, Joshua, Jacob, girl Chantelle, Hester

Rev. Charles O'NEIL ....pg 447, 1813 – Aug 1815, estate acct

   Isaac, Polly, Harriet

William DUVALL .... pg 449, 16 Aug 1815, inv & appr

   Mary, Ben, William, Phalmore, Charlotte, Emeline, Tom, Joshua

Wormly CARTER Sr. ....pg 452, 4 Sept 1815, inv & appr

   men Griffin, Simon, Joe, Tasker, Joe, James, Arthur, Paul, Simon, Dolly & child Beck, Beck & child John, Winney, Sarah, Judy, Edmund, Nutty, Simon, Stephen, Watt, Harriet, Easter, Chris, Martha, Carline, Sally, Abigail, Bridget, Moses, George

Gerard SPINKS ....pg 453, 11 Aug 1815, will

   Harry, Mima, Silby, Essex to wife Ann SPINKS and after her death to son Gerard SPINKS; boy Anthony, girl Liddy to daughter Susannah SPINKS; boy Lamore (Samson?), girl Mary to daughter Winiford CREAMER

Helen G. HUIE.................................... pg 456, 20 July 1814, will

   woman Molly & rest of negroes & slaves to be sold

Benson DAVIS...............................pg 457, 2 Oct 1815, inv & appr

 men Jacob, Henry, boy Moses, woman Charlotte, woman & children, old woman

Martha BRIDWELL........................pg 461, 6 Nov 1816, inv & appr

 woman 28 years, boy 10, boy 8, girl 7, girl 3

Arthur L. ROBINSON .... pg 463, 15 June 1815, inv & appr

 boy

Helen G. HUIE...............................pg 464, 6 Oct 1815, inv & appr

 Molly & 2 children, Eliza, Jesse, London, Will

Redwood EVANS ....pg 466, 7 Nov 1815, inv & appr

 woman Sarah

James W. COLQUHOUN ....pg 468, 11 Oct 1815, inv & appr

 Ralph, Davy, Peter, Dinah & child, Fanny & child, Joe, Sandy, Peter, Charlotte, Susan, Kitty, Phillis, Maria

James ANDERSON .... pg 472, 8 Nov 1807, estate acct

 hire & sale of negroes

Alexander HENDERSON ....pg 475, 24 Feb 1815, will

 Jack & wife Dorcas & youngest child, Ben & wife Clara & her child James settled in lieu of Dower on my wife

Robert CARTER .... pg 479, 5 Dec 1815, inv & appr

 man 30 years, 2 boys 5 or 6, 3 women (1 old), 2 young, 2 girls

Mary BRUNDIGE..............................pg 480, 6 Nov 1815, inv & appr

 Will, Jess, Nelly, Harriet & child, Betsy, Sooky, Celia, Mary, Henry, Alfred, Robert, woman Paul 70, Jim

Sarah CHALMERS ....pg 483, 21 June 1813 – 20 Sept 1815, exec acct

 Mary, Suckey, Ben, Johnson, Anthony, hire of Dick, Ralph, Edmund

Gerard SPINKS .... pg 487, 4 Dec 1815, inv & appr

> man Harry, woman Sylvia, man Essex, woman Mimy, boy Anthony, girl Lydia, child Lemo, child Mary, boy Newton, man Sampson

David DAVIS .... pg 490, 5 Feb 1816, inv & appr

> woman & 2 children

Sarah B. MASON .... pg 492, 29 May 1815, inv & appr

> Will Dean, Web, Mary, Sally, Bett, Abb, Fanny 14 years, Kate 18

Ann EDWARDS .... pg 497, 9 Nov 1815, will

> Adam, Mary & her 2 sons Reuben & Aaron to be divided among my 3 children Gilbert EDWARDS, Ann H. EDWARDS, & Lucy EDWARDS

Daniel Webster .... pg 502, 23 Nov 1815, will

> to my wife Lucy Webster (whom I purchased from the late John MACRAE) & to my child James Webster their freedom

John CALVERT .... pg 509, 13 Mar 1816, inv & appr

> man Jesse, girl Betty

William DAVIS .... pg 510, 30 May 1815, inv & appr

> men Joseph, Aaron, woman Eave, fellow Moses

Beverly R. WAGENER .... pg 521, 1808 – 3 Apr 1816, trustee acct

> negro hire, Sylvanus sold

Sarah DADE .... pg 539, 26 Feb 1816, inv & appr

> Tom, Aaron, Lige, Henry, Tasco, Dinah, Judy, Arthur, Kate, Mary, Fanny, Richard, Betsy, Amanda, Daphne, Mema, old Jim

Gerard SPINKS .... pg 542, Dec 1815 – 3 Apr 1816, estate acct

> Phil, paid crier for negroes; children sold; Sampson sold; all at public auction in Dumfries

Mary NEALES .... pg 543, 23 Oct 1815, inv & appr

Dick, Ben, Job, John, Bob, Aaron, Charles, Lewis, Peter, Westwood, Madison, Ben, Cate, Cary, Fauny, Malinda, Nancy, Polly, Susannah, Washington, Elizabeth, Dinah

Dr. George GRAHAM .... pg 545, 6 Mar 1816, inv & appr

men Will, Sam, Daniel, Emanuel, John, Moses, Alfred, Jane & 2 children, Ann & 2 children, boy Jesse

WILL BOOK L
1816 – 1823

Thomas HARRISON .... pg 1, 7 Oct 1816, inv & appr

    Sylvanus, Frank, Bob, Phillip, Israel, Diggs, Betty, Behethlin, Lydia, Sucky, Lib, Eliza, Polly, Anna, John, Matilda, Maria, Sarah, Amy

William TYLER Sr. .... pg 9, 14 Sept 1816, will

    negroes to be equally divided

Margaret FEAGAN .... pg 11, 25 July 1815, inv & appr

    Benjamin, Lucy

Margaret FEAGAN .... pg 12, 6 Jan 1817, acct of sales

    woman to W. _ WASHINGTON; man to William GREEN

Richard BRENT .... pg 14, 2 Aug 1815, inv & appr

    Nelly, Edmund 20, Jonas, Peter, George, Patsy, Becky, Lucy, Nace, Esther, child, Elick, Nutty, Thornton, Dick, Washington, Louisa, Hannah, Mary, Milly, Jim, Caroline, child Phil, Moses, Nelly, Dyer, Daniel, Liddy, Katy, Rachel, twin girls, Fanny, Katy, Ned, Belima, Simms, Joshua, Robert, Betsy, Dick, Lucy, Joe, Simon, Aaron, Scott, Hannah, Betty, Bill, Carter, Matilda & child, Helen & child, Charles, John, Simon, Leoisa, Henny, Jim, Sarah, Lucy, Jenny, Tom, Aaron, Kate, Milly 2 years, Clara, Charity, Isabell, child, Eve, Billy, Isaac Cook, child, Rachel, Armistead, Harry, Charles, Fanny, Charlotte, Letty, Kitty

James G. EVENS .... pg 19, 5 Nov 1816, inv & appr

    men Osburn, Ben, James, boys Nace, Dempse, Peter, women Pricilla, Terry, Ceclia

Charles TYLER .... pg 26, 6 June 1815, inv & appr

    George & family, George, Lucy & 3 children Franky, Robert, & Anderson; George, Reuben, Henson, Abraham, Tomas, Joshua, Daniel, Bud, Jim, Dick, Richard, George, Dennis, Anthony, Charles, Moses, Billy, Michael, Henson, Godfrey, Dennis, Owens, Nelly, John Parton, Sandy, Nancy, Julius, Grace & children Eliza & Henry, old

Bill, Jerry, Jinny, Jinny & 4 children Mahala, Abigail, Mary, & Nat, Jenny & 2 children Sally & Syphuse, Nancy & child Davy, Mima & child John, Nelly & child Isaac, Aggy & child Oaradise, Nelly & child Aggy, Charity, Anna, Cloe, Milly, Molly & children Ann & Betty, Beck & child Henry, Jenny, Nelly, Patience, Susan, Joan, Charity, Beck

Prudence GWATKIN .... pg 30, 29 Aug 1816, will

all negroes to be set free: Lewis, Sarah, Charlotte

Susannah FEAGAN .... pg 31, 2 Aug 1816, will

girl Sarah to Francis FEAGAN, boy Nat to Raughly FEAGAN, sons of my brother Henry FEAGAN

William MOUNT .... pg 32, 21 Nov 1816, inv & appr

Israel, Martin, John, Daniel, Peter, John, Neale, Michael, William, Milly, Hannah, Polly, Bridget, La_hny, Henry, Fanny, Gustavus

James FEAGAN .... pg 34, 13 May 1810, estate acct

sale of 4 negroes

Alexander HENDERSON .... pg 36, 24 Jan 1817, inv & appr

Reedy Creek:

young George, Simon, Pompey, Ben, Tom, Sam, Watt, Mariah & child, Hannah, Lucinda, Sal, Artimisia, Baulis, Lewis, Sydney, William, Betty & child

Cow Creek:

Daniel, Meg & child Charlotte, Sandie, Winney, Harriet, Melinda, Caesar, Rachel & child, Mary, Kitty, Elias, Julianna, Jenny, Eleanor, Davy, Elvira & child, Delia, Matilda, Adam, Obannion, Lockart, Edie, Jim Bunch, Lucy & child, little Bill, Lucy, Davy, Joshua, Bob, Betty, Daniel, Bond, little Betty, Anne, Bristoe, Darcus & child, Charity, Flora, Patience, Dick, Patty, Hannah, Shadrick, Towerhill, Jude & child, Fanny, Jack, Sylla, Gene, George, Peg, Milly, Horace, Louise, Jacob, Absalom, Jim, Sam, Dick, Charity, Caroline

Stephen Joy COMPTON .... pg 42, Feb 1813 – 11 Mar 1817, estate acct

John, slaves

Daniel KING ....pg 43, 20 Feb 1814, will

> negoes

Leonard BRASFIELD ....pg 45, 22 Mar 1817, will

> negroes at decease of wife be drawn for by my children: George, Thomas, Leonard BRASFIELD, Nancy WHEELER, Mariah, Lucinda, Betsy, & Julia BRASFIELD

John McCLENACHAN ....pg 49, 5 Apr 1815, acct of sales

> sale of negroes made at Hay Market 1 Jan 1816, Henry to James CAMPBELL; Simon, Fielding to Washington J WASHINGTON; John to Thomas HUNTON; Ben to Edward HARDEN; Spencer to James McCLENACHAN

John McCLENACHAN ....pg 52, 23 Mar 1815, inv & appr

> John, Spencer, Sam, Simon, Ben, Fielding, Henry, John, Bill, Hannah, Betty

John McCLENACHAN ..... pg 53, 5 Apr 1815 – 23 Nov 1816, estate acct

> sale of negroes 3 Jan 1816; old negro to be kept by ___ MEALON

James GRAHAM ....pg 55, 17 Dec 1812 - , adm acct

> Elias to John WHITE?, girl to Thomas B. SINCLAIR?

(Note attached to pg 56: pp.57 to 85 torn out)

James WYATT.................. pg 88, 19 Nov 1813 - 17 June 1814, estate acct

> Tom hired, negroes hired & sold; Daphne & child sold

Robert THURMAN ....pg 90, 11 Oct 1817, will

> boy Amos to son Thomas; Barnett, Nat, Daniel to son Sanford; man Henson to son John; Silvey, Jesse to daughter Catharine; Ann & her child Sinah to daughter Peggy FEWELL; Nell, Isaac to son James; girl Mariah to grandchildren Elizabeth FEWELL, William FEWELL, & Robert THURMAN son of John

Ann Linton NESBETT..pg 93, 10 Oct 1817, will

> boy Charles to be sold; 2 negroes of niece Maria LESLEY were sold & replaced by Bill & Albert; man John, woman Cate & her son George

& her young child to be sold; the rest of the negroes to friend John LINTON in trust for my brother James NESBETT until his death then to niece Maria LESLEY

Basil BRAWNER .... pg 95, Dec 1812, will

boy Ned to son William BRAWNER; girl Celia to son John BRAWNER; girls Hannah, Mary to daughter Sarah GAINES; girl Dinah, boy Jerry to daughter Nancy GAINES

John MACRAE .... pg 99, 1812 – 12 July 1817, adm acct

John; Harry perished in a snow storm; Abraham, Jim, John, Harry, old Billy, old Amy, Suky, Judith, Polly, Argyle, Grace, Dennis, George, Daniel, Mary Ann, Matty & her children Rachel & Tom, William, Courtney, Jesse, Maria, Addison, Nace, Sam, Kitty

Basil BRAWNER .... pg 112, 5 Jan 1818, inv & appr

man Daniel George, Lewis, Jesse, E Saw (Esau?), Henson, Letty, Mary, Jane, Friday, Kitty, Elisa, Mariah, John, Fanny, Sharlot, Harry, Charity, Dennis, Ann, Sandy, Daniel, Isaac

Gerard SPINKS .... pg 120, 2 Sept 816, inv & appr

Essex, Harry, boys Anthony, Newton, Lemo, Sylvia, child Mary, Mima, girl Lydia, Sampson

Gerard SPINKS .... pg 123, 8 Oct 1816, estate acct

2 slaves delivered to Winifred KIEMOR, 7 sold to A.S.; Sampson, boy Newton sold

Townshend DADE .... pg 128, 31 Oct 1814 – 17 Dec 1817, estate acct

negroes hired; Davy, Laurence (slave?), Harry, Sophia in child bed, old Jenny, Thornton, Phil, Kiziah gave birth, Solomon a cripple

William DAVIS .... pg 138, 20 June 1815, estate acct

Moses in jail, sold

.... pg 140, 20 June 1815, acct of sales

man Joe, woman Eve to Uriah BYRNE; Moses to James KELLY

Robert THURMAN ....pg 141, 27 Feb 1818, inv & appr

> men Jesse, Nat, Daniel, lad Isaac, boys Bama, Henson, Amos, girls Sylvia, Mariah, Ann & her child Siner

Leonard BRASFIELD .... pg 156, 2 June 1817, inv & appr

> Henrietta, Clara & child, Wilson, Mary, Evelina, Polly, Moses, Simon, Matilda

William GREEN .... pg 158, 18 Dec 1817, inv & appr

> Ben, Elijah, James, Maria, Winna, Syrus, Juliann, Milly, Nancy

John DeBELL .... pg 164, 12 Jan 1818, acct of sales

> man Sanders to Dorcas DeBELL; man James, Priscilla & child to Jeremiah DeBELL; boys Harry, Thomas to William BYRNE; man Jonathan to James BEATTY; boy William, girl Jane, boy Willis to John HADDUX Sr.

Charles TYLER .... pg 169, 8 June 1815 – 14 Feb 1818, estate acct

> Jerry, George, Bob, Job sold?

John FERGUSON ....pg 175, 3 Nov 1817, inv & appr

> men Will, Tom, boys James, Dave, Lonon, man Dick, woman Sharlot

.... pg 176, 11Dec 1817, acct of sales

> six slaves were divided amongst the representatives & not sold

John MACRAE .... pg 184, 4 Oct 1813- 23 Apr 1815, estate acct

> Jack died, slaves to be divided; Sukey to Mrs. HUNTER; Dennis to Capt MACRAE; Nancy, Dennis, Jack, Addison, Judith, black man, George, old Sukey, Nace, Polly, John

James SETTLE .... pg 191, 17 Mar 1815 – 3 Nov 1817, estate acct

> Ellis to Francis SETTLE; Tyler (slave?)

Joseph HUBER ....pg 197, 3 Feb 1817, inv & appr

> Jenny, Joy & child, Nancy, Natt, John, James, William, Caroline, George, Frederick, Charles

Joseph DEAN .... pg 221, 15 Apr 1815, will

slaves & servants to wife Hannah DEAN

Susanna FEAGANS .... pg 223, 5 Aug 1818, inv & appr

Polly aged 30 or 40 & child Jack, man about same age not hired by Gracy FEAGANS in Fauquier Co.; Fanny 50; there is one woman & child which appears not to have been named in the will of Francis FEAGANS the father of Susanna

Matthew W. BROOKE .... pg 225, 11 Sept 1818, inv & appr

Hannibal, William, Humphrey, Siller, Peggy & children Kitty, Polly, Judy, Charles & Henry; Rose & children Nancy, Rosetta, Jennette, Jackson, & Judy

Elizabeth WHITING .... pg 227, 6 Feb 1815, will

valuable negroes of my own to son George B. WHITING; girls Rachel, Cortney to oldest granddaughter Elizabeth How (Howe?) LITTLE; Hampton a son of Sarah to grandson Francis Henry WHITING; Alfred a son of Polly to grandson William Henry LITTLE; girl Nelly daughter of Patty to granddaughter Elizabeth Braxton WHITING

William GREEN .... pg 229, 16 Dec 1817 – 25 Sept 1818, estate acct

sale of Mima, Syrus, Julian, Milly, Elijah, Ben, Jim & his wife Maria, Nancy

Daniel KING .... pg 239, 10 Oct 1818, inv & appr

men James, Ben, boy Jesse, girls Sophy, Moriah, Emmala, woman Winnie

John GIBSON .... pg 240, 1807 – 5 Oct 1816, commissioner's acct
.... pg 243, 7 Aug 1807 – 24 Dec 1816, estate acct A

midwife for Juba's daughter, Sam; paid George GRAHAM in full of 3 Judith of Mrs. DOUGLAS of children (Judith has 3 children?); slaves sold from Slaty Run; funeral of old Nanny; old London, Peter, boy, old Hannah,

.............pg 254, 10 Aug 1807 – 7 June 1813, estate acct B

Charles, sick woman, sick man, Aaron, Daniel died; young child, midwife for Juba's daughter, 40 slaves & 2 plantations in Pr Wm Co, 21 slaves & 2 plantations in Fairfax Co
.... pg 263, 23 Dec 1807, Prospect Hills sales

Peter to Henry FAIRFAX
....pg 265, 4 Feb 1871, Dumfrie sales

Charles to Tolemiah RHODES; Sampson to William E. BECKWITH; Loue to James COCHRAN; George to Robert THURMAN; Ben to Quinton RATCLIFF; Juba no bid; Sarah, Agnes, Elsey, Junnie, Henny all with 2 children each to Samuel SPRAGGINS; Clay with 2 children to Simon LUTTRELL; boy Africa to Richard COLVIN; boy Lundy to Thomas HOMES; girl Maria to James GRADY; Hannah & 2 children, girl Lucy to Seth COMBS; Fanny & 2 children to Russell WIGGINTON; boys Jennins, Stephen to William E. BECKWITH
.... pg 266, 30 Nov 1809, Slaty Run sales

slaves selected for MACKEYS directed by will: Cyrus, Vincent, Stephney, Moses, Jenny & child, Hannah & 2 children, Anny
.............................pg 269, 5 Apr 1813, Dumfries sales

Ned, Phil, Easter & child, Mima & 2 children, boy Harrison, girl Betsy to Daniel Carroll BRENT; Anthony to James REID; John to Bazil BRAWNER; Delia & 2 children to William BRAWNER; Jesse to Daniel M. CHICHESTER; Aaron to Richard BRENT; Moses to George _HAD, Lydia & child, boy Barney to Thomas THURMAN; Harry to Gerald ALEXANDER Jr.; Charles to Samuel PURCELL; Dorcas & 2 children to Stephen KING; girl Charlotte to Ellis GRAVET; Milly to W.A.G. DADE; boy James to Joseph HUBER; Cloe & 2 children to Col. Gerald ALEXANDER; girl Easter to Joseph SIMPSON; girl Cumford to James TURLEY; boy Edmond to Daniel C. BRENT; girl Matilda to Reason HASLO_; Mary & child to Cossom HORTON; girl Harriet to Philip WEBSTER; boy Henry to Robert CHISLEY; girl Sucky to William WILLIAMSON; girl Winna to Charles SCOTT; Ned to John SPENCE; Will to Samuel COLE; old Willoughby & wife Nelly to Hedgeman MURPHEY

Solomon ELWELL .... pg 270, 4 Dec 1878, inv & appr

Tom, girls Amy, Sarah, boys William, Richard, small girl Jane

Maryann CAVE .... pg 273, 4 June 1818, inv & appr

Polly, girls Ellen, Sinah, Mary

William BROWN .... pg 275, 12 July 1818, will

negroes to be divided among my surviving brothers John BROWN, Benjamin BROWN, & Richard BROWN after my mother's death

John McMILLIAN .... pg 276, 6Apr 1878, comm acct

hiring of slaves; support of 2 slaves, 1 now dead, the other crippled, little girl now hired out

Robert LUTTRELL .... pg 283, 2Apr 1812, will

1/6 slaves to wife Nancy LUTTRELL & after her death to be divided between my 3 daughters Melenday, Jane, & Peggy; 1/6 of slaves each to son Simon LUTTRELL, son Thomas LUTTRELL, daughters Melenday DAVIS, Jane LUTTRELL, & Peggy LUTTRELL

Catherine CARTER .... pg 285, 9 Nov 1818, inv & appr

Dolly, Moses, Becky

Robert LUTTRELL .... pg 286, 10 Mar 1819, inv & appr

old man Adam, men George, Thomas, boys Sanford, Alfred, Daniel, Samuel, Jesse, George, Arch, Henry, Gerard, Dennis, Lewis, William, Simon, women Sarah, Amy, Agathy, Betty, Selia, Delphy, Mary, Agatha, Judith, girls Betty, Matilda, Mahala, Fanny, Betty, Nelly, Charlotte, Sophy

.... pg 288, debts due

Simon LUTTRELL, John F. DAVIS for negro hire

Samuel JACKSON .... pg 289, 8 June 1815 – 29 Apr 1819, estate acct

girl Julia to/from? George W. JACKSON

Martha JAMES .... pg 291, 23 Aug 1814, will

negroes from my mother may be hired out for 5 years & my boy Carl MITCHELL & the money…to son Westwood Wallace JAMES. I free the said negroes after that hire of 5 years.

Dr. Solomon EWELL .... pg 292, 30 Jan 1819, estate sale

    Matilda to Sarah B. EWELL

John CARTER .... pg 295, 9 June 1819, inv & appr

    man

John STUMP .... pg 295, __18__, will

    (Stafford, Harford Co, Maryland)

    all the black servants owned by me shall be manumitted and discharged from all servitude and service...the males at 21, the females at 18...except Simon & his wife Urania & their child Henry & children who are now with my son William & who are now willed to my wife Cassandra to be free or otherwise at her discretion

James CAMPBELL .... pg 298, 6 Jan 1818 – 1 Sept 1819, estate acct

    James CAMPBELL's bond for the purchase of a negro, negroes sold, hire of Fielding & girl

James CAMPBELL .... pg 300, 22 Jan 1818, acct of sales

    Stephen, old Sally & daughter Nelly to ___

James CAMPBELL .... pg 301, 20 Jan 1818, inv & appr

    Felding, girl, old woman Sally

Dr. Thomas THORNTON ....
.... pg 307, 27 June 1817 – 4 Dec 1819, estate acct

    Dick hired from Mrs. WEEMS

Rev. Thomas HARRISON ....pg 310, 1 Jan 1815 – 1 Jan 1819, estate acct

    Sheriff levy for 1 slave; Betsy, Matthew, Matilda & child, Henry, Cecelia, Sally, Frank, Norman, Henry, Maria, Charlotte

Samuel PURCELL .... pg 323, 12 Feb 1820, inv & appr

    men Jeffry, Tim, boy William, Betty & child George, boys Joe, Sampson, girls Anny, Nelly, Alcy & child John

Richard BRENT .... pg 324, 1 Jan 1815- 14 July 1819, estate acct

> negroes for sale, Peter; girl Liddy to Major TOLSON; sale of 48 negroes, Nutty's child Mary, Carter? to William BRENT Jr.; boy Edmond from Brenton to Mrs. Euphan BRENT; Bill, Dicky, Ned sold to Col. GRAGHAM; George from Brenton to Mrs Euphan BRENT

James W. COLQUHOUN ....
................................pg 333, 24 May 1815 – 1 Jan 1820, estate acct

> Laxy, man Peter, Davy, Dinah & children, boys Joe, Sandy, girl Kitty, woman Fanny & children, Sharlotte; old man Ralph died

Elizabeth NORMAN .... pg 344, 12 Sept 1820, inv & appr

> man Ely, woman Catharine

Elizabeth NORMAN .... pg 348, 22 Aug 1820, acct of sales

> Ely to James NORMAN; Cate to Patsy NORMAN

Philip SPILLER .... pg 352, 13 July 1820, will

> man Bartley, girl Mahaley to wife Dianer SPILLER; Jane to be free after my wife's decease

Sibellah PEYTON .... pg 354, 21 Oct 1814, will

> all negroes to brother John LINTON in trust for my daughter Nancy GWYNN

Thomas NEWMAN .... pg 355, 28 Dec 1820, will

> Reuben, Nell, lad John to son Elias NEWMAN; Ann, Mima, Wilson to son Thomas Jett NEWMAN; Patt & her children, Jack to daughter Nancy Jett NEWMAN; Isaac, Phillis to daughter Mary SPINDLE; Sally, Stephney to James BROWN in trust for daughter Sarah BROWN; Harry, Thornton, Eliza to son William Jett NEWMAN in trust for daughter Sarah BROWN; son Tom, Betty & their children Charles, Charlotte, Jim, & George to son William Jett NEWMAN; Jack, Milly & their children Maria, Reuben, & Margaret to daughter Catherine Newton NEWMAN; Tom, Winney, Moses, Jenny & her children Esther, Rachel, & Betsy to daughter Peggy NEWMAN; Ned, Lucy, Peg & her children Mary, Lewis, Penny, & Juliet to daughter Eleanor NEWMAN; personal property negroes, Jess & his wife & children to be sold

John DeBELL ....pg 358, 7 Aug 1817, inv & appr

    Saunders, Jonathan, James, William, Henry, Thomas, Willis, James, Priscilla, Lizett

James GRINSTEAD ....pg 359, 7 May 1821, inv & appr

    Libby 70 years, Sam 35, Ben 12, Mariah 10, Mary 6

John McCLENACHAN ....pg 360, 11 Jan 1820 – 3 Jan 1821, estate acct

    Sam, old Hannah his wife, Bell sold

Townshend DADE ....pg 362, 1 Jan 1818 – 28 Apr 1821, exec acct

    Solomon, George Turtle, Kizzy & 4 children, Davy, Jenny over 90 years died, George Turtle, Sophia, George Blackstone, Daniel

    A: Davy, George Blackstone, Daniel, Tom, George Turtle, Sophia & child, Esther, Phil, Thornton

    B: old Jenny lived with STORKE

    C: Davy, George Turtle, Thornton, Tom, Esther, Phil, Kizzy & 2 children, Sophy & 2 children, George Blackstone, Solomon

    D: Davy, Tom, George Turtle, Thornton, Daniel, George Balckstone, old Phil, Sophia & 2 children, Solomon, Esther, Kizzie & their children

    E: Davy, Tom, Daniel, George Balckstone, Thornton, George Turtle, Kizzie & Esther & family put out, Sophy & children out with clothes, Solomon, old Phil

    Harry & old Penny dead; Sarah, Brooks, Suckey, Winney, Molly & child, Martha, Betty & her child Townshend, Johnston, Evelina, Sally, Ben, Lucinda, Polly or Mary, Bonaparte, Frankey & child, Jane sold; Matilda, Thompson, Sophy, Anne, George Washington, Araminta to B.W. STOCKE & wife; Fanny, Franklin, Jacob, Maria to West ASHTON & wife; Phil, Davey, Daniel, Tom, Solomon, Abram called George, old woman Kezial to John H. WASHINGTON for division with himself, Langhorne & Laurence DADE; Davey, Nat to Langhorne DADE; Matilda & several children... recovered in a lawsuit; old Esther, George Blackstone, Kezial (a legacy to M. WASHINGTON) & son Thornton called Tom & several of her other children, Sophia & 2 children born since T. DADE's death to dower of widow Chadwalada DADE; son Langhorne chose boy Davy Nat & afterwards sold to Dr. William ALEXANDER

John McCLENACHAN ....pg 370, 2 Nov 1819, inv & appr

   Sam 40 years, Bill 21-27, old John, old Betty, old Hannah

John McCLENACHAN ....pg 371, 3 Jan 1821, acct of sale

   William Cary

....pg 371, 1 Jan 1820, acct of sale

   Sam & old Hannah his wife

Thomas NEWMAN............................. pg 371, 9 Apr 1821, inv & appr

   man York, Ned, Jim; family: Tom, Betty & 6 children, Jack, Milly & 7 children, Tom, Jenny & 4 children, Jesse, Sally & 2 children, Peggy & 4 children

Sally H. PLUMMER ....pg 376, 14 Feb 1821, will

   woman Nelly to niece Sally PLUMMER the daughter of Benjamin & Margaret PLUMMER

Thomas LARKIN .... pg 379, 26 Apr 1821, inv & appr

   men Aaron, George, Harry, Will, David, boys Benjamin, Solomon, James, Henry, Daniel, Beike, 1 Charles, 2 Charles, woman Betty, Priscilla & child Andrew, Susan, Charlotte & child Harriet, Eliza, Lucy, Lettice, Mary, Sophia, Aaron, Mildred & child Patty, Kezia, Sally, Mariah, Hester, Lydia, Moses, Peggy, Winney, Lucy, Storke, Tener, Rebecah, Fanny, William, Sarah & child Peter, Delpha, Winney & child Betsy, Daphney, Amy

Hannah CARTER..pg 381, 12 Sept 1809, will

   woman Ealsy to be free

Jesse BARRON .... pg 387, 1813 – June 1819, estate acct

   A: negroes, Dolly, old Cloe

   C: to have young woman or boy 14 or 15 for a good price

   D: Jenny, Dick

   5: Dolly, James, Dick, Lucy; Dolly sold

Josias STONE .... pg 392, 2 Oct 1821, inv & appr

    Judah, Charles, Mary, Charlotte, Rachel & child Samuel, Bennett, Lucinda, Lydia, _eamen, _inia, Thomas, Sandy, Maria, Indian, Matilda, George, Winney

Elizabeth HORTON .... pg 399, 1 July 1809, will

    woman Hester & her children Silas & Moses to granddaughter Peggy H. MADDOX

Bernard GALLAGHER .... pg 400, 29 Aug 1821, will

    Lucy, Fanny, Jim to wife Margaret GALLAGHER & at her death divided among all the children; girl Harriet to daughter Eliza S. PEYTON; Sarah to daughter Mary; girl Jane to daughter Ann; Emily to daughter Margaret; remaining negroes to be hired out

John BRONAUGH .... pg 402, 20 Oct 1821, will

    negroes to be sold

Charles SLADE .... pg 405, 25 Dec 1810, will

    boy George to obtain his liberty in 12 years from this date; any other person of color I may have to be free at age 27

Edward E. CARTER .... pg 407, 20 Nov 1820, will

    slaves to brother Shirley

John WRIGHT .... pg 409, 1 Jan 1815 – Oct 1820, estate acct

    negro

George FLORENCE .... pg 412, 6 Dec 1821, will

    woman Mary Sr., man Reuben to wife Eve

Sally CAMPBELL .... pg 414, 3 Nov 1821, will

    Matilda & her children Adeline, Mary, Fanny, & Eliza to daughter Sarah B. CAMPBELL

Ann SPINKS .... pg 415, 1 Dec 1821, will

    girl Mary to be sold

John S. SMITH.................... pg 416, 3 Dec 1821, inv & appr
    men Luke, Jack, woman Hannah
Thomas NELSON .... pg 417, 20 Dec 1803, will
    Robert 16 years to daughter Elizabeth Stonestreet NELSON
Thomas NELSON .... pg 419, 7 Jan 1822, inv & appr
    men George, James, girl Eliza
Ann SPINKS .... pg 421, 18 Jan 1822, inv & appr
    Mary about 7 years old
William ARNOLD .... pg 422, 4 Dec 822, inv & appr
    woman
Martin MADDUX .... pg 426, 3 Dec 1821, inv & appr
    man James, girl Matilda, old man
William CUNDIFF.................... pg 430, 7 Jan 1822, inv & appr
    Cesar, Adam, Randall, Levi, Harry, London, Edmond, Fanny, Matilda, Cynthia, Violet & child Hannah, Benjamin, Charity, Franky & child Isabella, John, Judah, Anny, Sally
John M. TYLER.................... pg 433, 7 May 1821, inv & appr
    men Daniel, Anthony, Bob, boys Julius, John, Grayson Carter, girls Evelina, Cloe, women Esther, Nancy, Mima, Rebecca
John M. TYLER.................... pg 435, 14 Dec 1821, acct of sales
    Bob to E. BOOKE Jr.; Anthony to R.B. TYLER; John to L.G. THORNTON; Julius to Charles HUNTON; Nancy to Richard A. BRITT; Esther & 4 children to William B. TYLER
William ROACH.................... pg 441, 2 Apr 1822, estate acct
    negro
George FLORENCE .... pg 446, 7Jan 1822, inv & appr
    girl Lucy, boy Ben, girls Mary, Emily, Ann, man Reuben, woman Mary, boy Gerard

Joseph HUBER ....pg 452, 11 Sept 1818 – 14 Mar 1822, estate act

   man John

Phillip SPILLER .... pg 455, 10 Mar 1821, inv & appr

   Jane, man Bartly, girl Mahala, boy Moses, child Craven

Phillip SPILLER .... pg 457, 3 June 1822, acct of sales

   boy Moses, child Craven

Phillip SPILLER .... pg 458, 5 Mar 1821, allotment

   Jane, man Bartly, girl Mahala to widow Dianer SPILLER

James REID................................pg 459, 9 Aug 1821, inv & appr

   man Anthony

Hendly BARRON .... pg 466, 15 July 1822, inv & appr

   Charity, Lucy & child, Adam, Sandy, Harry, Frederick, George

Richard ALLEN .... pg 470, 2 Feb 1815 – 1 Jan 1822, estate acct

   Scipio sold, Jesse

Elizabeth CARTER ....pg 477, 5 Aug 1822, will

   slave families to be kept together when divided among sisters Mrs. Robert HOOE & Mrs. HENRY & the children of my deceased sister Mrs. BRUCE

Henry BREWER ....pg 479, 2 Sept 1822, inv & appr

   girl Mary

Wormely CARTER .... pg 479, 19 Apr 1815 – 31 Dec 1821, estate acct

   negroes, 5 negroes sold, Simon, old Sally

Bernard GALLAGHER......................... pg 487, 6 June 1822, inv & appr

   Daniel Bull, John, George Chapman, Henry, John, James, George Coote, Fanny, Lucy, Sarah, Jane, Emily

William BROOKS................................ pg 490, 1 Apr 1822, inv & appr

   Shadrack, Elisha, Alfred, Lucy, Eliza, Phebe & child

Zachariah WARD ....pg 492, 22 Mar 1822, will

   negroes to wife Anna WARD

Augustin GAINS ....pg 495, 7 Oct 22, inv & appr

   men James, George, Aaron, Jerry, Sandy, women Dianna, Kitty, Lorenda, girl Maria, boys Hey, John

William GRAGHAM ....pg 499, 7 Nov 1821, inv & appr

   Rhemus, Sarah, George, Cesar, Dolly, Lucy, Daniel, Alsa, Betty, Priscilla, Susanna, James, Cesar Jr., Edmund

Jesse BARRON ....pg 502, 6 Nov 1822, estate acct

   negroes

William FLORENCE ....pg 503, 25 Oct 1822, inv & appr

   Jamson, Lucy, Chloe, Sharlotte, Jesse, Herrington, Sophia, Patsy, John, Lucinda

Joseph BROWN ....pg 508, 6 Jan 1823, inv & appr

   Lucy & child Harrison, Milly & children Fanny, Elizabeth, Mary, Lydia

Elizabeth CARTER ....pg 510, 2 Sept 1822, inv & appr

   men Alfred, Billy, Peter, Marshall, Jack, boys George, Beverly, Harrison, Davy, Alexander, Marshall, woman Suckey, girls Sarah, Betsy, Maria, Nancy, Betsy, Clary & child Jenny, Lucy & child Mary, Janny & child Marthy

George SMITH ....pg 513, 30 Nov 1822, inv & appr

   Isaac, Seth, big Daniel, little Daniel, Billy, Jesse, big Fanny, little Fanny, Lydia, Eliza, Jane, Dick

John BRONAUGH ....pg 527, 20 July 1822, inv & appr

   William Berry, Reuben, Lewis, Joe, Venus, Leah, Rebecca, Lucinda, Austin, Anne, Maryann & child, Henry, Moses, Leah

Dorcas DeBELL ....pg 536, 20 Sept 1821, inv & appr

   Sanders, Ann & child, Amy, Eliza, Winney

WILL BOOK M
1823-1827

(214 pages missing)

Dorcas DeBELL .... pg 1, 21 & 22 Sept 1821, acct of sales

    man Sanders to Elias MATTHEW; girl Amy to Jeremiah DeBELL; girl Eliza, woman Winney to Joel DeBELL

Joshua BUCKLEY .... pg 3, 11 Nov 1822, inv & appr

    man Peter, woman Linny, girls Rachel, Harriet

William BUCKLEY .... pg 6, 11 Nov 1822, inv & appr

    man Moses, woman Peg, girl Maria

Mark THARP .... pg 10, 8 Apr 1823, acct of sales

    man Jesse to Robert THURMAN; Jacob to Huriah BURN, Richard to Richard BRETT

Maryann CAVE .... pg 13, 13 July 1818 – Mar 1823, estate acct

    girl Sinah, Polly & children, Henry died, Gerard, Ellen, Henny

Alexander MUSCHETT .... pg 21, 8 Feb 1823, will

    ...slaves given to my wife by her father I give to said wife Luisa C. MUSCHETT & her heirs; George, John to son James Montifix MUSCHETT

Alexander COMPTON .... pg 23, 25 Apr 1823, will

    Jesse, Fanny, Peter, Henrietta, Davy to present wife Ann COMPTON by will of her mother

Presley DAVIS .... pg 24, 4 May 1823, inv & appr

    woman Docia, Susan & child Julian, man Aaron, lad Tom, woman Letty, boys Joe, Willard, Dennis

Hector ALEXANDER .... pg 25, 1 Jan 1823, will

> lad Richard to son Robert ALEXANDER; Jinney & son James to son William ALEXANDER; boy William to son John ALEANDER; woman with her youngest child & her daughter Mary to Constantin WHITFELL

Leonard BRASFIELD .... pg 27, 20 Aug 1820, estate acct

> legacies: woman & child to Maria BRASFIELD; boy to Lucinda BRASFIELD; girl to Elizabeth BRASHIELD; girl to Thomas BRASHIELD; girl to Leonard BRASHIELD; boy to George BRASHIELD; woman & child to Julia BRASHIELD; woman & child not divided by the commisoners sold

Thomas T. PAGE .... pg 31, 13 June 1822, will

> Bacchus & Mary to be free

Thomas HOMES Jr. .... pg 32, 7 July 1823, inv & appr

> Alexander, Sandy, Henry, Sally, Darcus, Charlotte, Susan, Daniel Sarah, Kellis, George

Timothy BUNDIGE .... pg 57, 7 Oct 1822, inv & appr

> man Austin, women Mima, Sally, Comfort, Jane & child

William MERCHANT .... pg 63, 8 July 1823, inv & appr

> woman __tty

James HOLLIDAY .... pg 65, 7 Sept 1821, will

> old woman Nelly not to be sold but to choose her master from my children; Sam, Dennis, London to be sold

James HOLLIDAY .... pg 67, 6 May 1823, inv & appr

> men Samuel, Dennis

William TYLER .... pg 71, 2 Dec 1816 – 26 Apr 1822, estate acct

> James, Cesar, Tom, Dick, Milly, Charity, ___, Alfred, Moses, old Ruth (midwife) Sumesette, Harry, Solomon, Esther & child, Milly, Ned, Ann, Eliza, Mary & child, Jim, Alfred, Ann, Polly & child, Esther & child, __icent sold, Harriet, Maria, Ezekiel, Fielding, Jack & 6 of his family sold, Matilda

(It appears that there are other negroes named, however, that information was covered with dark tape.)

Daniel FOSTER .... pg 84, 11 Dec 1822, inv & appr

> man Lewis, girl Maria

John STORKE .... pg 89, 3 Feb 1811, will

> fellow Sam who was given...Seymour HOOE by his grandmother Fran___ KE...to children Seymour Hooe STORKE, John, ___ JETT, Ann JETT, Mary Francis HOOE, & Susan ___, Thom__ ___ HOOE, John & William Jett STORKE

.... codicil, 3 Feb 18__

> boy George to son ___am Jett STORKE, girl Nelly to daughter Francis HOOE, girl Jane to daughter Susanna HOOE, girl Lettice

Matthew W. BROOKE .... pg 91, Sept 1816 – 25 Sept 1823, estate acct

> Nancy Buckner (servant), woman Ro__, Joshua, Michael, Nancy, Rose & children, Hannibal, William, Isaac, boy H__, Phil

Charlotte, EWELL .... pg 94, 18 Sept 1823, inv & appr

> Daniel, Sandy, Francis, Prue, Tom, Delia & child, Harriet & 2 children, Eliza, Margaret, John William, Cecelia & child, Lucy, Armistead, Elenor, Maria

Sarah EWELL .... pg 100, 3 May 1816, will

> Charles, Mary to niece? Frances H. HAISE daughter of Sally E. HAISE under control of trustees brother Charles ELWELL & Bertrand E. TRENIS

Charles EWELL Jr. .... pg 102, 9 Oct 1823, will

> Fanny, Jim, Williamson, Loisa & child Nelson, Beck & child Jane to be hired out; Letty, Chris, Kitty leaving my wife the choice of 2 small maids; 1/3 of the hires of my slaves to my wife, the remainder to be divided between my children Sarah Ann EWELL, Joseph F. EWELL, Edwin H. EWELL, & Lucy EWELL; 3/8 to daughter Lucy EWELL, 2/8 to each of my sons Joseph & Edwin EWELL, Sarah Ann EWELL; the increase of negroes named shall be free at age 25, & their increase at the same age; Nelson & Jane should be included in the old slaves but the increase; division of slaves to be made between wife & children

under the guardian; slaves to KY if wife, children, & guardian remove to the land there
.... pg 104, 20 Oct 1823, codicil

slaves to choose to be free or remain slaves at age 25

Thomas MAHENNY .... pg 106, 26 Oct 1822, will

...my son Jack a slave in possession of Mrs. Sarah WEEDON...

William MOUNTS .... pg 108, __, inv & appr

Bill, Michael, Bartly, Kneel (Neal?), John, Bridget, Alfred, Harriet, Mortin, Marian, Hannah, Eliza, Ambrow, Henry, Dafny, Lias, Richard, Mahala, Paul, Gusty, Robert, Jane, Israel, Peter, Martin, Milly, Daniel, Fanny

William BURNES .... pg 110, 12 Nov 1823, inv & appr

David, Edward, Jane, Oliver, Henry, Kitty, Ann, Jemmima, London, Charles, John, Jenny, Jesse

Maria HAMILTON .... pg 119, 1 Dec 1823, inv & appr

young man William, boys Lewis, Fredrick, Tro_lous, Robert, girls Louisa, Mary, Cordelia, Judy, Fanny & 3 children, small boy Peter

Stephen Joy COMPTON .... pg 121, 2 Feb 1813, inv & appr

man Henson, woman Liddy, girl Malicia

Benjamin CARNEY .... pg 136, 15 Jan 1824, inv & appr

men James, Wallace, boy Harry, Suke & 2 children, woman Rachel, Rose & 2 children, Phillis & 2 children, woman Moll

Nehemiah LYNN .... pg 139, 16 Nov 1822, will

(crossed out) girl Caba? to daughter Eleanor? R. LYNN

John BRONAUGH .... pg 144, 11 Dec 1821 – 1 Jan 1824, estate acct

Charles, Mary Ann & her 3 children Henry, Thomas, & Alex; Jack?, Billy sold, removal of slaves from Fairfax for Dr. BRONAUGH, Billy, Reuben, Lewis, Venus & her 5 children young Liah, Becky, Lucinda Sally, & Anna; Joe

Richard DAVIS .... pg 157, 4 Jan 1824, will

> John to son Richard; Phil to son Alexader; Suky & her 2 children William & Henry to daughter Elizabeth RANDOLPH; Diza & her 3 children Jane, Mary, & Charlotte to daughter Jane RENOE?

James HOLLIDAY .... pg 160, 7 June 1824, acct of sales

> Sam to Daniel COLE, Dennis to Nelsen TOTSON

French JOHNSON .... pg 163, 2 Feb 1824, inv & appr

> man, 2 girls

Jesse WARDER .... pg 164, 3 Nov 1823, will

> James, Jack, Mariah to wife Milfoard WARDER & after her death to my children Mary STONEL, Jr. WARDER & his wife, William WARDER, Walter WARDER, Elizabeth WARDER

William GREEN .... pg 170, 30 Jan 1824, will

> woman Jane to daughter Ann MORRISS; woman Hannah to daughter Elizabeth EVES; man Wilson to son William GREEN; girl Harriet to daughter Nancy GREEN; girl Evaline to daughter Lavina; girl Mary to daughter Lucinda GREEN, boy Daniel to son Thompson GREEN; boy Dennis to son Wesley GREEN; boy Jesse to son Townshend ___ GREEN; woman Matilda to son Staunton GREEN; boys George, Frank to be sold

William BUCKLEY .... pg 172, 4 Nov 1822 – 24 Apr 182_, estate acct

> negro sold by William FLORENCE; negroes

William SMOOT .... pg 175, Oct – 2 Nov 1821, estate acct

> sale of man Will, boy Jack, woman & child

Alexander COMPTON .... pg 176, 5 Aug 1823, inv & appr

> Dove Hill:
>
> Lucy & her 3 children Abraham, Minta, & Clarissa
>
> Poplar Hill:
>
> men Harry, Dick, Andrew, girl Judy

Alexander COMPTON..................pg 179, 10 Dec 1823, acct of sales

  Poplar Hill:

  men Harry, Andrew, boy Abraham to Martha E. PEYTON; man Dick to Hannah GRAHAM; Lucy & 2 small children to Thomas B. HAMILTON; girl Judy to John WILKENSON

Gilbert J. MOXLEY.....................pg 186, 1 Aug 1824, estate acct

  boy James sold

Elizabeth CARTER..........pg 197, 14 Oct 1822 – 3 July 1824, estate acct

  slaves, Sall

John POTTS...............................pg 202, 1 Dec 1823, inv & appr

  man Addison, women Eve, Matilda, boy Charles, woman Anne, girl Fanny, man George, child Betty, child Tom, girl Hutcha

John L. SMITH.........................pg 205, 30 May 1821 - 1824, estate acct

  crying sale of negroes

John L. SMITH.......................pg 207, 20 Dec 1821, acct of sales

  man to Peter SMITH; old man to John SMITH

Nehemiah LYNN......................pg 112, 5 Mar 1824, inv & appr

  Wallis, Cate

Rutland JOHNSON........................pg 221, 2 Nov 1824, inv & appr

  men Richard, Frank, Anthony, Bill, Isaac, George, boys Frank, Peter, William, John, Amos, women Sally, Sarah, girls Ann, Harriet, Rachel, Milly, Martha, Eliza

Henry DOGAN ....pg 226, 3 Mar 1824, inv & appr

  men Moses, Philip, boys Nelson, _ry, men William, George, Travers, Daniel, boys Tom, Elijah, James, Charles, Marshall, woman Janny, Jemima & child girls Sarah, Mary, Suckey, Cordy Hannah, Maria, Clary, Margaret

Thomas GREEN..................................pg 229, 5 Nov 1824, will

  Dick, Nat, Sandy to son Thompson GREEN

William MOUNT ....pg 232, 23 Feb 1825, inv & appr

> Peter, Michael, Hannah, Lea, Richard, Mahala, Charles, Henry, Martin, Dafney, Ambrose, Paul, Gusty, Liza, Robert, Jane, Israel, Martha, Bridget, Harriet, Alfred, Moten, Maria, Milly, Francis, John, Bartly, William, Daniel, Kneal (Neal?)

Thomas GRAHAM .... pg 233, 21 Feb 1825, estate acct

> man

John POTTS ....pg 234, 10 Mar 1825, acct of sales

> Addison, George, Eve, Charles, Amie, Fanny to Maryann POTTS

Dr. William GRAHAM .... pg 238, 7 Nov 1821, acct of sales

> Cesar, Betty & child to Presley FOLEY; Daniel, Remus & Sarah his wife to Charles HUNTON; Lucy to William HARRISON; Susan James to James JENNINGS; small boy Cesar to Thomas P. NOLON; Priscilla to Thomas B. SINCLAIR; George, Dolly to Stuart _. THORNTON

Jesse WARDER ....pg 255, 30 July 1834, inv & appr

> James, Jack, Maria

Elizabeth LYNN ....pg 257, 4 June 1824 – June 1825, estate acct

> Billy

David RENOE... pg 259, 14 Dec 1812, inv & appr

> girl Nell

David RENOE.....................................pg 261, 15 Dec 182_, acct of sales

> girl Nelly to Nancy RENOE

Elizabeth LYNN................................. pg 265, 24 June 1823, acct of sales

> old woman _rah? to Joseph R. LYNN

Alexander HENDERSON .....pg 267, Jan 1817 – 30 Dec 1823, estate acct

> old Sue, Ben & several other old slaves; Juba, Chloe, Molly, man Elliott, Cleary, servants to Pignut, old Molly & children, man Jerry taken from _. HARRISON, Winney, old Jenny, Billy, Simon, Bill, Daniel, Daniel, Clara, Betty, ...for William BURCH slave; Jim,

Stephany, Jeffrey, Winney's child, Isaac, John, Sally, Simon, boy Jim, slaves from Wood County, Juba, Abraham M. SCOTT balance of price of 89 slaves, Jenny, Nancy

The Pignut Estate .... pg 295, Feb 1819 – June 1823, estate acct

hands, cash paid _.H. HOOE for Chloe; Clara, Ben, old people, Polly & child, Isaac, Nancy & child
.... pg 302, 5 June 1824, recap

hire of John G. HENDERSON's negroes

William MOUNT .... pg 305, 3 June 1816 – 1 Jan 1820, estate acct

Bill
.... pg 311, 29 Jan 1820 – 1 Jan 1824, estate acct

Bill

William GRAHAM .... pg 319, 29 Sept – 7 Nov 1821, estate acct

woman

Maria HAMILTON .... pg 324, 20 Jan 1821 – 1 Jan 1825, estate acct

negroes

John LINTON .... pg 326, 2 June 1823 – 1 Jan 1825, estate acct

Betsy & child, boy Ben to John L. HARRISON; Alfred, Cornelias to Mary WILLIAM; Bob to A. HOWISON; Harriet & child to T. TOWNSHEND; Henry to Samuel THOMAS; old Billy to Mrs. BREWER; Fanny to J.W. TYLER; Cely to J. CARRICO

William WIATT .... pg 331, 20 Oct 1817 – 7 Jan 1825, estate acct

Daniel
.... pg 333, 10 Mar 1825

Mahala WIATT received girl Milly; Malissa WIATT received girl Patience…part of their legacies

Dorcas DeBELL .... pg 334, 21 Sept 1821, estate acct

negroes

James McCLENACHAN ....
.... pg 336, 20 Aug 1817 – 31 May 1821, estate acct

   cash paid John McCLENACHAN for his wife

Robert LUTTRELL .... pg 338, 8 Apr 1819 – 1 Jan 1822, estate acct

   infirm woman, woman & child

James H. HOOE .... pg 343, 19 May 1825, inv & appr

   Bradley Farm:

   man Billy, boy Robert, woman & child Tom, woman & child Lidia, Cenale & 4 children Elijah, William, Anthony, & Mary; girl Mary, man Charles, young man Billy, boy Bob, girl Kitty

   Page Land:

   men Dick, Aaron, John, Sarah & 4 children Ben, John, Harriet, & Ann, old Cate, Jenny & child Charles, Kitty, Ned

   Bull Run Farm:

   woman & 2 children Lidia & Seale, woman & son Tom

William J. NEWMAN .... pg 347, 23 Nov 1824, inv & appr

   girl Charlotte, boys George, James, men Tom, Alan Pimbay, woman Betty, man York, woman Sally

Elizabeth CARTER .... pg 353, 20 Jan 1821 – 16 July 1825, estate acct

   negro, division of negroes, Billy

John BROWN .... pg 358, 3 Jan 1825, inv & appr

   man Phil, girl Eliza, Sarah, Ellen, Peter, Mary, Sophia, Ara, Howson, Rose

George BOSWELL .... pg 360, 15 Sept 1825, inv & appr

   Nancy & 2 children, Charlotte

Maria BRASSFIELD .... pg 364, 20 Oct 1825, will

   girl Fanny to sister Elizabeth BRASSFIELD

Maria BRASSFIELD ....pg 368, 14 Nov 1825, inv & appr

   girl Fanny

Thomas GREEN ....pg 369, 26 July 1825, inv & appr

   men Lewis, Harry, boy Walter, Anny & child, girl Anny, boy Noah, man Dick, Winney & child, boy Sandy

Edward GWATKIN .... pg 371, 24 Dec 1825, will

   Hagar, Emma, Charles, Addison, Washington to brother James & sister Francis

Constance CORNWELL ....pg 373, 14 Sept 1825, will

   Letty, Piney & her 2 children Elizabeth & Albert to grandson John CORNWELL oldest son of my daughter Catherine, if he attempts to sell any of the slaves they shall be free

William SHAW .... pg 376, 2 Jan 1826, inv & appr

   Phil, Joe, Charlotte & 2 children Beverly & Caroline, Maria, Sarah, Robert, Matilda & 2 children Rebecca & Henry, Charity, Lucy & 2 children Grandison & Pamela, big & little James, Fanny, Priscilla, Ben, Sandy

Daniel FOSTER ....pg 378, 8 Sept 1824, inv & appr

   Lewis, Mariah

Edwin GWATKIN .... pg 380, 6 Jan 1826, inv & appr

   boys Charles, Washington, Adison, woman Hagar, girl Emma

Richard DAVIS ....pg 383, 6 Feb 1826, inv & appr

   men Jim, Harry, woman Polly, Alsy & 2 children, Diza & 3 children, Sucky & 2 children, boys Jeffrey, Lewis, Phil, Edmond, John, girl Betty

Sarah ELWELL.......................pg 387, 5 Nov 1823, inv & appr

   Fancy, Jane, Mary, Fanny, Stephen

Bernard HOOE .... pg 389, 2 Apr 1826, inv & appr

> George, Lucy, Stepney, Gowin, Swam, Sam, Barnet, Presley, Charles, Moses, Tom, Sandy, Hannah & child, Jacob, Mary Ann, Moses Jr., Gustavus, John, Judah & child, Charles Jr., Winney, Amy, Nelly, Dinah, Lucy Jr., Moten, Milly, L_ny, Patience, Hannah Jr. & child, Jenny

George F. HUBER .... pg 392, 1 Mar 1826, will

> all slaves to wife Verlinda HUBER & after her death girl Eliza to Ann Eliza STANGLE; rest of slaves to John STANGLE

James NEWMAN .... pg 394, 19 Apr 1826, inv & appr

> man George, woman Judy, boy Bob, woman Harriet, girl Courtney, boy Tom, little girls Caroline, Tammy, man, Tony, girls Ann, Edia

Mary ANDERSON .... pg 399, 3 Apr 1826, inv & appr

> man William, woman Winney, boys William, Henry, girl Mary

Charlotte EWELL .... pg 403, 25 Jan 1826, will

> a servant Eleanor I purchased at the Belair sale, Frederick & his sister Mary to sister WEEMS for the benefit of M.L. WEEMS & F.M. WEEMS

John POTTS .... pg 406, 1824, estate acct

> hires

Timothy BRUNDIGE ...... pg 407, 17 Sept 1822 – 17 Jan 1826, estate acct

> Jess, John, man Austin, woman Comfort, girl Jane

.... pg 414, Sept 1822 – Jan 1826, estate acct

> Austin, man Austin, woman Comfort, woman Jane

Jesse SCOTT .... pg 426, 6 Nov 1822, will

> girls Fanny, Mary, boy Sandy to be emancipated at age 36 to wife Clarinda; men Jesse, Samuel, old woman Dolly to wife Clarinda; at wife's death boy Sandy to son James W. SCOTT in place of boy sold given to him by his aunt Orela MADDOX; at wife's death Jesse, Mary to son William L. SCOTT, Jesse is never to be sold out of the family but to be maintained by the estate

William WHEELER .... pg 429, 16 Mar 1826, inv & appr

    Jenny. Henry, Eliza, Jude, Evelina, Simon, Rosetta, Washington, Louisa

Thomas BRASSFIELD .... pg 432, 20 Dec 1823, inv & appr

    girl Polly

Thomas BRASSFIELD .... pg 433, 22 Dec 1823, acct of sales

    girl to Lucinda & Elizabeth BRASSFIELD

Jesse CORNWELL .... pg 437, 6 Dec 1825, inv & appr

    Frank 22 years, Betsy & 2 children Mahala & Jane; Betsy & her children in a suit in Superior Court of Prince William Co.

Constance CORNWELL .... pg 439, 6 Dec 1825, inv & appr

    Privey, Elizabeth, Albert, 1 infant, Lettice

William FRENCH .... pg 440, 30 Aug 1826, inv & appr

    Roger, West, Simon, Alexander, Thomas, Benjamin, Joshua, Gerard, Moses, Thornton, Jonathan, Caleb, Albert, Orange, Haywood, James, Toliver, Washington, Lucinda, Hester, Terry, Charlotte, Clary, Charles, Lorinda

Jane ALEXANDER .... pg 444, 4 Nov 1825, will

    Aron, Cloe, Sandy, Elic, Eliza, Vina, Caroline to daughter Sidney ALEXANDER

Robert THERMAN .... pg 451, 7 Aug 182, inv & appr

    men Jesse, Daniel Nat, Isaac, Barnett, Henson, woman Amy, girls Silvy, Mariah, Siner, boy George

Thomas THERMAN .... pg 453, 23 Sept 1826, inv & appr

    boy Phill, man Jacob; Elizabeth THERMAN has her life interest in Jacob by A. CONTRAST between her & Thomas THERMAN

William FLORENCE .... pg 457, 6 Nov 1826, inv & appr

    girl Ann

Dr. William S. ALEXANDER .... pg 458, 18 Nov 1826, inv & appr

> George, William, Mack, William, Daniel, Nelson, Henry, Louisa, Alice, Virginia, Cary, Mason, Jackson, Matilda, Bernard, Amanda, Richard

William SHAW .... pg 460, 30 Dec 1826, inv & appr

> men Philip, Benjamin, James Cook, James Peterson, Joe, Lucy & 3 children Granderson, Milly & Martha; woman Charity, Charlotte & 2 children, Caroline & Beverly; women Fanny, Sarah, boy Sandy, girl Maria, Matilda & 2 children Rebecca & Henry; woman Priscilla, man Robin

John BROWN .... pg 464, 25 Jan 1825, acct of sales

> men Fill (Phil?), Pug to Moses BOLWARE; woman Rose to Benjamin JOHNSTON; Sophia & 2 children to James LEGG; boy Peter to Charles S___; man Elijah to John LEACHMAN; Sarah & 2 children to Eli CRUPPER

John MILLS .... pg 469, 25 Nov 1826, inv & appr

> man Henson, boy Reuben, woman Winifred, girl Lucy, boy Amos, girl Harriet, woman Betty, Sharlot & 2 children

James GREEN .... pg 472, Oct 1826, inv & appr

> Simon 60 years, Simon's wife Sally 60, Dick, George, William, Nancy, Henry, Billy, Isaac, Abel, Sally & youngest child, Susan & child, Sara, Patsy & 2 children, Nelly, Elizabeth, Phillis, Simon 16, Harriet, Charity & child, Harrison, Adaline, Beverly & Frances two of Sally's children, Jane, Emmanuel, Charlotte, Ralph, Eliza

James GREEN .... pg 474, 20 Dec 1826, acct of sales

> old Simon & wife, old Sarah to George E. GREEN; Harrison, Jane to George H. NORRIS; Henry, Simon, Isaac to Lewis BERKELEY; Phillis to Peyton NAWAL; Sally & child to John H. CARTER

Benjamin DAWSON .... pg 479, 1 Dec 1825, will

> girl Mary to son Benjamin DAWSON in trust for daughter Nancy DAWSON; boy Daniel to son Benjamin DAWSON

Gainer FORTUNE..pg 480, 10 Oct 1826, will

>George, Lucy, Suck to daughter Caty DENNIS, Elizabeth, John to daughter Fanny CUNDISS; Manuel, Hannah, Jim, Ben & his mother Jane, left to my wife by her father, to daughter Polly FORTUNE; Cesar, Luzan to daughter Elizabeth JANNINGS; Henry, Carlene, Kate to daughter Lucy FORTUNE; Sam, Mary, Joe to daughter Nancy FORTUNE; Phil, Priscilla to son Thomas FORTUNE; Morris, Cealay to daughter Malinda BRAWNES

....codicil

>if the negroes in dispute left to my daughter Lucy FORTUNE are not recovered...

John LINTEN .... pg 482, 8 Apr 1823, inv & appr

>Fortune, Lewis, Adam, Matilda & child, Susan & boy child, Mary, Anne, Sally, Harriet & child, Alfred (dec'd), L__ Ann (dec'd), Bob

John LINTON .... pg 484, 14 May 1823, inv & appr

>old Billy 60 years, man Sam, Henry, Bob, boy Alfred, lad James Strout, boy Henry, lads Edward, Ben, _olydiro, Leige, child William, child Cornelius, little girl Cely, old woman Rachel, woman Mary, Betsy & baby, Eliza, boy Henry, George 3, Tom, Sophia, child Alexander, Manuel 40, boys Peter, Gustavus; Fanny 20, Maria 18, Harry 57, James 20, Sinah 26 & child, Cely 16, Kitty 15, Eliza 11, Louisa 10, Anthony 7, Leige 4, Betsy 5, Mary 3, Nancy

Gainer FORTUNE................................ pg 491, 8 Mar 1827, inv & appr

>Susan, Cate, Morrice, Priscilla, George, Philip, Hannah, Manuel, Mary, Caroline, Samuel, Cesar, Elisor, Clia, Henry, John, Susan Jr., Lucy, Joseph, James

George WILLIAMS ....pg 494, 4 Oct 1825, will

>boy Philip to grandson James A.M. MUSCHETT; boy Nat, girl Delia to grandson Jesse WILLIAMS; man John to son John W. WILLIAMS; the balance of slaves to be divided between my 4 children

Gerard ALEXANDER .... pg 495, 5 Dec 1826, div of slaves

>Kitty to Ashton ALEXANDER; Gerard, Frank to Gerard ALEXANDER; Matilda & child Henry to Needham L. WASHINGTON in right of his wife Sara; Ned to Griffin STITH in

right of his wife Mary dec'd; Nancy to Otho W. CALLIG in right of his wife Jane; Sarah & her 2 children Jerry & William to Sidney ALEXANDER

Benjamin DAWSON ....pg 497, 22 Feb 1827, inv & appr

boy Spencer, girl Eliza, woman Mary, boy Daniel, women Hannah, Celia, boys Gusta, Charles, Sandy

Benjamin DOUGLASS .... pg 500, 17 May 1823, will

Betsy to daughter Aminta Elizabeth MOXLY

Benjamin DAWSON ....pg 502, 1 Mar 1827, acct of sales

girl Eliza, boys Gusta, Charles, woman Carlia to George CHAPMAN; boy Spencer to Thomas FOSTER; woman & child to H.M. LEWIS

Willoughby Francis CANNON ....pg 504, 25 Oct 1823, will

Amy, Sam, Winney to nephew Barnaby CANNON; Charles, Jack, Loannah to nephew Luke CANNON; Abner & his sister Milly to be free; residue of negres in trust of nephews Barnaby CANNON & Luke CANNON Jr. for niece Ann LOWDON & her son John LOWDON

Moore HOFF .... pg 506, 24 May 1825, will

Eliza, Lucy, Harrison to daughter Pamelia; old Winney to choose her master

Henry DOGAN .... pg 507, 9 Oct 1824 - 1826, estate acct

girl Sarah, boy Tom, girl Cordy

William S. ALEXANDER .... pg 510, 3 Dec 1827, inv & appr

George, William, Mack, William, Daniel, Nelson, Henry, Louisa, Alsa & 4 children Virginia, Cary, Mason, & Jackson; Matilda, Amanda

WILL BOOK N
1827 - 1833

(Note: 214 pages missing.)

Thomas FITZHUGH .... pg 215, 20 July 1829, will

slaves heretofore given her to daughter Alice Thornton HEREFORD; man Jackson in addition to negroes heretofore given her to daughter Lucinda Helm RATCLIFF; same (but not Jackson) to daughters Susanna Conway BRYARLY, Mildred SHIP, Caroline Matilda FITZHUGH, & Elizabeth Conway NORTHEN; Sukey & her 2 children John & Amanda, Stephen, Lina to daughter Harriet Helen FITZHUGH; boy George to grandson Thomas Fitzhugh BRYARLY; Titus, Frank, David, Tom, Bartley, Ned, Nancy & her child Mary Ellen to son Daniel McCarty FITZHUGH

Thomas LUTTRELL .... pg 217, 7 Sept 1829, inv & appr

woman Jude & child Leanna, boys Frank, George, woman Agga, man Daniel

Matthew SANDERS .... pg 218, 12 Aug 1828, acct of sales

hired: Billy to Leonard SANDERS; Ginny to Thomas R. HAMPTON; Mary, Benton to Nancy SANDERS

William BROOKS............ pg 219, 1 May 1822 – 20 Oct 1829, estate acct

money from division of slaves

William RENOE .... pg 226, 4 Jan 1830, div of slaves

Fanny & child May, Martha, Moses, Jesse, Bazil, William, Page to William FLORENCE in right of his wife Louisa; Rachel, James, Harrison, Emily, Seqismond to Elizabeth RENOE; Celia & child Catharine, Henson, Daniel, Kemp, Mahala to George N.B. RENOE

Carr BAILEY .... pg 227, 25 Feb 1830, inv & appr

Simon, Lewis, Harry, Willoughby, Jona or Reuben, Tom, Milla, Drusilla?, Winna, Joshua, Andrew, Sally, Jane, Richard

Hezekiah MARTIN .... pg 230, 16 Jan 1830, inv & appr

   man Daniel, girls Lucy, Anne, woman Mima, Billy & wife Betty, woman & child (Violet)

Thompson GREEN .... pg 234, 8 Oct 1829, inv & appr

   man Lewis, boy Sandy, Phil

William TOMLIN .... pg 240, 1 Mar 1830, estate acct

   man

Alexander COMPTON .... pg 242, 2 Aug 1824 – 1 Jan 1826, estate acct

   cash to old Ned for fowls

Francis D. POMROY .... pg 244, 11 Jan – 12 Apr 1827, estate acct

   Wabler

John S. HARRISON .... pg 245, 12 Mar 1828 – 2 Nov 1829, estate acct

   George Cook, Charles, Mima, Phill, the hires of Richard ALLEN

Nathan HAISLIP .... pg 248, 16 Mar 1826 – 1 Jan 1828, estate acct

   Alfred

James JENNINGS .... pg 251, 28 Dec 1829, acct of sales

   girl Maria to E. JENNINGS

Thomas BEVERIDGE .... pg 260, 16 Jan 1830, acct of sales

   woman Charlotte to Henry A. BARRON

William L. SCOTT .... pg 262, 14 Apr 1830, will

   slaves to mother Clarinda SCOTT

Jane ALEXANDER .... pg 267, 17 Nov 1827, acct of sales

   young woman Eliza to G. William FOOTE; boy Sandy to George SMALLWOOD; Aaron, Cloe, Caroline to S. ALEXANDER

Jane ALEXANDER .... pg 271, Nov 1827, acct of sales

   (estate of Gerard ALEXANDER at Greenwood Farm)

division of negroes: Gerard, Francis to Gerard ALEXANDER; Kitty, Washington, Matilda & child, Stith, Ned to Ashton ALEXANDER; Sarah, Gerry, William, Callis, Nancy to Sidney ALEXANDER

Elizabeth GREEN .... pg 274, 5 July 1830, will

Amy & child, boy, Wat, small boy, Ferdinand to daughter Frances E. GREEN

Sandford THURMAN .... pg 275, 31 July 1826 - , estate acct

Phil, Jacob, Isaac, Henson sold (THURMAN vs THURMAN)

Judge William A. G. DADE .... pg 279, 7 Sept 1830, inv & appr

Ben 44 years, Billy 39, Henry 25, Lewis 23, Davy Parker 58, Adam 24, Uncle Davy, Bassett 27, George 18, Dennis 13, William of Penny, Charles of Fanny, Aaron 9, Gustavus 11, John of Sinah, Wallace of Fanny, Nelson of Kitty, Henry, Fanny & 4 children Matilda, Alcinda, Ben, & Virginia; Sarah Ann 13, Jane 14, Caroline 14, Amanda of Kate, Sinah & 3 children Murray, Cecelia, & Williamson; Lucy & 3 children Nancy, Mary, & Tasco; Kitty & 2 children Martha & Elizabeth; Penny & 2 children Caroline & Guynette; Betsy Maria, Mary Ann, Aunt Sophy, Aunt Kate, Aunt Milly

John LONG .... pg 283, 7Aug 1830, inv & appr

old woman

Matthew HARRISON .... pg 285, Jan 1808 – 8 Apr 1826, trustee acct

boy Henry, servants, negroes, Frank, Sam, Taylor, Ruth, Sarah, Sall, Bill, Eliza, Cate, Joan

.... pg 303, 8 Sept 1807 – Apr 1829, estate acct

Frank, Charlotte, Rachel, Andrew, Sawney, fee paid for division of estate, old man, Sam

James GREEN .... pg 315, 18 Aug 1828 – 20 July 1830, estate acct

girl Harriet, Nelly, Betsy, Eliza

Elizabeth GREEN .... pg 317, 9 Sept 1830, inv & appr

woman Amy, man Watt, boy Ferdinand, child Mildred

Jane CARNEY ....pg 319, 19 Aug 1830, inv & appr
> man James, Rose & child Manda, child Mary, Lucy, boy Tony, girl Milly

Thomas HOFF ....pg 323, 17 Oct 1830, inv & appr
> man Charles

William TOMLIN .... pg 325, 4 Nov 1828 – 27 Jul 1830, estate acct
> Joe

Richard H. PHILIPS .... pg 328, 1 Oct 1828 – 29 June 1829, estate acct
> George, Clem, Bob, Bill, Suckey & her children Sophia & Jane

Reuben CALVERT .... pg 340, 9 Nov 1825 – Dec 1827, estate acct
> negro

Nathan HAISLIP ....pg 341, Oct 1828 – 1 Aug 1830, estate acct
> Mason, Flora

Thomas I. NEWMAN ....pg 343, 15 May – 24 Dec 1829, estate acct
> Mima & child sold

Ellen Matilda DENT .... pg 344, 22 Jan 1831, will
> Phillis, Nelly, William, Judson, John to cousin Mary Frances Adeline THORNTON, wife of Stuart G. THORNTON, with request that Phillis goes to her daughter Caroline M. THORNTON, girl Nelly to daughter Ellen Matilda, boy William to Ellen's son Charles Edwin, & boy John to Ellen's son William Henry

A.M. BRISCOE......................................pg 348, 17 Aug 1830, inv & appr
> Robert, Francis

Alexander M. BRISCOE ....pg 350, 7 June 1831, acct of sales
> old Fanny to Thomas BRISCOE

Joseph R. GILBERT .... pg 353, 2 July 1831, inv & appr
> men John, Thomas, Sandy, woman Jenny, Luke

Richard NEWMAN .... pg 355, 6 May 1831, inv & appr

old man, woman & 2 children

W. George CHAPMAN ....
.... pg 356, 14 Dec 1829, inv & appr, Fauquier Co

Meadowville:

old Winney, old Hannah, old Jarrett, old Dick, Edmond, Milley, Mima & child, Mariah & child, Matilda, Scyntha, Bill, Rush, Eliza, Jeffy, Israel, Jim, William, Winney, Joshua, Lucy & child, Moses, Isaac, Silas, Alfred, Lucinda, Shadrack, Charity

Privado:

Lewis, Frank, George, Lucinda & child, Betsy, Anne, Mary, Susannah, Harriet

Cherry Hill:

Peter, Simon, Judy
....................................pg 358, 16 Dec 1829, inv & appr, Prince Wm. Co

Thoroughfare Farm:

Bill Curry, Bob, Winney & child, Matilda, Julianne, Jim, Priss, Tom, George, Ben, Letty, Harriet & child, Sarah Anne, Pug, Washington, John, Kitty & child, William, Susannah, Fredonia, Louisa & child, William (Pierce), Elias, Mary, Nancy, Abednego, Billy Buck, Abraham, Armistead, Dick, John, Simon, Jinney, Aggy & child, Celia, Martin, Peggy, Malvina, Hannah, Nat, Joshua, Gula, Harriet, Fanny, old Sukey

William FRENCH .... pg 365, 15 July 1831, inv & appr

West, Roger, Alexander, Thomas, Ben, Gerard, Moses, Thornton, Jonathan, Caleb, Albert, Washington, Charles, John, Penny, Lucinda Clary, Lorinda, Hester

Richard H. PHILIPS .... pg 367, 29 June 1830 – 29 Apr 1831, estate acct

Clem, George, Suckey & her 2 children, Bob, William

Dr. John SPENCE .... pg 375, Aug 1830, inv & appr

George White, George Osburn, Adison, Mary, Armistead, Mariah, Lavinia, George, John, Simon

Mary C. GALLAGHER .... pg 381, 1 Nov 1830, inv & appr
    Sarah, Moriah, James, Alfred

Nathan HAISLIP .... pg 381, 15 Jan 1830, estate acct
    Mason, Jack, Gabriel, Alfred, Toliver, Nelson, Tom, Flora

Martha E. PEYTON .... pg 383, 30 June 1831, will
    negroes to be hired out for 1 year and then emancipated

Joseph JONES .... pg 387, 31 Dec 1821, will
    slaves to wife Susanna

Clarinda SCOTT .... pg 389, 26 July 1830, will
    slaves to son James W. SCOTT

Alexander M. BRISCOE .... pg 390, 18 Aug 1830 – 6 June 1831, estate acct
    negro

Ellen M. DENT .... pg 397, 11 Aug 1831, inv & appr
    girl Phillis, man William, Judson, boy Thomas, girl Nelly

Judith CARTER .... pg 405, 2 Jan 1832, inv & appr
    man Tascoe, woman Beck & child

Garner FORTUNE .... pg 407, 16 Mar 1827 – 3 Nov 1831, estate acct
    hire of negro, Ciller, man Morris, George, Sam

William ROGERS .... pg 412, 23 Feb 1828, will
    man Vincent, woman Milly to son Reuben; boy David, woman Penny to daughter Susannah; girl Mary to children of daughter Fanny BENNET; boy George, girl Rachel to children of son William ROGERS; girl Julia to granddaughter Ann Maria BENNET; girl Maria to granddaughter Elizabeth ROGERS; girl Jane to granddaughter Martha ROGERS; man Hendly to choose his master

Temple FOUCHE .... pg 414, 3 Jan 1832, inv & appr
    Fanny & 4 children Frances, Catherine, Caroline, Sharlot

William RENOE .... pg 417, 1 June 1829, inv & appr

> men Daniel, James, Fanny & child, Aggy, Martha, Emily, Moses, Jesse, Harrison, Mahalia, Segismend, Kemp, Basil, Page, William, Henson, Celia & child Katherine, Rachel

Spencer BALL .... pg 426, 11 Jan 1831, will

> boy Robert son of Aggy to son Francis Waring BALL; choice of women to daughter Elizabeth Lucy CARTER; man Armistead to son Alfred BALL; woman Sukey daughter of Chloe to daughter Louisa BALL; woman Maria daughter of Sally to daughter Adeline BALL; daughter Frances Tasker LEWIS has in her possession woman Polly with her children who were sold by the sheriff & bought by ___ CARTER whom I hope will convey his title to my wife

David BOYLE .... pg 427, 29 May 1832, inv & appr

> Jesse, Billy, Priscilla, Mary, John, Nathaniel, Butler, Albert, Thomas

William BUCKLEY .... pg 443, 3 Aug 1849, estate acct

> Peggy, Maria

Sarah DADE .... pg 444, 10 Aug 1819, estate acct

> small girl Betsy, woman Huk retained by W.A.G. DADE or distributed with the other slaves?; the residue of the slaves were divided among the 3 other distributees Jane A.A. BAYLOR, Sally A. DADE, Eliza L. DADE

Josiah STONE .... pg 447, 7 Dec 1829, estate acct

> in the division of slaves: Samuel BOTTS, Charles STONE, Miss STONE, Fanny STONE, John STONE

Thomas HARRISON .... pg 460, 14 Feb 1816 - 1822, estate acct

> negroes, Bob, Scye, Lydia sold

William FRENCH .... pg 466, 5 Sep 1826 – May 1829, estate acct

> family of negroes sold

Hezekiah MARTIN .... pg 474, 16 Jan 1830 – 26 Oct 1831, estate acct

> old Billy, old Betty, Daniel sold; Violet & child Betsy, Lucy to Leanna MARTIN her dower

Elias B. MARTIN & others vs Leanna MARTIN .... pg 477, 3 Jan 1831, in Chancery

> ...slaves cannot be divided in kind...1/3 part of the slaves to Leannah MARTIN...the residue of slaves to be sold

Thompson GREEN ....pg 481, 10 Oct 1829 - 11 Nov 1831, estate acct

> Sandy sold to Daniel THORNBERRY; Louis?

James GREEN ....pg 483, 20 Jul 1830 – 16 June 1832, estate acct

> Eliza, Nelly, Betsy

William CARTER .... pg 485, 29 Feb 1828 – 1 Jan 1829, estate acct

> Sam, Bill; man James, woman Betty sold

William ROGERS .... pg 486, 9 May 1832, inv & appr

> Lewis the elder, Vincent, Bob, Winney & child Anthony, Sarah, Eleanor, children Mary, Hannah; Kitty, children Ca___, Lewis

Peter TRONE ....pg 488, 15 Aug 1832, inv & appr

> servant Harry, Charlotte, James, George, Milly & child, Willis, John, Sam, Izabella & child, Tom, Ann, Charles, Harrietta, Luke, Benjamin, Joseph

Sophia CARTER .... pg 492, 16 May 1832, will

> servants to sister Julia BERKELY & at her death to niece Sophia Carter BERKELY

Catherine C. ROE................................ pg 495, 13 Nov 1820, div slaves

> Nancy, Solomon, Henry, Ellen, Mary Jane, Alexander Marshall, Harriet, Washington, Adaline to Henry F. ROE; Robertson, Eleanor, John Beverly, Maria, Alfred to Ferdinand A. WEEDON; Milly, Westley, Bott, Margaret, Lewis to George WEEDON

David BOYLE.. pg 496, 1823 - 1830, estate acct

> Billy

Richard DAVIS .... pg 499, 4 June 1832, inv & appr

> Alcey & child Henry, boy John, girls Jane, Disy, Calary, Mary, Matilda

Joseph R. GILBERT .... pg 504, 25 Jan 1830 – 7 Aug 1832, estate acct

John, Luke, Tom, Sandy

Jane CARNEY ....pg 508, Aug 1830 - 21 July 1832, estate acct

woman Moll

Noah MADDOX .... pg 512, 23 July 1832, will

woman Eliza, man George, to wife Sarah MADDOX; Betty & 2 children may be sold but may not be taken a remote distance from her husband, if not sold to go to nephew Noah MADDOX son of Ignatious MADDOX; Baptiste & his wife Henny and their daughter Sarah to brother Allison MADDOX after the death of Sarah MADDOX; boys Sam, John the sons of Betty, girl Ann, boy Andrew to nephew James W. SCOTT; girl Harriet to nephew Thomas MADDOX son of Allison MADDOX after death of my wife; girl black Ann daughter of Baptists to nephew Joseph BRAWNER after death of my wife

Col. William ALEXANDER..................... pg 513, 1 Oct 1832, div slaves

Dishman, Kitty, Armistead, Sandy, Beverly, Susan, Charles, Joshua, Henry, Alice, Abraham, Westwood to William FOOTE; Aaron, Eliza, Jess, William, Mary, Douglas, Thompson, Peter, James, Matilda, Washington to Lawrence G. ALEXANDER; Frank, Nelson, Jacob, Sally, Lewis, Nancy, George, Jefferson, Fanny to Philip ALEXANDER; Francis & child in possession of P. ALEXANDER, Sally age 76 , Joshua to P. ALEXANDER

John G. RUBLEMAN ....pg 515, 26 Nov 1832, inv & appr

Vina & 3 children

Moses COCKRELL .... pg 517, 29 Jan 1833, div of slaves

yellow woman Fanny, black woman Fanny, Moses, Adalade, Alfred to Sarah COCKRELL; Daniel to William COCKRELL; Bernard to Thomas L. THURMAN in right of his wife; Melinda, Henry to Sarah COCKRELL; George to Benjamin COCKRELL; Francis to Hulah COCKRELL; Sanford to Mary COCKRELL; Edward, Reuben to Johnson COCKRELL; John to Jesse COCKRELL

Samuel JACKSON .... pg 518, 30 July 1819 - 2 June 1826, estate acct

David, Bob

Richard L. FOOTE .... pg 521, 14 Feb 1833, will

> Sprigg, Abram to sister Sarah L. FOOTE; Indy, Harrison to sister Helen _. FOOTE; Albert, Vina to, sister Elizabeth W. CHE_IG; interest in the servants coming to me at the death of Mrs. McNAMARA of Lancaster County to be divided between brothers Haywood FOOTE & William L. FOOTE; Daniel

Henry DOGAN .... pg 522, 7 Aug 1832, estate div

> slaves to be divided among Elizabeth DOGAN, Harriet BEEDLE, Jane HARRISON nee DOGAN, John DOGAN

> Lot 1: George, Eliza, Mimy & child, Margaret, Jane to Harriet BEEDLE; Lot 2: Travis, Nelson, Mary, Louisa, Mary Ann to Elizabeth DOGAN; Lot 3: Moses, Ira, Sukey, Jack to Allen HARRISON in right of his wife Jane; Lot 4: Daniel, Charles, Marshall, Maria to John DOGAN; Lot 5: Phil, James, Hannah, Clary, Will to William N. DOGAN

Gustavus B. TYLER .... pg 530, 23 Agu 1822, inv & appr

> men George, Richard, girls Cecelia, Aggy, boy Isaac

Gustavus B. TYLER .... pg 531, 1822, acct of sales

> Aggy to Peyton REID, Celia to E.A. BRITE

(pages 534 & 535 missing)

Susanna F. GRAHAM .... pg 536, 8 Sept 1827, will

> Joe, Charles, Daniel, Jenny to William Arthur HOOE son of Thomas B.C. HOOE; Jesse, Mary Ann to niece Susan Hooe SWEENY; Harrison, Nutty, Maria & her child Winney to Virginia HOOE daughter of nephew John HOOE; Nelly to Mary Elizabeth HOOE daughter of nephew Bernard HOOE; Alfred to Anna Maria HOOE daughter of Bernard HOOE; Leanah to Ellen HOOE daughter of Bernard HOOE; Felicia to Cecilia HOOE daughter of Bernard HOOE; Gengs to Albert RUSSELL son of Col. Albert RUSSELL; Manuel to John RUSSELL son of Col. Albert RUSSELL; Daniel to James RUSSELL son of James RUSSELL; John Parker, Elijah, Beck to nephew John HOOE; Henson to John Eugene SWEENY son of John H. SWEENY; Kitty, Virgin to John HOOE Jr. in trust for niece Ann C. HARRISON wife of John P. HARRISON; Harry, Aga to Maj. Charles HUNTON in trust for Ann Gailand HOOE wife of Thomas B.P.

HOOE; Franky, Anna to John HOOE, Jr. in trust for George SWEENY & Sarah B. SWEENY children of nephew Hugh SWEENY; Lewis to great-nephew Joseph Thompson HOOE son of Thomas B.P. HOOE; Cambridge to great-nephew Alfred Luckett HOOE, son of Thomas B.P. HOOE
.... memorandum

Cambridge to Gonynn PAGE is cancelled; Lewis to 2nd son of Fanny PRYOR is cancelled

WILL BOOK O
1833-1842

(pages 1 and 2 missing)

James GWATHIN.................................. pg 3, 2 Apr 1833, acct of sales

 Charles, Addison, Emily & child to L. HUTCHISON; Lewis to A. HARRISON; Washington to W. GRIGSBY; Harriet to James FEWELL; Moses to G. LATIMER; Matilda & child to M. DAVIS; Laura to Mrs. HITH; old woman to S. LYNN; old woman to M. HARRISON

Richard H. PHILIPS............ pg 8, 29 Apr 1831 – 31 Dec 1832, estate acct

 (C. Ann R. PHILLIPS infant child of R.H. PHILLIPS dec'd)

 Clem, Suckey & 2 children, George, Bill; Bob sold to Peyton NORVILLE, Will sold to J.M. SAUNDERS

Thomas BEVERIDGE ....pg 10, 1828 – 15 Oct 1830, estate acct

 Charlotte sold

William LEBERMAN............................pg 11, 7 Nov 1831, inv & appr

 Mary 30 years, Caroline 10, Martha 7, Albina, Tiberius 65

Robert H. HOOE.................................. pg 17, 27 Dec 1832, inv & appr

 Johnathan, Barsheba, William, Solomon, Letty, Beverly, Rachel, Thomas, Gerard, William, Daniel, Jiles, Henry, Dinah, Page, Jane, Carter, Spencer, Nelly, Sarah, Davy, Richard, Friday, Hester, Charles, Mary, Peter, Lucy, Leannah, Michael, Cate, Davy, Lewis, Edwan, Ellen, Mary Ann, Minty, Emanuel, Sarah, James, Anthony, Wallace, Richard, Kissy, Jesse, Clara, Caroline, Albert, Elias, Bernard, William, Bud, Dolly, Alexander, Thornton, Amanda, Juda, Lawson, Harriet, Moriah, Jehnah, Charles, William, Lawson, Ned, John, Philip, Charles

Robert LATHAM ....pg 21, 18 Feb 1833, will

 girls Celia who was originally called Tenar, Elija to wife Sarah LATHAM; boy Moses, woman Delilah, girl Harriet, boy Randle, old woman Ann to son John LATHAM; Nancy & her son Charles to grandchildren Robert Candiffs, Margaret Elizabeth, Lucy Ann,

Thomas Richard, & Susannah by son Robert LATHAM dec'd; Henry, Agnes, Jane, Esther, John to son Thomas LATHAM; Charlotte, Ann, Martha, James, Washington to daughter Lucy LATHAM

Sampson WINDSOR .... pg 22, 5 June 1833, will

boy David to son Alfred WINDSOR

Jane ALEXANDER .... pg 23, 1 July 1833, inv & sale

Aaron, Chloe, Caroline to L. ALEXANDER; lad Gandy to G. SMALLWOOD; Elisa to G.W. FOOTE

Richard NEWMAN .... pg 26, 2 Apr 1831 – Jan 1832, estate acct

Lilera & children sold

William C. MURPHEY .... pg 28, 15 July 1831 – June 1832, estate acct

Arch

Mildred FOX .... pg 32, 15 May 1833, inv & appr

man John, girl Nancy

Enoch RENOE .... pg 32, Apr 1828 – Apr 1830, estate acct

Seymore, old Dinner; old Solomon sold

Isaac BRIDWELL .... pg 35, 12 Mar 1833, will

girl Rose Ann, old Nancy to daughter Mary; girl Sophia to daughter Franey; Daniel, Elijah, Vinia to son Lewis, daughter Elizabeth & son Langhorne

Jane ALEXANDER .... pg 36, 1826, estate acct

Chloe, Aaron, Caroline to Miss Sid ALEXANDER sole heir of Jane ALEXANDER; Elisa

Temple FOUCHE .... pg 40, 5 Dec 1831, inv & appr

Harry 4 years 10 months, Milly 60

Temple FOUCHE .... pg 40, 21 Dec 1831, acct of sales

Harry to H. ROGERS; Milly to I.L. MARTIN

Fanny & her 4 children Jane, Katherine, Caroline & Charlotte to William COOMBS

James GREEN................pg 44, 16 Jun 1832 – 15 Sept 1833, estate acct
  Nelly, Betsy, Eliza & child sold
John LINTON ....pg 46, 1829 - 26 Feb 1833, estate acct
  Mary, girl Cely
Reuben CALVERT Jr. ....pg 50, 4 Jan 1831 – 6 Feb 1833, estate acct
  Lewis, Tom, slaves sold
Sarah KING............................pg 51, 7 Nov 1831 - May 1832, estate acct
  George, Ben, Jim
Daniel KING ....pg 52, Aug 1831 – 5 Oct 1833, estate acct
  negroes, old George sold
Alexander DAVIS .... pg 55, 9 Aug 1833, exec acct
  Phil, division of the negroes, Harry sold
William WHEELER................................ pg 57, 20 Jan 1834, inv & appr
  men Jerry, Simon, boy George Washington, Ebalina & child Margaret, women Eliza, Rozetta, girl Louisa, woman Judith
Robert LATHAM ....pg 59, 6 Mar 1832, inv & appr
  Nancy, Charles
Houson HOOE ....pg 63, 19 Oct 1833, will
  Britt, Eliza, Eliza Jr., Alexander, Olina, Grace, Lewis, Julian, Peter, Richard, Thornton to daughter Elizabeth; Charles, Charlotte, Kitty, Daphne, Emanuel, Mary, John son of Sucky, Jane, John, Hanson to daughter Jane; Buddy, Lavinia, Celia, Jerry, Mason to son James HOOE; Ben Sr., Ben Jr., Lucy, Tom, to son Edward HOOE; Austin, Caroline, Sooky, Antony to son Richard HOOE; Daniel, Sarah, Jesse in trust for son Houson
Emily FOX .... pg 70, 28 Aug 183_, estate acct
  slaves hired, sold, divided

George BRETT ....pg 72, 6 Mar 1834, acct of sales

   2 girls sold

Francis H. DUNNINGTON ......pg 81, Apr 1827 – 1 Jan 1832, estate acct

   Tom Brooks, Maria, Bonaparte, Caroline

C.C. ROE .... pg 84, 3 Feb 834, estate acct

   Nancy, Solomon, Henry, Ellen, Mary Jane, Alexander Marshall, Harriett, Washington, Alaline, (Adaline?) to Henry F. ROE; Robertson, Eleanor, John, Beverly, Maria, Alfred to Ferdinand A. WEEDEN; Milly, Westley, Bett, Margaret, Lewis to George WEEDON

Colin CAMPBELL.................pg 86, 1830 – 12 Aug 1831, estate acct

   Davy

Gustavus B. TYLER .... pg 87, 28 Dec 1821 – 6 Oct 1826, estate acct

   Milly, Isaac, Dick, George

George BRETT ....pg 89, 5 Feb 1831 – 16 Mar 1833, estate acct

   2? girls sold

Margaret GALLAGHER................. pg 90, 28 May 1833, will

   man George Chapman to daughters Ann, Margaret, & Julia GALLAGHER

Robert LATHAM ....pg 92, 29 Oct 1833, inv & appr

   Sharlotte & 3 children Martha, James, & Washington; Henry, Aggy & 3 children Jane, Esther, & John; Delilah, Cely, Eliza, Ann, Moses, Harriet, Randall

Houson HOOE ....pg 94, 18 Feb 1834, inv & appr

   men Thomas, Britt, woman Eliza, Eliza & child, Austin, boy Alexander, girls Selina, Grace, boy Lewis, girl Juliana, boys Peter, Richard, Thornton, man Charles, Charlotte & child, girls Catharine, Daphne, boys Manuel, John Henry, Henson, man Daniel, girl Cecelia, boy John, old men Mason, Anthony, Buddy, woman Lavina, boy Jerry, girl Lucy, Sarah, girls Jane, Mary, Caroline, men Ben, Jesse

George F. HUBER .... pg 101, Mar 1828 – 19 July 1830, estate acct

Henry, George & wife Polly, Eliza sold

Richard FOOTE ....pg104, 4 Aug 1834, inv & appr

Thornton, Nancy, Mary Ann, Catharine, Robert, Will, Pompey, Mason, Rolly, Charles, Friday, Reuben, Ben, Jesse, Davy, little Rolly, Davy, Charles, Manuel, Watson, Dick, Jesse, Washington, Daphne, Anna, Jinney, Fanny & child Henry, Harriet & child Robert, Enoch, Elias, big William, little William, Frederick, Joe, Reuben, Thomas, Wesley, Sydney, Phoebe, old Jinney, Emily & child Daniel, Elizabeth & child Joshua, Kizziah & child Lorenzo, Dinah & child Julia Ann, Ann, Matilda, Martha, Charlotte, Mary, Adelaide, Sarah, Eliza, Frances, Susan, Simon, Lucy, Albert, Lucy

Richard H. PHILIPS..............................pg109, 1 Jan 1833 - , estate acct

Suckey & children Jane & Harriet, Clemont, George

Charles E. DADE ....pg 111, 1 Sept 1834, inv & appr

Lewis, Burnnell, James Henry, David Parke, Nelson, Horace, Elizabeth, Kitty, Martha, Sophy, Mary, Heartly, Easter, William Henry, Betsy, Emanda, Henry Harris, Bassett

Richard DAVIS .... pg 115, 1 Oct 1832 - 1833, estate acct

woman & 4 children; girl Jane, Alice & 2 children Betsy & Henry, girls Disy, Clarissa, Matilda, Mary, John sold

Eleanor P. LYNN ....pg 117, 4 Oct 1834, inv & appr

Kitty & 2 small children

Catherine L. HANCOCK ....pg 119, 4 Oct 1832, will

(see also pg 189 & 267)

all slaves over 25 years of age to be free & slaves under 25 to be free when they attain that age
.... pg 120, 4 Oct 1832, codicil

Lucy Ann to serve my relation Frances B. GIBSON wife of John GIBSON Jr. until the age of 25; Emily & Dolly daughters of Kate, servant Lucy shall serve as above; Kate does not desire to be emancipated and will go to friend Mrs. Ann WARD

Augustine WEEDON .... pg 121, 6 Jan 1834, inv & appr

Jack, Tom, William, women Mariah, Nancy

John LYNN ....pg 124, 1 Sept 1834, inv & appr

Mary Taylor who was family; Mary Lynn & not return?

David JAMESON...................................pg 126, 13 Oct 1934, inv & appr

boy John

David BOYLE... pg 129, 5 Mar 1834, div of slaves

Billy, Mary, Albert, Thomas, John to Thomas M. BOYLE; Sylla, Jesse, Nat, Butler to Angelina K. BOYLE

Peter TRONE ....pg 130, 1 Oct 1832, estate div

Sarah A. TRONE, dower: George, Tom, James, Milly & child, Harriett; Lot 1: Willis to John. C. WEEDON; Lot 2: John to John TRONE; Lot 3: Sam to George WEEDON; Lot 4: Ann to James TRONE; Lot 5: Charles, Harry to Lucinda TRONE; Lot 6: Isabella & her child Sandy to William A. TRONE

George BRETT ....pg 134, 25 July 1831 – 11 June 1834, estate acct

2 girls sold

Thomas B. HOOE .... pg 136, 1834 – 1 Jan 1835, estate acct

Joe, Charles, Daniel, Janney, Leah, Nancy & 3 children, Lewis, Cynthia

Richard FOOTE .... pg 137, 28, 29 Aug 1834; sales

man Rolly to ALSOP

William ASHMORE ....pg 152, 15 Feb 1834, will

Moses, Melinda to wife Sarah M. ASHMORE; Melinda to daughters Betsy G. BERRYMAN & Sarah F. ALEXANDER after the death of my wife

....codicil, 2 Feb 1835

in place of Melinda substitute Nancy & her son Edward abt 2 or 3 years old & shall go as directed at wife's death

William ASHMORE ....pg 155, 2 Feb 1835, inv & appr

> Lucy & child Ella, John, Malinda, George, Matilda, Lenora, William, Mary, Peggy, Joseph, Joshua, Solomon, Moses, Julian, Milly, Jacob, Junius, Nancy, Edward

George F. HUBER ....pg 157, 4 Mar 1835, inv & appr

> man Addison, George, Henry, Eliza, Polly

David BOYLE .... pg 162, 8 May 1832 – 2 Feb 1835, estate acct A

> Mary & children, Scilla, Nat, John, Oliver, Billy King, Albert, Tom, Jesse, John

William TOMLIN .... pg 170, 27 July 1830 – 15 Mar 1832, estate acct

> Joe

Lucy LATHAM .... pg 171, 11 Dec 1833, inv & appr

> Charlotte & her 3 children Martha, James, & Washington; Ann

Benson DAVIS ....pg 185, 12 Mar 1835, inv & appr

> man Harry, Loney, Barnett, woman Charlotte, Ruth, Mahaly & child

Catharine HANCOCK ....pg 189, 4 Oct 1832, will

> (see also page 119 & 267)

Sarah COURTNEY .... pg 194, 24 July 1833

> man Charles 43, Aggy 64 years to Chapman G. CLARK

Willoughby W. TEBBS .... pg 195, 24 Dec 1832, inv & appr

> Sandy, Dick, Charles, Bainbridge, Hannah, Martha & child, Harry, Elijah, Enoch, man James, boy James

Sally LINTON .... pg 207, 6 Aug 1835, codicil

> slave of late husband to pass to granddaughter Sarah E. LINTON; John W. TYLER to purchase my servant Matilda, wife to Luke Johnson, so that she may remain with her husband

Robert HAMILTON..........pg 208, 9 Sept 1835, inv & appr

   men Jacob, Griffin, women Dolly, Beck, Caty, girl Cornelia, woman Betty

Willoughby W. TEBBS..pg 215, 15 May 1835 – 1 Jan 1834, estate acct

   Enoch sold; Charles, Dick, Sandy, Elijah, Harry, Bainbridge, Jenny, Hannah, Ann

Henry L. DAVIS..........................pg 221, 2 Nov 1835, inv & appr

   girl Julet (Juliet?)

William LYNN..............................pg 222, 10 Nov 1835, inv & appr

   woman Moll

Carr BAILEY...............pg 223, 15 Oct 1831 – 23 Nov 1832, estate acct

   Lewis sold

John S. HARRISON..........pg 227, 2 Nov 1829 – 2 Nov 1835, estate acct

   old Mima, Nancy

William WHEELER................. pg 234, 18 Feb 1836, estate acct

   Jerry, Evaline & child, woman Elisa, boy George, woman Rozetta, girl Louisa

John P. ROLLINS ....pg 236, 13 Aug 1835, will

   Esther & her children Edmand & an infant to sisters Sally WHITE & Nancy ROLLINS

Cornelius SKINNER .... pg 238, 5 June 1834, will

   woman & children previously given to her to daughter Elizabeth TAYLOR

Jesse CORNWELL .... pg 239, 31 Dec 1825 – 7 Mar 1836, estate acct

   Frank

Richard FOOTE .... pg 254, 11 Feb – 30 July 1836, estate acct

Jesse, Fele?, man Harry, boy Watson belonging to estate sold, girl Martha, man William, Frederick, Jenny, Charlotte, Dinah & child; Rolly belonging to estate of R. FOOTE dead sold, Elizabeth & 2 children, boys Washington, Richard, girl Mary sold, Joe sold; Enoch, Ann sold to _._. FOOTE; Emily & 2 small children sold, Nancy, Adelaide sold to Dr. F.F. CHEVIS; Jesse sold, Charles sold, Matilda sold, Davy sold, William to be sold in Mississippi to B. SIMMS; Manuel, Elias, Phoebe & child, Ben, William, Davy, Charles, Jesse, old Reuben, young Reuben, Pompey, Friday, Thomas, Lynda, Jinny, Anna, Harriet & 2 children, Fanny & 3 children

Jesse WARDEN .... pg 265, 6 June 1836, estate acct

Jack, Mariah Sr., Andrew, Mary, Mariah Jr., Caroline

Mary to Richard STONNEL in right of his wife; Mariah Jr. to John WARDEN; Jack, Caroline to William STONNEL in right of his wife; Andrew to Walter WARDEN; Mariah Sr. to Richard WARDEN in right of his father

guardian encourgaged to sell slave of Richard WARDEN abt 11 years old – slave abt 40 years old - worth more now then when Richard reaches age 21

Catherine HANCOCK............................pg 267, 4 Oct 1832, will

(see also pg 119 & 189) Discussion follows will.

Michael CLEARY .... pg 270, 19 Sept 1836, inv & appr

Tom, Polly, Robert, Betty, Louisa, Henry, Joe

Richard FOOTE .... pg 272, 7 Nov 1836, div of slaves

Lot 1: man Reuben, Reuben Jr., girl Sarah, boy Richard, old woman Sidney, Harriet & her child to Helen FOOTE; Lot 2: man Elias, Fanny & child, man Jesse, girl Eliza, boy Robert to William L. FOOTE; Lot 3: Kizziah & her child, girl Frances, boy Thomas, man Ben, old man Pomprey to Hayward FOOTE; Lot 4: woman Phoebe, boy Wesley, girl Susan, boy Lorenzo, men Emanuel, Friday to James B.C. THORNTON in right of his wife Sarah L. THORNTON; Lot 5: man Davy, women Jinny, Anna, man Charles to Francis T. CHIVIS in right of his wife Elizabeth W. CHIVIS

Thomas P. HOOE ....pg 273, 12 Aug 1836, will
   old man Stepney to J. Seddon MASON

Phillip D. DAWES ....pg 275, 9 Oct 1832, inv & appr
   man Jerry

Thomas P. HOOE ....pg 283, 26 Sept 1836, inv & appr
   man Stepney

David JAMISON ....pg 287, 21 May 1834 - 1836, estate acct
   John, James sold

Truman TOWNSHEND .... pg 296, 3 Apr 1837, inv & appr
   girl Martha, woman Joan, girl Maria, boy Henry

Thomas TURNER .... pg 308, Nov 1832 – 1 Dec 1836, estate acct
   Winney

Caroline KINCHILOE .... pg 311, 18 Mar 1837, inv & appr
   man Jesse, boy Dennis

Matthias COLE .... pg 315, 3 Apr 1837, inv & appr
   woman Sarah, man Sanford

Elizabeth FOSTER ....pg 316, 20 Feb 1827, will
   Charles of husband's estate sold to son Isaac FOSTER replaced with Aaron

Jonathan REEVE...................................... pg 320, 2Sept 1837, inv & appr
   women Charity, Mariah, young man William, boys Silas, Charles, girl Jane, small boy Tom, small child Susan

Elizabeth G. BERRYMAN ....pg 322, 28 July 1836, will
   man Rolly, woman Milly to husband Alexander BERRYMAN

Dade HOOE ....pg 332, 1820, will
   Richard, black John, Charlotte & her children Ann & Jesse, Bob, Lily, Sarah, Harry, John, Osborne, Caty, Maria, Mack, Manuel, William to

wife; remaining slaves after the life estate of my wife to be divided between son Dade HOOE & George James HOOE; Nancy, Arthur, Lucy, Cooper, Sinah, Alsy, James, Washington to John HOOE Jr. in trust for daughter Lucy DANIEL wife of Richard DANIEL; Caroline & her son Charles, Polly, William, little Richard, Albert, Mary, Townshend to John HOOE Jr. in trust for daughter Mary HOOE wife of Francis Townshend HOOE

Elizabeth FOSTER ....pg 337, 15 Nov 1837, inv & appr

woman Alley, man Henry, woman & child, girl Jinny, boys Billy, Martin, old man Dick

Sarah LINTON ....pg 343, Oct 1835 - 15 Aug 1837, estate acct

Tom

Robert HAMILTON............ pg 345, 6 July 1835 - 4 Dec 1837, estate acct

girl Cornelia sold

Elizabeth GREEN ....pg 348, Oct 1830 – 24 Nov 1837, estate acct

Wats

Cornelius SKINNER ....pg 350, 8 Sept 1836, inv & appr

woman Winney, men Alfred, Andrew Jackson

Cornelius SKINNER .... pg 352, 15 Sept 136, acct of sales

man Alfred to Bernard BUCKNER; man Jackson to John W. PATTERSON; woman Winney to Frances ROSSOW

Willoughby W. TEBBS...
.... pg 355, 15 May 1835 – 14 Nov 1836, estate acct

Bainbridge sold; Elijah, Sandy, Charles to H.B. POWELL; Richard, Ann, John to Charles SIMAN; Martha & 2 children, Jane, James to William BYRNE; Dick, Hannah; Harry sold

William ASHMORE .... pg 358, 7 Nov 1836, div slaves

George, Lonora, William, Lucy, Ellen to Frances E. ALEXANDER; Solomon, Mary, Matilda, Joshua to Alexander BERRYMAN

Charity WEIR .... pg 362, 23 Mar 1838, will
   girl Mary to son Alexander WEIR

William WIATT .... pg 363, 2 Nov 1835, estate acct
   girl to John ROSSEN & wife

Catherine L. HANCOCK ....
.... pg 365, May 1814 - 31 Mar 1838, estate acct A

Margaret L. HANCOCK ....
.... pg 373, 31 Oct 1834 - 31 Oct 1838, estate acct B

   Abraham, boys Edwin, Joseph, Washington, girls Arrilly, Lucy, Ann, Dolly, Richard, Oliver, Humphrey, Phil, Lewis, Bob, Peter, Leannah, Daniel, Joe, Sandy, Willis, Sampson, John, Anna, William, Rebecca, Price, Ganderson, Charles, Henson, Richard, Arena, Joseph, Solomon, Andrew, Sally, Lawson, Mary Ann, Susan, Judy, Louisa, Molly & son Andrew 4 years

.... pg 381, 25 May 1835 -, estate acct C – D

C.L. HANCOCK .... pg 382, Nov 1834 – 31 Mar 1838, E
   Leannah, John

Catherine L. HANCOCK ....
....pg 383, 1836 - 1837, hires of slaves F

   Peter son of Rose, Sinah daughter of Rose, Abraham son of Nan, Nelly daughter of Maria, George son of Nan, Phillip son of Lavinia, Daniel son of Jenny, Humphrey son of Hannah, Milly daughter of Jenny, Amy daughter of Sinah, Jenney, old Lewis, Mary 52 years & has children, Betsy 40-50 & children, Harriet 30-40 & has children, Martha 30, Rose, Molly 30 & has children, old Lavinia; Nelson an emancipated slave

.... II

   1-Betsy, 2-Peter, 3-George, 4-Phillip, 5-Millford, 6-Humphry, 7-Milly, 8-Molly 9-Abraham, 10-Lewis, 11-Martha, 12-Mary, 13-Jenny, 14-Harriet, 15-Lavinia, 16-Amey, 17-Daniel

   There does not appear to have been advances to Sinah, Nelly, & Rose, 3 of the emancipated slaves

emancipated slaves of said estate entitled to equal distributable portions...
..................................pg 387, Apr 1838, Commissioner's Statement

recap of estate accounts A - F

Richard P. SCOTT ....pg 392, 31 Dec 1834 – 15 June 1837, estate acct

...going to Maryland for slaves & returning with same; Billy, woman & children sold

Cornelius SKINNER........pg 401, 24 Feb 1837 – 13 Aug 1838, estate acct

Briscoe, Rolly (slaves?)

James HOOE ....pg 402, 10 Oct 1838, will

Jerry to sister Jane HOOE to be freed after 10 years

Philip ALEXANDER.................................pg 403, 6 Aug 1831, will

old Anthony to wife Frances B. ALEXANDER; woman Matilda, girl Sylla to daughter Frances WORK

William SMITH .... pg 408, 7 Jan 1839, inv & appr

Moses

James DOWELL .... pg 410, 16 Jan 1838, inv & appr

girl Ann, boy Charles

William LONG....................................... pg 414, 20 Dec 1837, inv & appr

old woman Winney Jackson

James HOOE... pg 420, 2 Apr 1839, inv & appr

old Mason, Levinia

James HOOE .... pg 421, 2 Apr 1839, acct sales

old Mason to William ROACH; old Levinia to Samuel TANSILL

Sarah C. CALVERT...pg 422, 21 Aug 1839, will

Lewis, Henny, William to son Robert A. CALVERT; Ned, Delia, Julia to son Robert A. CALVERT in trust for daughter Chloe Ann COOPER wife of Benjamin COOPER

George TENNILLE .... pg 443, 5 May 1838, will

> James, Jeffrey, Celia & her child to son James D. TENNILLE; Silas, Garret, Martha, Mary & her child to son Alexander TENNILLE; Harrison, George, Maria, Nelly & her children Robert & John to grandson George A. DOUGLAS

John UNDERWOOD .... pg 444, 29 July 1840, inv & appr

> woman Harriet

Capt. John UNDERWOOD .... pg 457, 17 June 1839, acct of sales

> Eliza Ann to John ALLISON

Jacob LANGYHER .... pg 477, 24 Sept 1840, inv & appr

> woman Milly, man Tom, boy James

Strother RENOE .... pg 483, 8 Apr 1841, inv & appr

> men Armistead, Edmond, Daniel, Adam, Nathan, Godfrey, Robert, Joseph, Chat, old Joseph, Charles, women Jane, Dicy, Viney, Charlotte, Harriet, boys Spence, Wallace, girl Emily, Jane & children Mary 3 & Charles 1, Harriet & children Peter 5, Amandy 4, & Lyia Ann 1

William ROSE Sr. .... pg 485, 23 Mar 1841, will

> Sucky & her children Francis, Sandy & James to be sold; Lou, Milly & her infant child Julia Ann to wife Mary ROSE; boy James to son William; boy Ellick to son Israel; boy George to son Robert; boy Charles, girl Lucy Ellen to daughter Juliet; girl Hannah to daughter Mary THOMAS; girl Mary __ to daughter Levina BYRD; Sarah Jane to son Robert in trust for daughter Sarah S. SPENCER

Strother RENOE .... pg 489, 10 June 1841, inv & appr

> old women Lucy, Charlotte, men Daniel, Adam, Chatt, Nathan, Godfrey, Robert, Edmon, Joseph, Armistead, old Joseph, Charles Cooper, woman Winney, Harriet & child, Jane & 2 children, boys Spence, Willis, Peter, girl Amanda, Dicy & boy, girls Emily, Whitney

George A. COLLIS .... pg 494, 14 May 1841, acct of sales

> man Bob to M. COLLIS

William SELECMAN ....pg 505, 1 July 1841, estate acct
    Alvina, Tibe, Caroline

Reuben CALVERT ....pg 510, 1 Jan 1833 – 1 Jan 1836, estate acct
    man Tom

James NELSON .... pg 517, 6 Dec 1841, inv & appr
    Daniel, Milly, Maria, Ned, Christopher, Dennis, Lewis, Sarah, Joshua, Sam

George ROBERTSON .... pg 521, 6 Dec 1841, inv & appr
    Malinda

Ann HOOE... pg 523, 29 Jan 1842, inv & appr
    women Hannah, Martha, girl Fanny

Samuel MILSTEAD................................. pg 528, 10 Jan 1840, inv & appr
    Priscilla age 47, Artimacy 9, Mary Adalin 2, Sandy 27, white Tom 22, big Tom 47, Cornelius 15, William 13, James 12, Anne 21 & her child, Louisa 45 & her child, Albert 9, Mahaly 7, Emma 9, Edward 5, Lydia 6, John 3

WILL BOOK P
1842-1850

(pages 1 – 140 missing)

Daniel FOSTER .... pg 143, 18 Apr 1825 – 18 Apr 1843, estate acct

    Maria, Lewis sold, York, Sophia, Mary

Thomas DAVIS .... pg 153, 15 May 1843, will

    boy Lewis to son Jesse W. DAVIS; woman Harriet to son William W. DAVIS; boy Bob to daughter Sarah WINDSOR; girl Martha to daughter Fanny TANSILL & at her death to grandson Thomas TANSILL; Patty & child Mary Jane to daughter-in-law Sophia DAVIS wife of son Hugh W. DAVIS; boy James to son John W. DAVIS; boy Jesse to daughter Harriet KEYES

Eliza L. DADE .... pg 155, 5 Aug 1844, will

    Esau to niece Roberta SLYE; man Richard, girl Susan to Marian G. SLYE; boys Davis, Thomas to Gwynnella P. SLYE

George ATKINSON .... pg 159, _ Dec 1844, inv & appr

    man Albert, boys George, Charles, Osborn, girl Prissey, boy Albert, woman Hannah, Henry

Euphan BRENT .... pg 166, 25 Mar 1845, will

    Evelina & her youngest child Kitty Chin to daughter Euphan STARK

George ROBERTSON .... pg 167, 1843 – 28 Sept 1844, estate acct

    negro sold

Richard GILL .... pg 175, 22 Apr 1845, inv & appr

    old woman Peggy

Ann S. GILL .... pg 176, 22 Apr 18_5, inv & appr

    Hester & child

Richard GILL .... pg 177, 22 Apr 1845, acct of sales

    old Pegga to Mrs. ROUCH

Ann S. GILL.. pg 182, 20 Apr 1844, will
   Hester & child to niece Ann Eliza SANDERS

George SMITH............... pg 186, 23 Sept 1841 – 17 Sept 1844, estate acct
   negros sold from W. HAM___'s estate; Fanny, Nancy, Isaac, Billy, Lydia, Joe, Charles, Daniel, Eliza

Robert WEIR................. pg 195, 13 Oct 1842 – 1 May, 1844, estate acct
   negro

John HUTCHISON................ pg 200, 1843 - 5 Feb 1845, estate acct
   Phil to be sold in Alexandrea

Sarah B. DAVIS... pg 207, 10 Feb 1842, will
   Tom, William, Robert, Abram, Charles, Sally Helen, Lucy Ann, Sarah, Frances, Wellington, Amanda, Charlotte, Mary, John, Ann, Maria to husband Hiram D. DAVIS

Ann S. GILL.. pg, 209, 22 July 1845, inv & appr
   boy Newton

James M. TYLER .... pg 216, 20 Aug 1845, inv & appr
   Michael 40-45 years, Nathan 30-35, George 25, William Sr. 19, William Jr. 16, Henry 14, Nelly 60, Grace 55, Rachel 15, Samuel 10, Cannah 9, Charity 40 & 4 of her children Mary 6, Washington 4, Francis 3, & infant boy

George ATKINSON............................. pg 220, 1 Oct 1845, estate acct
   Michael, Armistead

Cooper CHANCELLOR .... pg 232, 29 Dec 1845, inv & appr
   Jeffrey, Lorenzo, Daniel, William Sr., Henry, Thornton, Turner, Cornelius, William Jr., Benjamin, Moses, Iamus, Lucy, Letty, Milly, Easter, Nelly, Jane, Amanda, Mima, Milze, Ann, Stanton?, Elis, Mildred, Winne, Levi, John C., Mima, Louisa, Amelia, Calvin, Paleshane, Jules, Lanra?, Susan, James, Jane, Jesse, Parthany, Charles, Albina, Manuel, Emily, Custus, James K.P., Caroline, John, Nancy, Andrew, Sophia, Lolly, Mary

Herman D. DAVIS .... pg 234, 12 Jan 1846, will

> girl Sarah to be sold; Martin & his wife Sully, Lucy Ann, Charles Washington, Amanda, Charles, Abram, Mary, John, Ann, Mariah, Priscella shall be free; Thomas Jackson was sold…to be redeemed & be free; …young servants Charlotte, Mary, John, Ann, Mariah, Prescilla…

Cooper CHANCELLOR .... pg 241, 2 Dec 1845, estate div

> Lot 1: Milly, Mima, Ann, Celi, Mildred, Jeffrey, Melze, Stanton to Patsy A. CHANCELLOR; Lot 2: Lorenzo, Parthany, Albina, Manuel, Emily, Curtis, James K.P. to Jane CHANCELLOR; Lot 3: William, Nelly, Jane, Nancy, Letty to Catharine CHANCELLOR; Lot 4: Thornton, Winna, Levi, John C., James, Menos to Mary NELSON; Lot 5: Turner, Caroline, John, Charles, Andrew to Matthew PRIEST; Lot 6: Moses, Louisa, Milia, Calvin, Paleshane, Julia to Elizabeth CHANCELLOR;

Herman D. DAVIS .... pg 243, 3 Feb 1846, inv & appr

> boys Charles, Abraham, Marten, girl Sarah, boy Wellington, girl Charlotte, Sally & infant, Lucy Ann, Amanda, John, Mary, Maria, Priscilla

John HOOE Jr. .... pg 250, 25 Nov 1845, inv & appr

> men Reuben, Richard, woman Nancy, Mary & child, boys Paris, Bill, girls Sally, Laurinda, old woman

Sarah TASKE .... pg 254, 15 Feb 1846, will

> Clany (Clary?) to be free

Euphan BRENT .... pg 255, 12 Jan 1846, inv & appr

> Evelina & youngest child Kitty divided to Mrs. STORK; Charles, Henry, Dick, Eugenia, John

Jules W. COCKRELL .... pg 256, 26 Jan 1846, acct of sales

> man Daniel to I.J. COCKRELL

Ann S. GILL .... pg 259, 2_ Apr - 19 July 1845, estate acct

> woman died, child

Euphan BRENT..pg 260, 21 Jan 1846, div slaves

Caroline, Kitty her youngest child to Mrs. Euphan STORK; boy Charles to John R. WALLACE trustee for Mrs. George WASHINGTON & children; boys John, Henry to James W. WASHINGTON; boy Dick, girl Eugenia to John R. WALLACE trustee for William WASHINGTON

Catherine MERCHANT..........................pg 261, 13 Feb 1845, inv & appr

Sukey & child

John GIBSON ....pg 271, 19 __ 1845, will

Emily & her 2 children Ellen & Addison, Mary & her 2 children James Henry & Edinburg, Martha & her 2 children Robert & Lucy, Matty, Kitty, Lousa, William Chin, John Chin, Jesse Chin & all children & grandchildren of Patty Chin, Julian & Angelena children of Harriet to wife Frances B. GIBSON, Patty & Harriet belonged to wife before marriage; Sarah Chin & her 2 children; George Crump to be free; balance of slaves to wife Frances B. GIBSON; …increase of slaves after death of C. ___ to be free…

Susan Ann FRENCH.. pg 276, 13 May 1846, will

Lucinda to sister Martha _. ADANNBERG

Samson RECTOR ....pg 277, 15 Aug 1846, inv & appr

old Maria

George CARNEY...pg 279, 12 July 184_, will

woman Delia & child Ann Catherine to daughter Nancy CARNEY wife of William CARNEY; man Sam, woman Anaky to daughter Fanny CARNEY; woman Artametia to daughter Silbina MOORE; man Gilbert & his mother Seally to son George F. CARNEY; Fanny, Sophia to serve single daughters; girls Adellen, Susan & her child to daughter Sophia CARNEY; woman Mahala, Ben, girl Ann Mariah to daughter Betsyann BEATTY; little boy James son of Anaky, little girl Martha to son Ninneonad CARNEY; Rachael & her? boy Charles to be sold; woman Betty to be free; Shadrach & wife Patience to choose master

John THURMAN ....pg 281, 22 Nov 1846, will

man Calvan to be sold

Sarah B. JONES ....pg 283, 18 Nov 1846, inv & appr

   old woman Allis, young women Margaret, Matilda, boy Henry, girl Betty, boys William, Mortimer

Sarah B. JONES ....pg 284, 21 Mar 1847, acct of sales

   women Allis, Margaret, Matilda, boy Henry, girl Betty, boy Billy, Mortimer to Thomas K. DAVIS

Phoebe NEWMAN ....pg 287, 22 Sept 1846, will

   George, Harriet to nephew James T. NEWMAN

Diana SPILLER .... pg 288, 1 Apr 1843, will

   Jane, Mahala, Henry, Armistead to be set free & offspring of Jane & Mahala born after deed of emancipation 7 Dec 1832

George BRADFORD .... pg 288, 25 Feb 1847, sales

   2 __ slaves to John FARR

Benjamin PRIDMORE .... pg 290, 14 Jan 1846, will

   negroes

James M. TYLER ....pg 293, 20 Aug 1845, acct of sales

   William Sr., William Jr., Henry to Mrs. NELSON; Nathan, Charity & 4 children to B.E. HARRISON; _nnett, Hannah to Joseph BREWIN; Grace, Nelly to H.B. TYLER

(pages 300 to 321 missing)

Benjamin COLE .... pg 324, 20 May 1854, will

   America to wife Prudence COLE

William A. WEAVER ....pg 325, 26 Nov 1846, acct of sales

   Hannah, Joshua, Sinah to Jane WEAVER

Benjamin PRIDMORE ....pg 329, 25 Oct 1847, inv & appr

   man Jackson, Daphney, Billy, Bob, Thomas, Eliza & child, Amand & child, Henny, Henry, Sarah, George, Aaron, Eli, Sina, Mahala, Fanny, Margaret Jane, Reuben, Wesley, Alfred, Amos, Emily

Henry FAIRFAX ....pg 333, 21 Sept 1840, will

> girl Matilday to daughter Mary; Mary to daughter Sary Ann; Emeline to daughter Sofhian wife of Mr. BOTS; servants, slaves to wife Elizabeth & at her death to children Martha LINDSAY & John WALTON

Margery BARRON ....pg 346, 11 Nov 1847, inv & appr

> Adam, Sally, Andrew, Amanda, Weaver, George, Jenny, Lavender, Lucy, Margaret, Jane, Annie

Euphan BRENT .... pg 361, July 1845 – Mar 1846, estate acct

> woman Milly, child of Evilisca, Dick, Eugenia, John; man Herbert sold, boy Charles

John F. REID .... pg 365, 4 Dec 1847, inv & appr

> man Charles, Charlotte, Emanuel, John Jackson, John Henry, Reilly & infant, Virginia, William, Ben, Addison, Frances, Chances

William FAIRFAX ....pg 367, 24 Mar 1848, inv & appr

> old man Charles

William FAIRFAX .... pg 367, 24 Mar 1848, acct of sale

> man Charles to Letty FAIRFAX

Phoebe NEWMAN .... pg 370, 3 May 1847, inv & appr

> man George

John HOOE Jr. ....pg 370, 27 Nov 1845 – 26 Nov 1847, estate acct

> 2 old slaves, boy Billy, boy Paris, girl Sally; Reuben, Nancy sold

Redman FOSTER .... pg 375, 30 May 1848, will

> all slaves, Sam, Lena & her 2 youngest children, big Henry, John to wife Margaret FOSTER; after death of my wife; Malinda, Lewis, Jasper, Cheshire to niece Elizabeth LIPSCOMB daughter of Daniel FOSTER dec'd; Kitty, Eliza, Arthur, Martin, Julia to niece Mary Mildred FOSTER daughter of James FOSTER; Agga, Aliss to nephew William P. FOSTER son of Daniel FOSTER dec'd; Albert, Harrison to nephew James FOSTER son of James FOSTER; Rolly to niece

Susan Amelia FOSTER daughter of James FOSTER; big Henry & John shall be free after death of my wife

John LEE .... pg 377, 15 June 1848, will

woman Luend to Jane Matilda MATTHEW wife of Henry P. MATTHEW; boy Polk to Mary CLARK; remaining slaves to children of Mary CLARK: Richard A. CLARK, Thomas A. CLARK, Solomon CLARK, John CLARK, William H. CLARK, & Mary E. wife of Matthew A. LEE; man Anthony to remain with Richard A. CLARK; Sucky & her daughter Henny to James ROBINSON; Henny wife of Nathaniel Harris be set free; Jamina & her children Dianer & Pendleton at liberty to live with her father James Robinson

Sarah TENNILLE .... pg 381, 18 Nov 1846 – 1 Aug 1848, estate acct

negroes

John GIBSON .... pg 385, 6 Nov 1846, inv & appr

George Crump 61 years free by will, Philip, Luke 52, Cyrus 32, Bartlett 61, Randolph 45, John Chellon 29, Armistead 33, George Hill, old Lewis, Thomas Henry 70, John William 14, Rachel 44, Maria 36, Maria Randolph & children Laura 17, Rosa 15, Douglas 13, Cora 11, Oscar 9 Albert 7, Frederick Howard 4, & Harriet 2; Lucinda 18 & her child Phillis 1 yr 7 mos; Matilda 32 & her children Julia 14, Eliza 10, Cecelia 8, George Berkeley 6, Leumales 4, Maria Frances 3; Lucy Ann 23 her child George Dallas 2; the family of Patty & John Chin to Mrs. Frances B. GIBSON by will; Emily 38 & her children Ellen 20 & Addison 18; Mary 36 & her children James Henry 13, & Edward Edinbrough 7; Catharine Elizabeth 31, Martha Jane 29 & her children Sarah Philips 14, Robert 4, Patsy 2, & Howard 8 mos; Susan 26 & her children Olivia Douglas 8, Mary Virginia 4, & Charles Edward 7 mos; William Henry 27, John 24, Jesse 13, Julian 27 son of Harriet, Lucy Locket 4, Tippet 17, Ned 18, Buck 18, Fanny, Balantine 5, Sam 13, George, Ratter, young Bett, Billy Button, Snass?, old Bett, Dandrige, Molly Richards

Benjamin COLE .... pg 387, 10 Nov 1847, inv & appr

woman America, child Martha

John F. SELECMAN .... pg 392, 3 May 1848, inv & appr

men Hensey, George, Robert

John SHUMAN .... pg 396, 17 May 1847, inv & appr

 man Calvin

John THURMAN .... pg 397, 17 May 1847, acct of sales

 man to Thomas S. WRIGHT

Philip G. WEBSTER .... pg 398, 5 Mar 1849, will

 before division: slave property to Matilda SIMPSON, Lucy BRAWNER, William B. WEBSTER

Isaac HEATH .... pg 400, 20 Jan 1849, will

 girl Mary to daughter Fanny HEATH after death of wife Sally HEATH; the residue of negroes to be sold after death of wife

Mary F. SINCLAIR .... pg 401, 21 Jan 1849, will

 Tom to be free?; Maria to Margaret SINCLAIR; Kitty, to be hired out; Jim & Jr. free at 30 years old

John LEE .... pg 403, 29 Aug 1848, inv & appr

 old men George, Anthony; Albert, Martha, Ludwell, Frank, Theoderick, Vaububau, William, Betsy & child Dallas, Addison, John, Harrison, Nat, Hatty, Polk, Chlor & child, Mary & child, Otoway, Moor, Alfred, Tasco, Bladeu, Jack (Isack?), George, Hannah, Susan, Janinsa, Deanna, Pendleton, Heuy; Louisa, Jack, Jacob, Jane in the hands of Henry MATTHEW

Lydia PRIDMORE .... pg 408, 18 Apr 1849, div of dower

 Thomas to Mary D. PRIDMORE; Amanda & child to James A. SPINDLE & wife; Margaret to Emiline LEE; Jane to Margaret Virginia LEE; boy Aaron to Sarah C. PRIDMORE; Salina to Martha Ann PRIDMORE; Humphrey Jackson to Mary D, PRIDMORE; Daphney to James A. SPINDLE

Isaac HEATH .... pg 411, 25 May 1849, inv & appr

 Davis 45 years, Reuben 14, Easter 5, Mary 10, woman 41 & child 2

William BRAMER .... pg 418, 29 June 1846, will

 wife Susan BRAMER her choice of either of my women

Mary B. CRAIG .... pg 423, 15 Aug 1842, will

   Mary, Julia Ann to husband William M. CRAIG

Lydia PRIDMORE .... pg 432, 30 Oct 1849, acct of sales

   Jackson, Daphney kept by Mary PEIDMORE

Benjamin COLE .... pg 438, 28 Oct 1847, estate acct

   America sold

Henry FAIRFAX .... pg 453, 2-5 Nov 1849, inv & appr

   Troy, Daniel, Barney, Adison, F. Williams, Lannon, Armistead, George, Lewis, Maria, Harriet, Elizabeth, Susan, Caroline, Clara, Fanny, Peter, Mason, Jim, Harry, F. Simpson, Gilbert, Charles, John, Alexander, Jarard, Ann Wood, Travis, Ann Fisher & child Laura, Lucinda, Elisa, Martha, Sally

Francis M. TRAVIS .... pg 461, 1 Oct 1849, inv & appr

   man Elijah, women Ebaline, Sally, boy Billy, girls Hannah, Amanda

Richard ARRINGTON .... pg 467, 22 Jan 1850, inv & appr

   Reuben, Humphrey, Volmore, Worden, Evelina & child, John Henry, Harriet, Joseph, Redman

Richard ARRINGTON .... pg 468, 24 Jan 1850, acct of sales

   servants hired until 1 Jan 1851: Reuben, Volmore, Humphrey, Worden, woman & child to George W. ARRINGTON; Redmond to John W. SIMPSON

Gerard MASON .... pg 476, 14, 15 Feb 1850, sales

   General Washington to Thomas MASON

Gerard MASON .... pg 480, 20 Jan 1850, inv & appr

   Abraham, Edward, Na__, P__, Hannah, Caroline, Milly, Benjamin, John, Mary, George, Charles, Alf__, Be__, D__

WILL BOOK Q
1851-1858

Benjamin PRIDMORE............pg 2, 1 June 1849 – 3 Apr 1851, estate acct

    2 negroes

Benjamin H. PRIDMORE.....pg 4, 20 Mar 1849 – 3 Apr 1851, estate acct

    boy Reuben sold

Samuel LATIMER...........................pg 16. 29 Nov 1857, inv & appr

    Thomas, Jeul, Dick, Wallas, Nelly, Chalod?, Harry, James, Mary

John HUTCHINSON.............pg 19, 5 Feb 1847 – 2 Feb 1851, estate acct

    Malinda 28 & her 5 children William 7, Matilda 5, Henry 4, Irail (Israel?) 2, & an infant 3 months old; Cornelia 22 & her 2 children Lewis 4 & Milly 2 sold

Richard ARRINGTON..............................pg 25, 30 Oct 1851, estate div

    Valmore to George W. ARRINGTON; Humphrey to Martha A. ARRINGTON; Redmond to John W. SIMPSON & Catherine A. his wife; Joseph, Samuel to Caroline D. ARRINGTON; John to Mary Jane ARRINGTON; Harriet to Lucinda F. ARRINGTON; Reuben, Evelina & ___ to Ann ARRINGTON widow

Jefferson P. AUSTIAL................ pg 26, July 1849 – Jan 1851, estate acct

    Harry

William ALLEN.................................... pg 27, 20 Jan 1850, will

    Robert, Lucinda to wife; Martha, Mary to daughter Catherine; Sophia, Eliza one of Jane's children to daughter Elizabeth

Theron W. NEWMAN .... pg 30, 15 – 16 Mar 1852, inv & appr

    Tom, Moses, Esther, Mary & 2 children Sarah & James Henry, Laura?, Charles, Susan, Matilda & child Franklin, Henry, John, Marner, Matt, Ann & infant child, Phebe, Courtney, Rachel & child Vincent, Maria, Betsy & 2 children Harriet & Margaret, Martha, Minna, Nelly, Jain (Jane?) Fanny, Rebecca, Nelson

Redmond FOSTER ....pg 39, 9 Aug 1848, inv & appr

    Agga Chapman, Henry Chapman, Wilson, Mary Jane, John, Sam, Lina & child, Malida, Jasper, Kitty, Martin, Agga, Albert, Rolly, Nelson, Kate, old Dick, Maria & child Wallace, Jesse, Addison, Mildred, big Henry, Anna, William, Lewis, Chester, Arthur, Julia, Aliss, Harrison, York, Eliza

Ann WARD.................pg 79, 24 Oct 1851, will

    negroes

John LEE .... pg 80, Jan 1848 – 3 Aug 1850, estate acct

    negro

Dianna SPILLER................. pg 93, 23 Jan 1847 – 5 Feb 1851, estate acct

    Henry, Jenny, Hezekiah

Peyton NORVILLE........... pg 95, 24 Aug 1849 – 1 Dec 1850, estate acct

    Dick, Victoria, Anna & child

Redmond FOSTER .... pg 100, 23 Aug 1848 – 3 July 1850, estate acct

    Nelson, Jesse, Kitty, Martin, John, Henry

William ALLEN................. pg 104, 28 Dec 1852, inv & appr

    Jack Turner, Sandy, Ludd, Robert Cook, Milton Monroe, Henry, James, John, Jesse, Martha, Mary, Eliza, Jane, Lucinda Turner, Ann Cook, Frances, Margaret

William BRAWNER..................pg 107, 15 Nov 1849, inv & appr

    Nead, Delia, Willaby, Silas, Anthony, Harriet & child, Barnett, Frederick, Friday, Ellen, Amanda, Roberta

Bernard GALLAGHER Jr. ....
.... pg 114, 15 Sept 1845 – 16 June 1851, estate acct

    Fanny

Prudence COLE................. pg 117, Feb - 14 Oct 1852, estate acct

    negro sold

John N. TOLSON..............pg 118, 20 Apr 1851 – 3 Mar 1852, estate acct

> servants sold; Moses, man William, Polly & child, man Temple, Jane, woman Laurinda

Joseph JOHNSON...................................pg 145, 10 Sept 185_, inv & appr

> man Tony, Ceny, woman Maria, men Beverly, Phil, women Franky, Nancy, Louisa, girls Mary, Sharlett, Lucy, Malinda, Virginia, boy Addison, girl Laura

Richard VANPELT...pg 148, 18 Sept 1851, will

> Daniel to be free after death of wife Polly VANPELT

Alfred BALL...pg 158, 22 July 1853, inv & appr

> Ned, Nany, Sally & child Elija, Moses, Washington, Samuel, Henry Grimes, Armistead, Jemina & child Armistead, Manuel, Nat, Lavinia, Lydia & 2 children William & Alfred, Sarah, Mary, Charles, Maria, Harrison, Luan, Henry, Willie & child Susan, Cloe, Ezekiel, Leticia, Betty, William Berry, Mary & child William, Sam, Robert, George, Martha, Dick, Mima & child Hulda, Judith, Elijah, small boy Jacob, Jacob age 42, Armistead's son George, Harrison's son Daniel, Esau, old Cerda, Mahala & child, Frederick, Armistead, Hunton

John LEBERMAN.........pg 165, 18 May 1848 – 15 Apr 1850, estate acct

> George

Mary E.M. WHEELER........pg 167, 1 Jan 1845 – 1 Mar 1849, estate acct

> George

John C. BARBEE.. pg 171, 11 June 1853, will

> to my brother Andrew D. WROE & James M. BARBEE & my sister Elizabeth W. BARBEE & Mary C. BARBEE my boy Henry & interest in boy Marshall but mother is to have the use of them during her natural life

Lucy Ann WILLIAMS..................................... pg 173, 20 June 1853, will

> Tom, Mary to daughters Emma J. WILLIAMS, Sarah M. WILLIAMS, & Margaret R. WILLIAMS

William ALLEN .... pg 175, 7 Jan 1853, div of slaves

> Sandy, Margaret, Jesse to Lydia ALLEN; Lot A: Henry, Ann, Martha to Alexander T. ALLEN; Lot B: James, Frances to Charles W.C. HUNNINGTON; Lot C: John, Jane, Mary to Robert B. MERCHANT

Anna Maria WARD .... pg 178, 2 Dec 1853, will

> ...Catharine Comor a free woman formerly a slave belonging to the estate of Moses HANCOCK...

Flora WILLIAMS .... pg 178, 11 Nov 1853, will

> Maria, Evelina, Catharine, Louisa to choose their children's master or mistress

Alfred BALL .... pg 179, 27 Dec 1853, div of slaves

> ½ slaves to Sarah E. BALL widow, the residue divided equally between Fanny LEWIS wife of John LEWIS; Elizabeth L. CARTER, Louisa WEIR wife of William I. WEIR, & Adaline BEST wife of H. BEST
>
> William Perry, Mary & child William, Sam, Robert, George, Martha, Dick, Ned, Nancy, Sally & daughter Eliza, Moses, Washington, Samuel, Armistead, Thornton, Frederick, Willie & child Susan, Betty, Mima & children Hulda & Alfred, Judith, Maria, Levinia to Sarah C. BALL widow; Harrison, Susan, Henry, Chloe, Daniel to Adaline BEST wife of H. BEST; Armistead, Jemima, Manuel, Nat, Mary to Fanny LEWIS wife of John LEWIS; Henry Grimes, Lydia & children William & Alfred, Sarah, Charles, Ezekiel to Elizabeth L. CARTER; Jacob, Elijah, boy Jacob, Letitia, Mahala & child, George Taylor to Louisa WEIR wife of William I. WEIR; old woman Corda, Esau to William I. WEIR

William A. DEAVER .... pg 189, 25 Nov 1846, inv & appr

> Hannah, Joshua, Sinah

William BRIDWELL .... pg 191, 10 Feb 1854, inv & appr

> boy Burk, girls Sophia, Susan, boy Jeff, man Hysom, old woman Rose

John GRAHAM .... pg 193, 7 Sept 1850, will

> wife to choose 2 slaves; slaves to be sold at her death

Flora WILLIAMS .... pg 203, 3 May 1854, inv & appr

   Mariah age 37 & infant, Meggy 16, Lunnon 9, Martha 7, Jane 5, George 2, Evelina 24, Richard 6, Catharine 22, James 1, Laura 14

Elizabeth W. BARBEE .... pg 205, 14 Dec 1853, will

   girl Mary to my mother, at her death to be divided between brothers Andrew D. WROE & James BARBEE & sister Mary C. BARBEE; boy Marshall to them also

John GRAHAM .... pg 206, 23 May 1854, inv & appr

   women Phyllis, Amy, Cardone, Alcy, Lucy, boys Joshua, Moses, Beverly, Aron, John, Thomas, Charles, Eliza

Charles G. CANNON .... pg 212, 9 July 1854, will

   Jesse, Jim, Sam

Richard B. TYLER .... pg 213, 5 Aug 1839 – 31 Dec 1841, estate acct

   Charles sold

Richard B. TYLER .... pg 218, 4 Aug 1840 – 1 Jan 1854, reformed estate acct

   negroes

William H. DOGAN .... pg 221, 19 Aug 1854, inv & appr

   men Jeff, Arthur, Clara & 2 children Betsy & __, woman Sarah, Mina, boys John, Jesse, girl Amanda, Margaret & child George, girl Matilda, Julia & child, boy Bob, girl Susan, boy Gusta, man Philip, girls Francis, June, woman & child George William, man James, girls Henrietta , Georgiana, boy James Polk, girl Leanna

Richard T. MITCHELL adm of Charles HUNTON .... pg 223, 1 Jan 1854, comm report .... pg 224, 7 June 1850 – 7 June 1851, estate acct

   ...slaves sold...slaves purchased

Charlotte M. MITCHELL ...pg 224, 2 Jan 1843 – 7 June 1851, estate acct

   slaves purchased by Charles HUNTON

Theron W. NEUMAN .... pg 244, 26 Dec 1854, div of slaves

> Tom age 70, Moses 45, Esther 52, John 18, Louisa 13, Frank 5 to Sarah E. NEUMAN; Mary 29, Adaline 1, Sarah 6, Susan 9, Wamer 15, James 4, Rebecca 10 to T. Wallace NEUMAN; Betsy 38, Matt 12, Winney 19, Harriet 4, Margaret 6 to James T. NEUMAN; Ann 48, Courtney 11, Charles 11, Fanny 11, Jane 12 to William B. NEUMAN; Rachel 44, Maria 10, Vincent 6, Martha 21, Alfred 3, Nelson 8 to Emily H. NEUMAN

Col. John M. WASHINGTON .... pg 246, 30 Dec 1854, inv & appr

> Horace, Kitty, Louisa, Louisa Scott, Roberta, John Scott, Lucy, Fanny, Francis and child Charles, Jennie, Susan, Lydia, Elizabeth, Anna, Webster, Lockman, Gusty

.... pg 246, 29 Sept 1854, inv & appr

> Fanny, Nelly, George, Spencer, Jenny & child Hubbard, James, John, Rose, Evelina & child Baily Washington, Mary Francis, Enfield, Philip Cattell, Charles, Senett, James Robert, Daniel, Georgiana, Polly, Luther, Sarah Ann, Mary Evelena, Eliza, Henry

Theron W. NEWMAN ..... pg 258, 19 July 1853 – 4 Mar 1854, estate acct

> Dennis, Mary & children, Betsy & 4 children

.... pg 263, 4 Mar 1852 – 4 Mar 1853, estate acct

> Ann, Betsy & 4 children

Philip G. WEBSTER .... pg 272, 9 July 1852 – 16 Nov 1854, estate acct

> negroes sold

Zachariah WARD .... pg, 275, 2 Nov 1822 – 1 Nov 1831, estate acct

> George; man Davy, Elija sold

Alexander M. BRENT .... pg 281, 2 Oct 1849 – 2 Feb 1854, gdn acct

> Jim, Matilda

Virginius K. BRENT .... pg 284, 2 Oct 1849 – 2 Feb 1854, gdn acct

> Hannah, Phoebe, Ned

Robert N. WEIR, wife, children ....
....pg 287, 1 Jan 1851 – 1 Jan 1853, estate acct

   Rachel & 4 children, boy Bob

....pg 288, 1 Jan 1853 – 1 Jan 1854, estate acct

   Rachael & 3 children, her infant died, Robert

Sarah E. WEIR ....pg 292, 29 July 1843 – 31 Dec 1848, gdn acct

   George, Lewis, Jackson, girl Maria

Lucy C. WEIR ....pg 295, 3 Mar 1843 – 31 Dec 1848, gdn acct

   Henrietta, Isaac, James; difference in value of negroes disbursed

John N. TOLSON .... pg 297, 4 Dec 1854, inv & appr

   women Charity, Priscilla, Willis, Anna & child, Jim Smith, Sally & child, George, Dudley, Temple, James, Eliza, Sidney, Georgiana, Rebecca, Harriet, Sarah, Henry, Charity, Simon, Web, Ben, Billy

   Dudley, Anna & child, Eliza, Sidney, James, Ben to Mrs. Margaret TOLSON her dower

   Lot 1: Willis, Sally & child, Charity; Lot 2: Jim Smith, Georgiana, Sarah, Web; Lot 3: George, Rebecca; Lot 4: Temple, woman Charity, Simon; Lot 5: Henry, Priscilla, Billy, Harriet

   Willis, Sally & child, Charity to Amia N. TOLSON; Jim Smith, Georgiana, Sarah, Web to Richard D. SHACKLET with wife Mary T. TOLSON; George, Rebecca to Margaret E. TOLSON; Temple, woman Charity, Simon to James W. TOLSON; Henry, Priscilla, Billy, Harriet to John N. TOLSON

Catherine N. NEWMAN ....pg 304, 7 Mar 1855, will

   Reuben Dean, Charles Dean to nephew Crawford CUSHING; boy Thornton to nephew Charles. Q. CUSHING; man James Dean to nephew Thomas N. CUSHING; Maria, Milly, Hoffman, Charles, & infant boy, Caroline, Eliza, Milly, John be divided between nephews Crawford CUSHING, Henry C. CUSHING, Charles L. CUSHING, Thomas N. CUSHING after the death of Christopher C. CUSHING & Eleanor CUSHING his wife

Sarah ELWELL..................pg 315, 25 Nov 1823 – 9 Feb 1824, estate acct

Fanny & 2 children; Stephen sold

Col. John M. WASHINGTON...................pg 316, 5 Nov 1855, estate div

Eliza, Susan, John, Enfield, Lydia, John Scott, Lucy – set aside for payments of debts

Emelina & child Bailey, Rose, Louisa Sr., Louisa Jr., Daniel, Horace, Lockrun, Willy?, James, Robert, Luther to widow Mrs. WASHINGTON

off Polly Scott a charge of

Lot 1: George, Webster, Jenny, Hubbard, James, Mary Frances, Charles, Elizabeth, Fanny Jr., Anna, Mary Evelina to William T. WASHINGTON

off Fanny a charge of

Lot 2: Spencer, Gusty, Frances Scott & child Martha, Charles, Jenny, Henry, Janet, Sarah Ann & child Betsy Bell, Philip Catlett, Georgiana, Roberta to H.W. Macrae WASHINGTON;

old Nelly put at nothing

Catherine N. NEWMAN .... pg 321, Sept 1855, inv & appr

men Reuben, Charles, James, women Maria, Caroline, Eliza, Nelly, Milly, boys John, Charles, Hoffman, Infant, boy Thornton

Richard ATKINSON........................... pg 327, 21 May 1855, inv & appr

Ruth Ann, Neabsco (slaves? books? animals?)

Richard ATKINSON........................... pg 332, 12 Feb 1856, inv & appr

George, Charles, Tobias, Bill Dinten, Jake, Priss?, Catharine, Ellen, Mary, Hannah

Joseph FARROW... pg 335, 4 Dec 1855, bottom

...appraised a negro man Henry...

Lydia ALLEN .... pg 336, 6 Mar 1856, div slaves

> Sandy Turney, Jesse to Charles W. DUNINGTON & Catherine M. his wife; Robert Cook to Alescandez? I. ALLEN; Lucinda Turney, Margaret to Robert MERCHANT

William ALLEN .... pg 337, 13 Mar 1856, inv & appr – D.C.

> Robert Cook, Sandy Turney, Lucinda Turney, Margaret, Jesse

John F. REID .... pg 337, Nov 1854, inv & appr

> Charlotte aged 60, China 10, Kitty & child Charles, Francis 10-12, Martha 7, William 14, Addison 12, Benjamin 14, Manuel 27, Charles 56, John 30
>
> Kitty & child Charles, Francis, Manuel to Redmond FOSTER in right of his wife; Charles, John, Addison, Martha to Redmond FOSTER guardian for John F. REID; Charlotte, China, William, Benjamin to P.D. LIPSCOMB guardian for Richard J. REID

Alfred BALL .... pg 346, 2 May 1853 – 1 May 1854, estate acct

> Armistead, Sam, Henry, Maria, Washington, Mary, Fred, Thornton, Ned & wife, Cloe

Alfred BELL .... pg 349, 2 May 1854 – 1 May 1855, estate acct

> negroes

Thomas A. GAINES .... pg 355, 26 May 1856, inv & appr

> man Henry, Wallace, Bill, Jess, Lucien, women Cily, Margaret & child, Martha, Rose

Charles E. NORMAN .... pg 356, 13 Nov 1855, inv & appr

> dwelling house: woman Cynthia, girl Caroline

Thomas WILKINS .... pg 372, 13 Sept 1856, inv & appr

> Peter, Rose & 2 children, woman Sarah, girls Minta, Ophelia, boys Ben, Sam

Ann BRITT .... pg 374, 9 Jan 1857, will

> Judy & son Lewis to William L.B. WHEELER

Lawson RECTOR .... pg 385, 16 May 1856, inv & appr

    Maria 65 years, Martha 27, Amanda 7, Lafayette 5 or 6

....pg 387, div slaves

    woman Martha to be sold; woman Maria to Margaret RECTOR widow; boy Lafayette to Isaac BRIDWELL in right of his wife; girl Amanda to Silas BIRDWELL guardian of Susan E. RECTOR

Richard STONNEL .... pg 390, 14 Jan 1857, will

    boy George to son Robert Francis; man Thomas to be free

Joseph JOHNSON .... pg 391, 27 Dec 1856, div of slaves

    Beverly, Philip, Franky, William to Emily E. JOHNSON; Nancy, Lucy, Rose to Joseph B. JOHNSON; Louisa, Melinda, Susan to Annie M. JOHNSON; Mary, Addison, John to Sarah E. JOHNSON; Charlotte, Virginia, Laura to George W. JOHNSON

Asa DAVIS ....pg 394, 26 Feb 1857, inv & appr

    Clarissa, Lydia, Sandy

George H. COCKWELL ....pg 395, 4 Feb 1857, inv & appr

    woman Betty

John GRAHAM Sr. ....pg 398, 7 Jul 1856 – 6 May 1857, acct of sales

    man Moses, boy John to William B. BRAUNER; Caroline & child, women Phillis, Amy to Sarah E. MOUNT; man Aaron, boy Tom to James H. SIMPSON; girl Eliza to Francis S. GRAHAM; boy Peter to Robert R. GRAHAM

Mary S. GWATKIN .... pg 409, 3 Dec 1857, will

    Charlotte, Lucy, William to Christopher C. CUSHING

Lawson RECTOR .... pg 418, 1 Oct 1857, estate div

    girl Martha to William TOLSON and wife

Richard STONE .... pg 419, 16 Mar 1857, inv & appr

    Thornton, Randall, old Maria, Ann Maria, Caroline, Amanda, Martha, Helen, Charley, Amanda the younger, Harriette, Andrew, Catherine, Edmania, Margaret, Luther, Henry

Isaac HEATH .... pg 426, 12 Jan 1855, estate sale

> men Dennis, Reuben, boy Manuel, woman Anna to Charles HEATH; girls Sarah Jane, Easter to A.L. GRIGSBY; boy John to T.R. DAVIS

Louisa C. MUSCHETT .... pg 433, 29 Mar 1856, will

> _n, Eliza, Martha, John, Henry, Susan, Werden after 3 years I give them & their increase their time forever; Martha McClain & her child Winney Ward their time forever; Robert Fairfax; Emily & her children James, Winney, Sally, Susan, Robert, Samuel their time forever; Sandy, Thomas, Wellington, ___ the son of Mary; Rachel & her children Mary, Thomas their time forever; Ellen; Mary Clark to be taken care of; Maria, Meggy, ___ Maria's son, Martha, Maria's daughter Mary Jane, Nan__, Lucretia; Evelina, Richard their time forever; Catharine & children, James, Charles; Laura & her increase their time forever; inherited servants from my son's estate their time forever; all to choose their master for 3 years, all given money to leave the state after 3 years; Mary & her youngest child to be cared for and their time forever

Richard ATKINSON .... pg 436, 12 Dec 1857, inv & appr

> men Charles, Albert, George, William, Jacob, Priscilla & young child, girls Ellen, Mary, Catharine, boy Thomas, Hannah & boy

Mary S. GWATKIN .... pg 437, 11 Jan 1858, inv & appr

> women Charlotte, Lucy, man William

Richard STONNEL .... pg 438, 16 Mar 1857, inv & appr

> Thornton, Randall, old Maria, Ann Maria, Caroline, Amanda, Martha, Helen, Charley, Amanda the younger, Harriett, Andrew, Catharine, Edmonia, Margaret, Luther, Henry

Richard O. SHIRLEY .... pg 446, 16 Jan 1858, inv & appr

> Jane & child Peter, women Martha, Mildred, girl Charlotte, boys Henry, Arthur, girls Lucy, Georgiana

Mary B. CANNON .... pg 449, 17May 1858, inv & appr

> man George Bowling, woman Scintha (Cynthia?), old Henny

William ROACH .... pg 450, 2 Apr 1858, inv & appr

    Sandy 50 years, Chin 45, Thomas 14, Ann 25 & her son Charley 8; Eliza 8 willed to Margaret ROACH; Cely 60, Emily & 2 children (boy & girl), young woman Mary, Clene 10

Sanford THURMAN .... pg 451, 9 May 1857, will

    1/3 of slaves to be equally divided between children of Ann E. NEWMAN formerly Ann E. FEWELL after death of wife Franny A, THURMAN; 1/3 of slaves to William S. FEWELL; 1/3 of slaves to Thomas T. FEWELL

WILL BOOK R
1858 - 1872

Wantsford EVANS .... pg 1, 10 May 1860, will

   Jesse, Sam, Jim to be set free

.... codicil

   ...Jesse has departed from this life...2/3 of my property to Helen & her children for Jesse's sake and 1/3 to Jim Jesse's brother...

Gustavus A. HUTCHINSON .... pg 4, 21 Mar 1865, will

   Charity & child to Henry B. HUTCHINSON in trust for sisters Louisa & Julia Ann

Roy W. HORTON .... pg 5, 23 Feb 1864, will

   boy Jeff to son Russel E. HORTON; girl Martha to son Meredith W. HORTON

T.I. HARRISON .... pg 7, 1 May 1860, will

   all servants except Sam be hired out; woman Jane to serve her mistress until age 33 & then freed; as the servants arrive at age 28 they are to be set free; possible slaves – Eliza & her youngest daughter Harry, Dorsey, James, Harry

Josiah WILLCOXEN .... pg 23, 10 Dec 1861, inv & appr

   old man Henson, Ellen, Alley, Thomas, Palestine, Martha, Celina & child, Mary Ellen & children, boys William Henry, Robert, John, girls Hester Ann, Kate, Jinnie

Christopher WINDSOR .... pg 63, 20 Feb 1857, will

   my boy John to son James Thomas WINDSOR; Margaret, Martha & 2 children to sons John Richard & James Thomas WINDSOR; slaves of John Richard to be held by James Thomas & not to be sold

William BRIDWELL .... pg 88, 3 Feb 1854 – 5 Feb 1855, estate acct

   servants

William HOGAN .... pg 95, 4 Nov 1854 - 4 Nov 1855, estate acct

   servant

Theron W. NEWMAN .... pg 96, 4 Mar 1854 – 4 Mar 1855, estate acct

   Henry, Nelly, Fanny, Louisa, Phoebe, Rachel, Missy, Matilda & child, Jane & child, John, Betsy & 4 children, Mary & 4 children

Theron W. NEWMAN .... pg 99, 4 Mar 1855 – 4 Mar 1856, estate acct

   Ann, Nelly, Moses, Jane, Henry, Matilda, Rachel, Courtney

Joseph JOHNSON .... pg 102, 8 June 1852 – 1 Jan 1857, estate acct

   Louisa Maria, old man Anthony (dec'd?)

Mary A.M. SHAW .... pg 107, 19 Dec 1848 – 1 Dec 1850, estate acct

   old woman Priss

Robert M. WEIR, wife, & children .... pg 116, 1 Jan 1854 – 1 Jan 1856, gdn acct

   girl Rebecca, Rachel & dec'd child, boy Robert

Hugh DAVIS Sr. .... pg 124, 26 Aug 1843 – 16 July 1846, estate acct

   Emily sold

Charles E. NORMAN .... pg 128, 5 Nov 1855 – 3 Nov 1856, estate acct

   servant

William REACH .... pg 133, 9 Apr 1858, acct of sale

   woman Celey to R.C. GLASCOCK; woman Mary to William BRAWNER; girl Jane to Richard COOPER

Elizabeth CHANCILLOR .... pg 135, 14 June 1858, will

   woman Fanny to niece Eliza J. NELSON; men William & John Henry to be hired out for 20 years & then choose their own masters

Sanford THURMAN .... pg 136, 12 Nov 1858, inv & appr

   men Isaac, Lewis, Henry, boys Martin, Preston, Richard, Reuben, girls Jenny, Sally, boys York, Sam, woman Lucy, Ann & child, Caroline, Ellen & child, boy Albert

Benson LYNN .... pg 141, 7 Jan 1859, acct of sale

    woman to Levi C. LYNN

Benson LYNN .... pg147, 14 Jan 1869, inv & appr

    man Frederick, woman Frank

John GRAHAM .... pg 154, 24 Feb 1859, estate sale

    men Beverly, Joshua to D.M. PALLIE; woman __llis to H.L. GRAHAM

Thomas H. GALLAHER .... pg 158, 28 Apr 185_, inv & appr

    Harrison Jackson, Henry Jackson, William Jackson, woman Susan, Sinah

Thomas H. GALLAHER .... pg 162, 24 Apr 1859, acct of sales

    woman Sinah, girl Susan, man Harrison sold until 11 May 1864, Henry sold until 17 May 1862, Albert sold until 18 Sept 1866 to Mrs. GALLAHER; John to be delivered 1 Jan 1860 to Brian GALLAHER

Ann P. LEACHMAN .... pg 193, 17 May 1855, will

    girl Melinda to son John T. LEACHMAN in trust for daughter Ann E. DICKINSON; my 2 girls Livy, Kitty to be divided between children Robert C. & John T. LEACHMAN & Sarah Ann FERWELL

Ann P. LEACHMAN .... pg 194, 26 Apr 1860, inv & appr

    Lenora & 3 children, girl Kitty

Jobe DAVIS .... pg 196, 28 Sept 1853, will

    Henry, Harriet to wife Anna (named wife Susan earlier); Elsy, Jenny to son William; Fanny & child Peyton to children of daughter Nancy GARNER; Ally or Alfred to children of daughter Betsy FORLY; Jane to daughter Susan MILSTEAD; Frank to daughter Ruth GOSSOM; Charley to son Josiah; Mason, Kitty, Wallis to daughter Matilda MADDOX; Dennis, Ellen to children of daughter Margaret COULTER; Sinar to daughter Linissy MILLS; Linssy to daughter Elizabeth DAVIS wife of Robert DAVIS

Jobe DAVIS .... pg 212, 30 June 1850, inv & appr

> Hennie, Harriet, Mason, Jane, Manuel, Catherine, Melze, Ellen, Jinnie, Laura, Wallis, Peyton, John, Laura, Charles, Francis, Sina, Alfred, Dennis, Ann

Edward HARDING & grandchildren ....
....pg 216, 19 Jan 1859 – 26 Mar 1860, trust acct

> Jim

Lucy A. WILLIAMS .... pg 223, Jan 1854 – 1 Sept 1857, estate acct

> boy Tom, girl Mary, man Jarrod

Sarah M. & Margaret R. WILLIAMS ....
....pg 227, 5 Oct 1857 – 1 Jan 1859, gdn acct

> Tom, Mary

Sarah M. & Margaret R. WILLIAMS ....
....pg 229, 1 Jan 1859 – 14 Jan 1860, gdn acct

> Mary, Tom

Cassin FOLEY .... pg 234, 29 Jan 1862, inv & appr

> man Charley, Eliza & child, Lucinda, Evaline, Edward, Ann

Ann BRITT .... pg 237, 16 May 1857, inv & appr

> boy Lewis, woman Judy

Thomas WILKINS ....pg 243, no date, inv & appr

> man Peter, girl Ophelia

Thomas WILKINS .... pg 243, 16 Dec 1856, acct of sales

> girl Sarah to William A. BAYANT; Rose & child to A.L. GRIGSBY; girl Minta to M__ SIMPSON; boys Ben, Sam to James W. WILKINS

Sarah A. TRONE......................pg 245, 20 July 1857, div dower property

> girl Milly to Austin B. WEEDON; George, Charles to John C. WEEDON; Harriet to John L. TRONE; Jim to Peter SMITH; Tom to George WEEDON; Jane to James TRONE

S.C. MUSCHETT .... pg 280, 1 Jan 1858 – 1 Nov 1866, estate acct

Maria & 3 children, Sally, Martha & child, Sania, Winnie, Evelina & children, Robert, Catherine, John & his wife Margaret, Sandy, Eliza, Susan, Sally & small girl, Meggie, Lunnon & small girl, Jonah & family, Sam, Rachel & child, Dick, Tom, Susan, Jane, Louisa & child, Martha & child, Eliza, Emily; Mary died

paid legacy under will: Catherine Chin, John, Eliza, Martha, Henry, Susan, Worden, Emily, James Gray, Winnie Powell, G.D. Powell, Lance Fenix, Sally Fitzhough, Susan, Robert, Samuel, Frederick, Maria Sanders, Lunnon Jr., Martha, Jane, Lucreta, Nancy, Martha M. Leon, Winney, Lunnon Sr., Sandy Clark, Evelina Mason, Richard, Charlotte, Margaret, Thomas Clark, Wellington Clark, Ellen, George Cook

Laura, Catherine Chin & her children James & Charles

S.C. MUSCHETT .... pg 288, 4 Jan 1858 – 4 Jan 1863, estate acct

Rachael, Ellen, Phil, Jim Gray, John, George, Winnie, Bob Fairfax

John BAYLY .... pg 318, 2 June 1861, will

Sal to son Richard P. BAYLY; Nancy to daughter Geraldine BAYLY; Mary Ann & her children Henry, Alfred, Ann, Jane, & Louisa to daughter Virginia, her husband secretly carried off Alfred & Henry & disposed of them – may have to go to court

Josiah WILCOXIN .... pg 341, 13 Dec 1861 – 1 Dec 1866, estate acct

boy Robert

Jobe DAVIS .... pg 354, 30 Aug 1860 – 3 June 1867, estate acct

boy

L.C. MUSCHETT .... pg 360, 1 Jan 1858 – 10 Aug 1867, estate acct

Maria & 3 children, Sally, Martha & child, Fanny, Laura, Winney, Evelina & children, Robert, Catherine, John & wife Margaret, Sandy, Eliza, Susan, small girl, Meggy, Nana, Lunnon, Jonah & her children, Sam, Rachel, Dick, Tom, Jane, Louisa & small girl, Richard's child, Mary died, Duffey

Legacy: Phil, Joan Fairfax, John, Eliza, Martha, Henry, Susan, Worden, Emily, James Gray, Winney Powell, G.D. Powell, Laura

Fenix, Sally Fitzhugh, Susan, Robert, Samuel, Frederick, Maria Sanders, Lunner Jr., Martha, Jane, Lucretia, Nancy, Martha M. Lean, Winney, Lunner Sr., Sandy Clark, Evelina Mason, Richard, Charlotte, Margaret, Thomas Sarkin, Wellington Clark, Ellen, George Cook, William, Emily for her children, Catherine Chin & her children Jane & Charles, Lunnore

Alexander COMPTON..............................pg 391, 30 Mar 1861, will

his choice of men Alec, Frederick, or Ewell to son Alexnder H. COMPTON

Roy W. HORTON............ pg 394, 1 Dec 1865 – 6 Nov 1867, estate acct

boy Tom, Henry

Meredith W. HORTON........ pg 398, 1 Jan 1855 – 28 Nov 1858, gdn acct

sale of negroes

Russell E. HORTON..............pg 400, 1 Jan 1855 – 8 May 1856, gdn acct

sale of negroes

James W. TOLSON.............. pg 408, 22 Nov 1861 - 2 Apr 1867, gdn acct

old Charity to be sold in Richmond, boy Simon to Mrs. TOLSON

Ann TOLSON ....pg 411, 9 Oct 1861 – 1 Jan 1867, gdn acct

Sally & children, Willis

C.C. CUSHING................. pg 423, 4 Sept 1865 – 2 Sept 1867, estate acct

negroes hired

Margarey E. TOLSON ....pg 445, 23 Nov 1861 – 2 Apr 1865, gdn acct

George, girl Becky

John F. DOGAN.................... pg 447, 1 July 1859 – 1 July 1866, gdn acct

Clara, John

Medora S. DOGAN............... pg 450, 1 July 1859 – 1 July 1866, gdn acct

Arthur, Bettie

William H. DOGAN .... pg 453, 1 July 1859 – 1 July 1866, gdn acct
Amanda. Matilda

Hennesta DOGAN .... pg 456, 1 July 1859 – 1 July 1866, gdn acct
Sarah, girl

Catherine E. DOGAN ....pg 459, 1 July 1859 – 2 Jan 1863, gdn acct
woman Mary, Frances

Ann M. DOGAN .... pg 462, 1 July 1859 – 6 Mar 1862, gdn acct
Georgiana

William J. WEIR ....pg 473, 5 Aug 1867 – 5 Aug 1867, estate acct
Arthur, Beverly, Albert, Philip (slaves or servants?)

Mary L. BUKELEY & children ....
..............................pg 504, 6 Sept 1860 – 4 Jan 1869, trustee acct
Jesse sold

Cassius CARTER .... pg 525, 27 Dec 1820, will
negroes to sister Shirley; Joe & his wife

Ann FLORENCE ....pg 526, 9 Feb 1860, will
Judith & her 3 children Lewis, Lucretia, & Granderson to niece Sarah Jane MANUEL

Henry D. LARKIN .... pg 527, 31 Dec 1858 – 31 Dec 1868, comm acct
man

John MILES ....pg 558, 30 Aug 1869, will
old fellow servant Henry German

Frederick P. BRAWNER ....pg 566, 2 Dec 1867 – 3 Dec 1869, estate acct
hired hands

Benjamin Ogle TAYLOE.....................................pg 583, 1 July 1856, will
servants to wife Phebe Warren TAYLOE

William M. LYNN .... pg 602, 20 Mar 1869, will

   …also my negro m____ Pa___ (Peach Blossom)…purchased of_._. SMITH & Sallie E. PEUGH to be equally divided between them…

George W. MATTHEW ....pg 642, 20 Dec 1865 – 4 Dec 1869, estate acct

   William Foley (negro hire)

Enoch FOLEY .... pg 688, 1866 – 1 Apr 1871, estate acct

   paid I.F. WHITING moving boy

Richard ATKINSON ....pg 731, 7 Dec 1857 – 7 Dec 1862, estate acct

   men Charles, Albert, William, George, Jacob

William M. LYNN .... pg 776, 15 July – 31 Dec 1870, estate acct

   girl, Bill, Jim, Bob

ADDENDUM

The following information is from the Lost Records Localities Digital Collection of the Library of Virginia, 1674 – 1894: http://www.virginiamemory.com/collections/lost

Gerard ALEXANDER Sr. .... pg , 19 Nov 1821, Deed

> Ellen, Fanny & 2 children Thornton & William, Juliet & her child Mary Anne in trust to James B. EWELL for Matilda Ann ALEXANDER; Gerard ALEXANDER Sr. to retain possession for life

William CARR .... pg , 23 Jan 1790, will

> slaves to wife until her death then Hannah & her children to daughter Betsy TEBBS; Agga & all her children Jack, William, Carr to son William CARR; Lucy & all her children Jim, Harry, & Viney to son John CARR; none of the slaves to be sold out of the family, if offered for sale they should be liberated; man Abner to be set free

Catesby COCKE .... pg , 30 June 1763, will

> Jack to son John Catesby COCKE; slaves to be hired

Michael DERMONT .... pg , 3 Feb 1730, will

> (found under Prince William Co but of Stafford Co)

> land left to wife Mary DERMONT & son Michael to be sold to purchase each a servant; man Charles W__ is to wife

Elizabeth GRAHAM .... pg , 7 Apr 1791, will

> child Sukey, boy Watt to granddaughter Elizabeth GRAHAM daughter to Walter GRAHAM; Betsy to granddaughter Elizabeth Mary WIATT daughter to William WIATT; woman Lydia & her children Alexander & Nancy to daughter Jenny GRAHAM

.... 2 Sept 1791, codicil

> boy Peter, girl Prycey to granddaughter Elizabeth GRAHAM daughter of Walls GRAHAM

John GRAHAM .... pg , 1 Mar 1783, will

> executors to purchase a girl 12 -14 years of age for daughter Jean GRAHAM; man Daniel Macrae to son Dr. William GRAHAM

Alexander HENDERSON .... pg , 24 Feb 1815, will

> ...farm...with all slaves in lieu of dower to wife...plus Jack & his wife Dorcus & their youngest child; Ben with his wife Clara & her child James; slaves in Fairfax made over in trust

John HOOE .... pg , 5 Jan 1798, will

> Moses, Jane, Daphne, Raphne, Solomon, George, Rose, Massey, old Ben, Hannah, Lolly, old Winney, Kitt to wife Ann HOOE; after her death to daughters Mary Ann THROGMORTON, Catherine O'LOCHLON, Sarah Burdett SWEENY, & Ann Frances HOOE; Bob, Sarah, Lucy & her children to son William HOOE; Abraham, Mingo to son Bernard HOOE; Winney, Pallas, Tom Parker, Ned, Sinah, Nelson Betsy, little Tom, Armistead to daughter Catherine O'LOCHLON wife of Cornelius O'LOCHLON; Lewis, Gilbert, Ester & her child Helen, Barey, Jesse, Joe, Nan to daughter Sarah Burdett SWEENY; Sam, Jacob, Charity, Lizzy, young Ben, Maria, Lucy, Syller, Rachel to daughter Ann Frances HOOE; Sarah, Aggy, Eliza, Beck, Frank, Ann, John, Felicia, Matilda, Virgin to daughter Susanna Fooke HOOE; Tommy to grandson John THROGMORTON

John LEE .... pg , 15 June 1848, will

> woman Luend & her children to Jane Matilda MATTHEW, wife of Henry P. MATTHEW; boy Polk to Mary CLARK; an equal distribution of remaining slaves to Mary CLARK's children: Richard A. CLARK, Thomas O. CLARK, Solomon CLARK, John _. CLARK, William H. CLARK, Mary E. wife of Matthew A. LEE; Anthony to remain with Richard A. CLARK; Sukey & her daughter Henny to James ROBINSON; woman Henny wife of Nathaniel Harris be set free; Jamima & her 2 children Dianer & Pendleton is at liberty to live with James Robison her father

INDEX

__icent, 94
_acher, 37
_anerlso, 21
_aussa, 41
_eamen, 89
_HAD: George, 83
_inia, 89
_nnett, 141
_oarzison: Edward, 8
_olydiro, 106
Aaron, 14, 15, 18, 21, 37, 39, 48, 51, 53, 57, 69, 70, 74, 75, 77, 83, 88, 92, 93, 101, 110, 111, 117, 122, 130, 141, 144, 156
Abb, 74
Abberilla, 49
Abednego, 113
Abel, 24, 105
Abigail, 1, 41, 72, 78
Abner, 27, 37, 107, 167
Abraham, 7, 12, 15, 17, 18, 19, 21, 22, 23, 25, 32, 33, 39, 43, 46, 47, 53, 61, 62, 64, 77, 80, 97, 98, 113, 117, 132, 139, 145, 168
Abram, 7, 19, 25, 48, 49, 87, 118, 138, 139
Absalom, 49, 78
Adalade, 117
Adaline, 105, 116, 124, 152
Adam, 1, 5, 12, 22, 23, 24, 36, 41, 42, 45, 48, 49, 50, 59, 60, 64, 74, 78, 84, 90, 91, 106, 111, 134, 142
ADAMS: Gavin, 47, 48; Jacob, 59; Susanah, 48
ADANNBERG: Martha, 140

Addison, 48, 64, 80, 81, 98, 99, 102, 121, 127, 140, 142, 143, 144, 148, 149, 155, 156
Adelaide, 125, 129
Adeline, 89
Adellen, 140
ADIE: Benjamin, 60
Adison, 102, 113, 145
Africa, 21, 83
Aga, 26, 118
Agatha, 19, 84
Agathy, 19, 38, 57, 84
Agcy, 41
Agg, 46
Agga, 12, 25, 65, 66, 109, 142, 148, 167
Aggy, 12, 20, 35, 49, 78, 113, 115, 118, 124, 127, 168
Agnes, 51, 83, 122
Ailacy, 40
Ailse, 18, 34
Alaline, 124
Alan, 101
Albert, 48, 79, 102, 104, 113, 115, 118, 121, 125, 126, 127, 131, 135, 137, 142, 143, 144, 148, 157, 160, 161, 165, 166
Albina, 121, 138, 139
Alce, 25, 49, 58, 69
Alcey, 116
Alcinda, 111
Alcy, 85, 151
ALEANDER: John, 94
Alec, 164
Alex, 40, 96
Alexander, 59, 92, 94, 104, 106, 113, 116, 121, 123, 124, 145, 167

ALEXANDER: Ashton, 106, 111; Col. Gerald, 83; Col. William, 117; Dr. William, 87; Dr. William S., 105; Elizabeth, 60; Frances B., 133; Frances E., 131; Gerard, 60, 106, 110; Gerrand, 54; Hector, 94; J.F., 30; Jane, 104, 110, 122; John, 3; L., 122; Laurence Gibbons, 67; Lawrence G., 117; Mary Stuart, 37; Matilda Ann, 167; Miss Sid, 122; P., 117; Phil, 66; Philip, 117, 133; Richard B., 58; Robert, 3, 94; S., 110; Sarah F., 126; Sidney, 104, 107, 111; Sigesmunda Mary, 67; William, 67, 69, 94; William S., 107
ALEXANDER Jr.: Gerald, 83
ALEXANDER Sr.: Gerard, 167
Alf__, 145
Alford, 66
Alfred, 41, 49, 53, 59, 62, 64, 68, 73, 75, 82, 84, 91, 92, 94, 96, 99, 100, 106, 110, 113, 114, 116, 117, 118, 124, 131, 141, 144, 149, 150, 152, 161, 162, 163
Alice, 23, 24, 25, 38, 41, 47, 60, 105, 117, 125
Alick, 40
Alicy, 40
Aliss, 142, 148
Alle, 45
Allen, 52
ALLEN: Alescandez I., 155; Alexander T., 150; Lydia, 150, 155; Richard, 69, 91, 110; William, 147, 148, 150, 155
Alley, 30, 131, 159

Allis, 141
Allison, 36
ALLISON: John, 134
Alliston: Bryant, 6
Ally, 58, 161
Alpherd, 59
Alsa, 92, 107
Alse, 39, 42, 46, 62
Alsey, 52
ALSOP, 126
Alsy, 102, 131
Alvina, 135
Amand, 141
Amanda, 74, 105, 107, 109, 111, 121, 134, 138, 139, 142, 144, 145, 148, 151, 156, 157, 165
Amandy, 134
Ambrose, 49, 99
Ambrow, 96
Amelia, 138
America, 40, 141, 143, 145
Americus, 40
Amia, 72
Amie, 99
Ammuzuow, 1
Amos, 34, 35, 49, 64, 79, 81, 98, 105, 141
Amy, 12, 13, 14, 20, 23, 25, 26, 33, 34, 38, 41, 58, 62, 64, 66, 68, 77, 80, 83, 84, 88, 92, 93, 103, 104, 107, 111, 132, 151, 156
Anaky, 140
Ancilla, 47
Anderson, 68, 77
ANDERSON: James, 49, 50, 73; Mary, 103
Andrew, 53, 63, 68, 88, 97, 98, 109, 111, 117, 129, 131, 132, 138, 139, 142, 156, 157
Angelena, 140

Anikey, 47
Ann, 2, 7, 24, 40, 41, 42, 49, 50, 54, 55, 60, 62, 64, 70, 75, 78, 79, 80, 81, 86, 90, 92, 94, 96, 98, 101, 103, 104, 116, 117, 121, 122, 124, 125, 126, 127, 128, 129, 130, 131, 132, 133, 138, 139, 145, 147, 148, 150, 152, 158, 160, 162, 163, 168
Ann Catherine, 140
Ann Maria, 156, 157
Ann Mariah, 140
Ann Rachel, 25
Anna, 36, 47, 53, 68, 77, 78, 96, 119, 125, 129, 132, 148, 152, 153, 154, 157
Annanica, 49
Anne, 16, 47, 52, 62, 78, 87, 92, 98, 106, 110, 113, 135
Annecha, 62
Annie, 23, 142
Anny, 30, 35, 41, 83, 85, 90, 102
Anthony, 14, 15, 30, 33, 41, 49, 52, 57, 65, 66, 70, 72, 73, 74, 77, 80, 83, 90, 91, 98, 101, 106, 116, 121, 124, 133, 143, 144, 148, 160, 168
Antony, 45, 123
Ara, 53, 101
Araminta, 53, 54, 87
Arch, 22, 69, 84, 122
Archy, 41, 49, 68
Arena, 132
Argyle, 64, 80
Armistead, 48, 64, 68, 77, 95, 113, 115, 117, 134, 138, 141, 143, 145, 149, 150, 155, 168
ARNELL: Elizabeth, 51
ARNOLD: William, 90
Aron, 104, 151

Arrilly, 132
ARRINGTON: Ann, 147; Caroline D., 147; George W., 145, 147; Lucinda F., 147; Martha A., 147; Mary Jane, 147; Richard, 145, 147; Wansford, 4
Artametia, 140
Arthur, 41, 60, 72, 74, 131, 142, 148, 151, 157, 164, 165
Artimacy, 135
Artimisia, 78
ASHFORD: Ann, 1; Michael, 1
ASHMORE: John, 3, 19; Sarah M., 126; William, 19, 126, 127, 131
ASHTON: Horatio Dade, 37; Laurence, 37; West, 87
Athena, 12
ATKINSON: George, 137, 138; Richard, 154, 157, 166
Atwell: Francis, 20
ATWELL: Ann, 25, 39, 41, 42; Charles, 25, 39; Hugh, 25, 41; Margaret, 25, 41; Mary, 25; Mary Lewis, 36; Thomas, 25, 39, 41; William, 25
Ausburn, 55
AUSTIAL: Jefferson P., 147
Austin, 69, 92, 94, 103, 123, 124
AWBREY: Francis, 6
Bacchus, 62, 94
Baccus, 52
Bach, 19
BAGLEY: Samuel, 18
Bailey, 154
BAILEY: Carr, 66, 109, 128
Baily, 152
Bainbridge, 127, 128, 131
Baker, 7, 49, 58
Balantine, 143

BALL: Adeline, 115; Alfred, 115, 149, 150, 155; Edward, 7; Francis Waring, 115; James, 57; Louisa, 115; Sarah C., 150; Sarah E., 150; Spencer, 115
BALLENDINE: Frances, 31, 36; Thomas, 36; Thomas William, 31
BALLENGER: Mary, 18
Bama, 81
Bangar, 3, 5
Banjar, 4
Baptiste, 117
Barbary, 19
BARBEE: Elizabeth W., 149, 151; James, 151; James M., 149; John C., 149; Mary C., 149, 151
Barey, 168
BARKER: Jane, 50; Joshua, 27
Barnaby, 21, 22, 39
Barnes, 22
BARNES: Mary, 45
Barnet, 103
Barnett, 46, 79, 104, 127, 148
Barney, 51, 83, 145
Barny, 21
BARRETT: Thomas, 69
BARRON: Hendly, 91; Henry A., 110; Jesse, 62, 64, 88, 92; Margery, 142
Barshaba, 41
Barsheba, 121
BARTER: Edward, 58
Bartlett, 33, 34, 143
Bartley, 86, 109
Bartly, 91, 96, 99
BARTON: Vallantino, 5
Bash, 39
Basil, 115
Bassett, 111, 125

BATES: Flemming, 50
Baulis, 78
BAYANT: William A., 162
BAYLOR: Jane A.A., 115
BAYLY: Geraldine, 163; John, 163; Richard P., 163
Bazil, 109
BEAN: William, 1
BEATTY: Betsyann, 140; James, 81
Beck, 17, 23, 24, 25, 27, 32, 39, 40, 41, 46, 47, 49, 58, 61, 62, 63, 72, 78, 95, 114, 118, 128, 168
BECKWITH: William E., 83
Becky, 40, 42, 77, 84, 96, 164
Bee, 36
BEEDLE: Harriet, 118
Behethlin, 77
Beike, 88
Belfast, 8
Belima, 77
Belinda, 36
Bell, 1, 87, 154
BELL: Alfred, 155
Ben, 9, 11, 12, 14, 15, 16, 17, 20, 23, 24, 25, 26, 29, 33, 34, 35, 36, 37, 38, 39, 40, 41, 42, 45, 47, 51, 52, 54, 55, 59, 60, 61, 62, 63, 64, 67, 68, 69, 71, 72, 73, 75, 77, 78, 79, 81, 82, 83, 87, 90, 99, 100, 101, 102, 106, 111, 113, 123, 124, 125, 129, 140, 142, 153, 155, 162, 168
Ben Jr., 123
Ben Sr., 123
Bender, 17, 40
Benjamin, 15, 37, 39, 43, 46, 68, 70, 77, 88, 90, 104, 105, 116, 138, 145, 155

BENNET: Ann Maria, 114;
   Fanny, 114
Bennett, 89
Benton, 109
Berkeley, 62
BERKELEY: Lewis, 105
BERKELY: Julia, 116; Sophia
   Carter, 116
Bernard, 64, 72, 105, 117, 121
Berry, 92; William, 149
BERRYMAN: Alexander, 130,
   131; Betsy G., 126; Elizabeth
   G., 130
Bess, 1, 5, 6, 8, 14
BEST: Adaline, 150; Adeline,
   150; H., 150
Bet, 38, 39, 65
Betey, 40
Betsy, 24, 33, 37, 40, 41, 49,
   55, 68, 73, 74, 77, 83, 85, 86,
   88, 92, 100, 104, 106, 107,
   111, 113, 115, 116, 123, 125,
   132, 144, 147, 151, 152, 154,
   160, 167, 168
Betsy Maria, 111
Bett, 16, 21, 23, 26, 36, 37, 74,
   124, 143
Bettie, 164
BETTS: Joshua, 18
Betty, 7, 11, 14, 15, 17, 20, 23,
   27, 37, 38, 40, 46, 49, 50, 52,
   53, 54, 59, 60, 62, 63, 64, 71,
   74, 77, 78, 79, 84, 85, 86, 87,
   88, 92, 98, 99, 101, 102, 105,
   110, 115, 116, 117, 128, 129,
   140, 141, 149, 150, 156
BEVERIDGE: Thomas, 110,
   121
Beverly, 46, 62, 92, 102, 105,
   117, 121, 124, 149, 151, 156,
   161, 165; John, 116
BIGBEE: George, 21

Bill, 23, 24, 26, 29, 31, 34, 41,
   46, 47, 50, 58, 60, 68, 69, 77,
   78, 79, 86, 88, 96, 98, 99,
   100, 111, 112, 113, 116, 121,
   139, 154, 155, 166
Billy, 21, 33, 36, 41, 45, 49, 60,
   64, 65, 77, 80, 92, 96, 99,
   100, 101, 105, 106, 109, 110,
   111, 113, 115, 116, 126, 127,
   131, 133, 138, 141, 142, 145,
   153
Billy Button, 143
Binah, 2
Birch: Billy, 49
BIRD: Margaret, 40; Thomas,
   16, 40; William, 19
BIRDWELL: Silas, 156
BLACKBURN: Bushrod W.,
   52; Col. Thomas, 16, 52;
   Maj. Richard Scott, 48
Blackston: G., 61
Blackstone: George, 68, 69, 87
BLACKWELL: Ann, 36;
   David, 37; George William
   Brent, 36
Bladeu, 144
Boatswain, 8
Bob, 8, 11, 12, 14, 15, 18, 24,
   30, 32, 33, 34, 35, 38, 39, 47,
   49, 50, 51, 52, 57, 63, 64, 65,
   69, 72, 75, 77, 78, 81, 90,
   100, 101, 103, 106, 112, 113,
   115, 116, 117, 121, 130, 132,
   134, 137, 141, 151, 153, 163,
   166, 168
Bolaz: Tom, 33
Boling: Tom, 34
Bolling: Sam, 49
BOLWARE: Moses, 105
Bonaparte, 54, 59, 87, 124
Bond, 78
BOOKE Jr.: E., 90

BOOTMAN: J., 66
Bosin, 38
BOSON: Rachel, 40
BOSWELL: George, 101
BOTS: Mr., 142
Bott, 116
BOTTS: Frances, 14, 17;
  Joshua, 14, 15; Samuel, 115;
  Susannah, 46; Thomas, 14
Bowling: George, 157
Bowson, 20
Boy, 2
BOYLE: Angelina K., 126;
  David, 115, 116, 126, 127;
  Thomas M., 126
Boyton, 40
BRADFORD: George, 141
BRADFORD Jr.: John, 8
Bradley, 68
BRAMER: Susan, 144;
  William, 144
BRASFIELD: Betsy, 79;
  Elizabeth, 94; George, 79,
  94; Julia, 79, 94; Leonard,
  79, 81, 94; Lucinda, 79, 94;
  Maria, 94; Mariah, 79;
  Thomas, 79, 94
BRASSFIELD: Elizabeth, 101,
  104; Lucinda, 104; Maria,
  101; Thomas, 104
BRAUNER: William B., 156
BRAWNER: Basil, 80; Bazil,
  83; Frederick P., 165; John,
  80; Joseph, 47, 117; Lucy,
  144; William, 80, 83, 148,
  160
BRAWNES: Malinda, 106
Braxton, 46
BRAZIER: Elizabeth, 34
BRENT: Alexander M., 152;
  Daniel C., 83; Daniel Carroll,
  31, 71, 83; Euphan, 137, 139,
  140, 142; Hannah, 36; Mrs.
  Euphan, 86; Richard, 71, 77,
  83, 86; Virginius, 152
BRENT Jr.: William, 86
BRETT: George, 124, 126;
  Richard, 93
BREWER: Henry, 91; Mrs.,
  100
BREWIN: Joseph, 141
BRICK: Benjamin, 23
Bridget, 15, 72, 78, 96, 99
BRIDWELL: Isaac, 122, 156;
  John, 47, 50; Martha, 73;
  William, 150, 159
Briscoe, 133
BRISCOE: A.M., 112;
  Alexander M., 112, 114;
  Thomas, 112
Bristoe, 33, 78
Bristol, 6
Bristoll, 5
Bristow, 18
BRITE: E.A., 118
Britt, 123, 124
BRITT: Ann, 155, 162; Richard
  A., 90
BROADWATER: Capt.
  Charles, 1; Charles, 1, 2, 5
BRONAUGH: Dr., 96; Francis,
  6; John, 89, 92, 96; Samuel,
  6, 8; Thomas, 6
BROOKE: B., 58; Cecelia G.,
  60; E., 66; Edmonia, 60;
  M.W., 66; Matthew W., 60,
  82, 95; Matthew Whiting, 60
BROOKE Jr.: Matthew
  Whiting, 59
Brooks, 48, 54, 59, 87; Tom,
  124
BROOKS: William, 91, 109
BROWN: Alexander, 32;
  Benjamin, 84; Betsy, 17;

Betty, 15; Catherine, 20; Elizabeth, 17, 20; George N., 70; James, 17, 86; John, 39, 49, 84, 101, 105; Joseph, 92; Levinia, 60; Lewburton, 17; Martha Lavinia, 60; Richard, 84; Robert, 17; Sarah, 20, 86; Thomas, 49; William, 20, 23, 50, 84; William W., 49
BRUCE: Elanara, 40; Eliza, 40; John, 40; Judith, 40; Landon, 40; Mary, 40; Mrs., 91
BRUNDIGE: Mary, 73; Timothy, 103
Bryant, 6
BRYANT: William, 29
BRYARLY: Susanna Conway, 109; Thomas Fitzhugh, 109
Buchanan: Joseph, 17
BUCHANAN: Joseph, 3
Buck, 14, 20, 21, 143; Billy, 113
BUCKLEY: Joshua, 93; William, 93, 97, 115
Buckner, 50; Nancy, 95
BUCKNER: Anthony, 20; Bernard, 131
Bud, 77, 121
Buddy, 123, 124
BUKELEY: Mary L., 165
Buliegh, 41
Bull, 91
BULLITT: Cuthbert, 33, 35, 43; Sophia C.M., 45
BULLOCK: Rachel, 4; Richard, 4, 5, 6; Sarah, 4
Bunch: Jim, 78
BUNDIGE: Timothy, 94
BURCH: William, 99
Burdett, 55
Burgus, 5
Burk, 150

BURN: Huriah, 93; Lydda, 49; Uriah, 49
BURNES: William, 96
Burnnell, 125
Burr, 67
BURROUGHS: Benjamin, 22, 23; Clement, 22, 23; John, 17, 22, 23; Joseph, 22, 23; Mary, 22, 23; Matthus, 22; Rachael, 45
Burton, 49
Butcher, 6, 14
Butler, 115, 126
BUTLER: Anne, 30; Helen, 39; Joseph, 30, 31; Laurance, 30; Lawrence, 23; William, 31, 60
Button: Sam, 47
BYRD: Levina, 134
BYRNE: Clary, 20; Derby, 70; Uriah, 80; William, 81, 131
Caba, 96
Cable, 22
Caesar, 5, 7, 11, 12, 16, 17, 21, 48, 65, 78
Calary, 116
Caleb, 58, 104, 113
CALLIG: Otho W., 107
Callis, 111
Calvan, 140
CALVERT: Eada, 31; Francis, 32; George, 42; John, 24, 32, 74; Mary, 13; Reuben, 11, 112, 135; Robert A., 133; Sarah C., 133
CALVERT Jr.: Reuben, 123
CALVERTZ: Obed, 55
Calvin, 138, 139, 144
Cambridge, 119
CAMPBELL: Colin, 124; James, 79, 85; John, 65; Rev.

Isaac, 21; Sally, 89; Sarah B., 89
Canab: Dick, 49; Harry, 49; John, 49
Candice, 24
Candis, 16
Cannah, 138
CANNON: Barnaby, 107; Charles G., 151; Francis, 107; Luke, 107; Mary, 11; Mary B., 157; Sarah Harrison, 34
CANNON Jr.: Luke, 107
Cardnecher, 4
Cardone, 151
Carlene, 106
Carlia, 107
Carline, 57, 72
Carlos, 41
Carne, 5
CARNEY: Benjamin, 96; Elizabeth, 46; Fanny, 140; George, 140; George F., 140; Jane, 112, 117; Nancy, 140; Ninneonad, 140; Sophia, 140; William, 140
Caroline, 38, 41, 77, 78, 81, 102, 103, 104, 105, 106, 110, 111, 114, 121, 122, 123, 124, 129, 131, 135, 138, 139, 140, 145, 153, 154, 155, 156, 157, 160
Carpenter: Morgan, 2
Carr, 167
CARR: John, 26, 167; William, 26, 39, 49, 65, 167
CARRICO: J., 100
Carshaba, 35
Carter, 77, 86, 121; Grayson, 90
CARTER, 115; Cassius, 165; Catherine, 84; Charles Landon, 40; David, 20; Edward, 48, 49, 53, 58, 63; Edward E., 89; Eliza Francis, 60; Elizabeth, 40, 91, 92, 98, 101; Elizabeth L., 150; Elizabeth Lucy, 115; Giles, 20, 25; Hannah, 88; J., 58; John, 85; John Fantleroy, 40; John H., 105; Judith, 40, 114; Landon, 40, 41; Margaret, 40; Mary, 30; Moore Fantleroy, 40; Robert, 20, 73; Samuel, 20; Sarah, 20; Sophia, 116; William, 20, 59, 116; Wormely, 91; Wormly, 40
Cary, 69, 75, 105, 107; William, 88
CASH: Elizabeth, 17; Katy, 63
Cat, 66
Cate, 7, 8, 11, 16, 19, 21, 22, 23, 24, 25, 29, 30, 33, 34, 39, 40, 43, 45, 50, 55, 57, 60, 62, 69, 75, 79, 86, 98, 101, 106, 111, 121
Catesby, 32, 49, 58
Cath, 23
Catharine, 86, 109, 124, 125, 150, 151, 154, 157
Catharine Elizabeth, 143
Catherine, 24, 31, 114, 156, 162, 163
Catlett: Philip, 154
Cato, 5, 24, 64
Catoc, 37
Cattell: Philip, 152
Cattron, 34
Caty, 40, 49, 53, 58, 128, 130
CAVE: Maryann, 84, 93
Ceal, 60
Cealay, 106
Cease, 51
Cebra, 29

Cecelia, 62, 85, 95, 111, 118, 124, 143
Ceclia, 77
Cecy, 55
Cela, 49
Celer, 60
Celey, 160
Celi, 139
Celia, 14, 16, 29, 30, 35, 47, 49, 55, 61, 65, 73, 80, 107, 109, 113, 115, 121, 123, 134
Celina, 159
Cely, 100, 106, 123, 124, 158
Cenale, 101
Centofy, 21
Ceny, 149
Cerda, 149
Cesar, 29, 90, 92, 94, 99, 106
Cesar Jr., 92
Cesh, 35
CHALMERS: Sarah, 65, 73
Chalod, 147
CHANCELLOR: Catharine, 139; Cooper, 138, 139; Elizabeth, 139; Jane, 139; Patsy A., 139
Chances, 142
CHANCILLOR: Elizabeth, 160
Chantelle, 72
Chapman: Agga, 148; George, 91, 124; Henry, 148
CHAPMAN: George, 107; Jenny C__n, 20; Joseph, 3; Nathaniel, 8; Sarah, 64; Susan, 64; Susanna, 20; Thomas, 20, 27, 34; W. George, 113
Charity, 17, 30, 35, 49, 58, 66, 77, 78, 80, 90, 91, 94, 102, 105, 113, 130, 138, 141, 153, 159, 164, 168

Charles, 3, 12, 14, 16, 19, 21, 23, 26, 27, 30, 32, 33, 34, 36, 37, 38, 39, 40, 41, 46, 47, 48, 49, 51, 52, 55, 57, 58, 60, 61, 62, 64, 67, 68, 69, 70, 75, 77, 79, 81, 82, 83, 86, 88, 89, 95, 96, 98, 99, 101, 102, 103, 104, 107, 110, 111, 112, 113, 116, 117, 118,121, 123, 124, 125, 126, 127, 128, 129, 130, 131, 132, 133, 134, 137, 138, 139, 140, 142, 145, 147, 149, 150, 151, 152, 153, 154, 155, 157, 162, 166, 167
Charles Edward, 143
Charles Fenton Mercer, 63
Charles Jr., 103
Charley, 34, 156, 157, 158, 161, 162
Charlie, 33
Charlotte, 12, 14, 15, 16, 17, 21, 22, 23, 24, 26, 27, 30, 33, 36, 39, 40, 41, 49, 51, 55, 58, 60, 62, 63, 68, 70, 71, 72, 73, 77, 78, 83, 84, 85, 86, 88, 89, 94, 97, 101, 102, 104, 105, 110, 111, 116, 121, 122, 123, 124, 125, 127, 129, 130, 134, 138, 139, 142, 155, 156, 157, 163, 164
Chat, 134
Chatham, 32
Chatt, 134
CHE_IG: Elizabeth W., 118
Chellon: John, 143
Cheshire, 142
CHESLEY: John, 47
Chessor, 46
Chester, 148
CHEVIS: Dr. F.F., 129
CHICHESTER: Daniel M., 83

CHICK: Ann, 25; Celia, 25; John, 25; Nancy, 55; Susannah, 25
Chin, 158; Catherine, 163, 164; Jesse, 140; John, 140, 143; Kitty, 137; Patty, 140, 143; Sarah, 140; William, 140
China, 155
Chiriss, 16
CHISLEY: Robert, 83
CHIVIS: Elizabeth W., 129; Francis T., 129
Chloe, 19, 22, 39, 40, 47, 49, 92, 99, 100, 115, 122, 150
Chlor, 144
Chris, 72, 95
Christopher, 135
Cila, 51
Cilla, 13
Ciller, 59, 61, 114
Cily, 155
Cinthy, 61
Cinthya, 63
Cisily, 72
Clany, 139
Clara, 25, 38, 41, 66, 73, 77, 81, 99, 100, 121, 145, 151, 164, 168
Clarissa, 49, 97, 125, 156
Clark, 163; James, 47; Joe, 47; Mary, 157; Sandy, 164; Thomas, 163; Wellington, 163, 164
CLARK: Chapman G., 127; John, 143; John _., 168; Mary, 143, 168; Richard A., 143, 168; Solomon, 143, 168; Thomas A., 143; Thomas O., 168; William H., 143, 168
Clary, 25, 52, 60, 92, 98, 104, 118, 139
Clay, 83

Cleary, 99
CLEARY: Michael, 129
Clem, 112, 113, 121
Clemont, 125
Clene, 158
CLEVELAND: Alexander, 24
Clia, 15, 106
Clio, 6
Cloe, 5, 6, 17, 21, 25, 33, 37, 40, 51, 62, 78, 83, 88, 90, 104, 110, 149, 155
Clowe, 40
Coal: Ben, 55
COCHRAN: James, 83
COCKE: Catesby, 167; John, 32; John Catesby, 167; William, 32
COCKRELL: Benjamin, 117; Hulah, 117; I.J., 139; Jesse, 117; Johnson, 117; Jules W., 139; Mary, 117; Moses, 117; Nancy, 49; Peter, 43, 49; Sarah, 117; William, 117
COCKWELL: George H., 156
Cole: John, 55
COLE: Benjamin, 141, 143, 145; Daniel, 97; Matthias, 130; Prudence, 141, 148; Richard, 70; Samuel, 83
COLERT: George, 65
COLLENS: Frances, 68
COLLING: Ann, 33
COLLIS: M., 134
COLQUHOUN: James W., 73, 86; Letitia, 33
COLVERT: Jacob, 30; Mary, 5, 30; Obed, 46
COLVIN: Richard, 83
COMBS: Seth, 83
Comfort, 94, 103
Comor: Catharine, 150

COMPTON: Alexander, 93, 97, 98, 110, 164; Alexander H., 164; Ann, 93; Marianne, 57; Stephen Joy, 78, 96
CONNER: Bryan, 2; Jean, 29
Constance, 32
CONTRAST: A., 104
Conway, 65
CONWAY: Lee, 51
Cook, 38; Ann, 148; George, 110, 163, 164; Isaac, 77; James, 105; Judy, 52; Robert, 148, 155
COOMBS: William, 122
Cooper, 25, 131; Charles, 134; John, 3
COOPER: Benjamin, 67, 133; Chloe Ann, 133; Richard, 160
Coote: George, 91
COPIN: William, 47
COPPEDGE: Baladwin, 16; Frances, 16
Cora, 143
Corbin: Letty Felicia, 60, 63
Corda, 150
Cordelia, 48, 57, 96
Cordy, 98, 107
Cornbon, 21
Cornelia, 128, 131, 147
Cornelias, 100
Cornelius, 50, 58, 106, 135, 138
CORNHILL: Francis, 39
CORNWELL: Constance, 102, 104; Jesse, 104, 128; John, 39, 102
CORSWILL: Ann, 20
Cortney, 82
CORTNEY: Sally, 13
COTTRELL: Frances, 42; Jeremiah, 42; Jesse, 42;

Moses, 42; Nancy, 42; Peter, 42
COULTER: Margaret, 161
Courtney, 36, 80, 103, 147, 152, 160
COURTNEY: Sarah, 127
Coxon, 35
CRAIG: Mary B., 145; William M., 145
Craven, 60, 91
CREAMER: Winiford, 72
CROOK: Zephariah, 12
CROSBY: Susana, 35; William, 53
Crump: George, 140, 143
CRUPPER: Eli, 105
Cubbo, 7
Cubit, 4
CULLINS: John, 11
Cumford, 51, 83
Cummey, 2
CUNDIFF: William, 90
CUNDISS: Fanny, 106
Cupid, 4, 7
Curry, 113
Curtis, 139
CURTIS: Christopher, 11
CUSHING: C.C., 164; Charles L., 153; Charles Q., 153; Christopher C., 153, 156; Crawford, 153; Eleanor, 153; Henry C., 153; Thomas N., 153
Cuss, 6
Custus, 138
Cuthull: James, 8
Cuzzy, 40
Cynthia, 90, 126, 155, 157
Cyrus, 47, 51, 62, 64, 83, 143
DACONS: Thomas, 9
Dacy, 24
Dade: Henry, 39, 67

DADE: Caduallader, 37; Chadwalada, 87; Charles E., 125; Charles Stuart, 37; Eliza L., 115, 137; Francis, 37; Judge William A.G., 111; Langhorne, 37, 87; Laurence, 87; Maj. T., 61; Maj. Townshend, 59; Mary, 37; Maryann, 45; Sally A., 115; Sarah, 37, 74, 115; Sarah Ashton, 37; Townshend, 37, 53, 54, 61, 68, 80, 87; W.A.G., 83, 115; William A.G., 59
Dafney, 99
Dafny, 96
DAGG: Thomas, 14, 21
Dainey, 64
DALE: Abraham, 12; Reuben, 12; Robert, 12, 13
Dall, 25
Dallas, 144
DALTON: James, 63, 67
Dan, 13
Dandrige, 143
Daniel, 1, 3, 4, 12, 15, 16, 17, 18, 19, 20, 21, 23, 24, 26, 27, 29, 30, 31, 32, 34, 37, 38, 39, 40, 41, 42, 45, 47, 48, 49, 50, 51, 53, 54, 57, 59, 60, 61, 62, 63, 64, 65, 67, 68, 69, 70, 71, 75, 77, 78, 79, 80, 81, 83, 84, 87, 88, 90, 91, 92, 94, 95, 96, 97, 98, 99, 100, 104, 105, 107, 109, 110, 115, 117, 118, 121, 122, 123, 124, 125, 126, 132, 134, 135, 138, 139, 145, 149, 150, 152, 154, 168
DANIEL: Lucy, 131; Richard, 131; Samuel, 49; Sarah, 42, 49
Daphine, 36, 40

Daphne, 11, 16, 40, 47, 60, 74, 79, 123, 124, 125, 168
Daphney, 17, 19, 24, 46, 54, 64, 66, 88, 141, 144, 145
Darcus, 30, 31, 33, 34, 51, 78, 94
Darkey, 23, 40
Darkins, 21
Darky, 68, 70
Dave, 69, 81
Davey, 54, 87
David, 3, 11, 14, 21, 22, 31, 36, 37, 45, 46, 49, 57, 62, 63, 67, 69, 70, 88, 96, 109, 114, 117, 122, 125
Davidson: John, 6
Davie, 14, 15, 29
Davis, 137, 144
DAVIS: Alexander, 123; Asa, 156; Benson, 73, 127; David, 74; Elizabeth, 161; Henry L., 128; Herman D., 139; Hiram D., 138; Hugh W., 137; Isaac, 42, 51; Jesse W., 137; Jobe, 161, 162, 163; John, 3, 32; John F., 84; John W., 137; Libbey, 59; Libby, 46, 70; M., 121; Melenday, 84; Moses, 59; Presley, 93; Richard, 97, 102, 116, 125; Robert, 161; Sarah, 65; Sarah B., 138; Sophia, 137; T.R., 157; Thomas, 137; Thomas K., 141; William, 36, 70, 74, 80; William W., 137
DAVIS Sr.: Hugh, 160
Davy, 20, 22, 30, 35, 49, 50, 51, 54, 59, 60, 61, 64, 68, 69, 72, 73, 78, 80, 86, 87, 92, 93, 111, 121, 124, 125, 129, 152
DAWE: Phillip, 58

DAWES: Phillip, 53; Phillip D., 130
DAWSON: Benjamin, 105, 107; Nancy, 105
DEAHERS: Thomas T., 8
DEALY: Ann, 70
Dean: Charles, 153; James, 153; Reuben, 153; Will, 74
DEAN: Hannah, 82; Joseph, 82
Deanna, 144
DEAVER: William A., 150
DeBELL: Dorcas, 81, 92, 93, 100; Jeremiah, 81, 93; Joel, 93; John, 81, 87
Delfery, 38
Delfy, 70
DELGARN: John, 19
DELGRIN: George, 17; James, 17; John, 17; Maryann, 17; Salley, 17; William, 17
Delia, 51, 78, 83, 95, 106, 133, 140, 148
Delila, 67, 68
Delilah, 49, 60, 121, 124
Delman, 40
Delmond, 40
Delmount, 19
Delph, 35, 68
Delpha, 88
Delphia, 60
Delphy, 39, 84
Delsy, 49
Dempse, 77
Denis, 48
Dennis, 13, 14, 15, 25, 36, 38, 39, 41, 59, 60, 62, 64, 67, 68, 69, 77, 80, 81, 84, 93, 94, 97, 111, 130, 135, 152, 157, 161, 162
DENNIS: Caty, 106
DENT: Ellen M., 114; Ellen Matilda, 112

DERMONT: Mary, 167; Michael, 167
Dianer, 143, 168
Dianh, 40
Dianna, 92
Dick, 1, 2, 6, 11, 13, 14, 16, 18, 21, 22, 23, 24, 25, 35, 37, 46, 48, 49, 52, 53, 57, 60, 62, 63, 65, 66, 67, 69, 71, 73, 75, 77, 78, 81, 85, 88, 92, 94, 97, 98, 101, 102, 105, 113, 124, 125, 127, 128, 131, 139, 140, 142, 147, 148, 149, 150, 163
DICKERSON: Edward, 62; Elizabeth, 62
DICKINSON: Ann E., 161; Frances, 53
Dicky, 86
Dicy, 134
Digen: Ann, 7
Diggs, 77
Dilsey, 58
Dina, 5
Dinah, 5, 13, 16, 17, 22, 23, 24, 25, 30, 31, 32, 33, 40, 41, 47, 49, 55, 57, 62, 63, 69, 73, 74, 75, 80, 86, 103, 121, 125, 129
Diner, 20, 25, 38, 50
Dinner, 122
Dinten: Bill, 154
Dishman, 69, 117
DISKIN: John, 23
Disy, 116, 125
DITTWILL: William, 39
Diza, 97, 102
Docia, 93
Dodson, 63
DODSON: Abraham, 5; Amey, 5; David, 5; Elijah, 5; George, 5; Greenham, 5; Joshua, 5; Thomas, 5

DOGAN: Ann M., 165;
  Catherine E., 165; Elizabeth,
  118; Hennesta, 165; Henry,
  98, 107, 118; Jane, 118;
  John, 118; John F., 164;
  Medora S., 164; William H.,
  151, 165; William N., 118
Doll, 8, 30
Dolly, 40, 41, 49, 62, 63, 68,
  72, 84, 88, 92, 99, 103, 121,
  125, 128, 132
Domingo, 48
Doratha, 27
Dorcas, 1, 14, 15, 27, 38, 73, 83
Dorcus, 26, 168
Dorkus, 21
Dorsey, 159
Douglas, 41, 42, 117, 143
DOUGLAS: George A., 134;
  Mrs., 82
DOUGLASS: Benjamin, 107
DOWELL: James, 133;
  Jeremiah, 53
DOWNMAN: Jabez, 16;
  Travers, 19; William, 50, 65
DOWNTON: Richard, 39
DRAKEFORD: Richard, 6
Drusilla, 109
Dublin, 8
Dudley, 61, 153
DUDLEY: John, 24, 30; Mary,
  24
Duffey, 163
DUNCON: John, 6
DUNINGTON: Charles W.,
  155
DUNNINGTON: Francis H.,
  124
DUVALL: John Pearce, 71;
  Sarah Elenor, 71; William,
  71, 72; William Henry, 71

DYE: Vicent, 34; Vincent, 36,
  38; William, 34, 38
Dyer, 77
E Saw, 80
Ealan, 39
Ealsy, 88
Ealy, 34
Easter, 50, 51, 59, 69, 72, 83,
  125, 138, 144, 157
EASTER: Giles, 6; Margaret
  Bert, 40
Easther, 13
Eave, 38, 74
Ebalina, 123
Ebaline, 145
Eda, 64
Eddie, 48
Edenborough, 62
EDGE: John, 3
Edia, 103
Edie, 78
Edinburg, 140
Edmand, 128
Edmania, 156
Edmon, 134
Edmond, 27, 37, 41, 65, 68, 70,
  83, 86, 90, 102, 113, 134
Edmonia, 157
Edmund, 48, 50, 51, 54, 57, 63,
  72, 73, 77, 92
Edwan, 121
Edward, 5, 8, 27, 45, 96, 106,
  117, 126, 127, 135, 145, 162
Edward Edinbrough, 143
Edwards: John, 8
EDWARDS: Ann, 74; Ann H.,
  74; Gilbert, 74; Lucy, 74
Edwin, 132
Elce, 37
ELDRIDGE: George, 2
Eleanor, 41, 49, 78, 103, 116,
  124

Elender, 38
Elenor, 22, 23, 35, 48, 95
Elgin, 16
Eli, 141
Eliah, 30
Elias, 78, 79, 113, 121, 125, 129
Elic, 104
Elick, 77
Elija, 40, 121, 149, 152
Elijah, 12, 13, 14, 19, 31, 50, 69, 81, 82, 98, 101, 105, 118, 122, 127, 128, 131, 145, 149, 150
Elinor, 31
Elis, 138
Elisa, 55, 80, 122, 128, 145
Elisha, 91
Elisor, 106
Eliza, 47, 49, 58, 59, 60, 61, 63, 64, 66, 69, 73, 77, 86, 88, 89, 90, 91, 92, 93, 94, 95, 96, 98, 101, 103, 104, 105, 106, 107, 110, 111, 113, 116, 117, 118, 123, 124, 125, 127, 129, 138, 141, 142, 143, 147, 148, 150, 151, 152, 153, 154, 156, 157, 158, 159, 162, 163, 168
Eliza Ann, 134
Eliza Jr., 123
Elizabeth, 23, 27, 39, 52, 75, 92, 102, 104, 105, 106, 111, 125, 129, 145, 152, 154
Eljah, 58
Ella, 127
Ellen, 49, 84, 93, 101, 116, 121, 124, 131, 140, 143, 148, 154, 157, 159, 160, 161, 162, 163, 164, 167
Ellender, 32
Ellick, 134
Elliott, 99

ELLIOTT: Mary, 13
Ellis, 70, 81
Ellzey, 37, 41
Elsey, 83
Elsy, 161
Elvira, 78
ELWELL: Charles, 95; Sarah, 102, 154; Solomon, 83
Ely, 86
Emancipated: Abner, 27, 107; Abram, 139; Amanda, 139; Ann, 55, 139; Antony, 45; Armistead, 141; Bacchus, 94; Betty, 140; Charles, 139; Charles Washington, 139; Charlotte, 78; Clany, 139; Daniel, 149; Daphney, 54; David, 45; Ealsy, 88; Elisa, 55; Fanny, 29, 103; Frank, 46; Frederick, 45; George, 50, 89; George Crump, 140, 143; Hannah, 55; Henny, 143, 168; Henry, 141, 143; Jack, 30; Jacob, 42; James Webster, 74; James Wilson, 55; Jane, 55, 86, 141; Jesse, 159; Jim, 159; Joan, 45; John, 139, 143; Lewis, 78; Lucy Ann, 139; Lucy Webster, 74; Mahala, 141; Mariah, 139; Martin, 139; Mary, 94, 103, 139; Mary Ann Starks, 68; Milly, 107; Milly Starks, 68; Nancy Taylor, 55; Nelly, 132; Nelson, 132; Patty Starks, 68; Polly, 29; Priscella, 139; Rachel, 51; Rose, 132; Roses, 50; Sally Starks, 68; Sam, 159; Sandy, 103; Sarah, 78; Sinah, 132; Sully, 139;

Thomas, 156; Thomas
Jackson, 139; William, 51
Emanda, 125
Emanuel, 55, 60, 75, 121, 123,
 129, 142
Emelina, 154
Emeline, 71, 72, 142
Emily, 89, 90, 91, 109, 115,
 121, 125, 129, 134, 138, 139,
 140, 141, 143, 157, 158, 160,
 163, 164
Emma, 102, 135
Emmala, 82
Emmanuel, 105
Enfield, 152, 154
Enoch, 53, 125, 127, 128, 129
Enock, 72
Ephraim, 34
Ephrain, 41
Esau, 80, 137, 149, 150
ESHEW: John, 40
Essex, 72, 74, 80
Ester, 40, 168
Esther, 12, 19, 20, 21, 25, 33,
 36, 41, 47, 48, 49, 55, 57, 60,
 64, 66, 68, 69, 70, 77, 86, 87,
 90, 94, 122, 124, 128, 147,
 152
Eugenia, 139, 140, 142
Evaline, 97, 128, 162
EVANS: Redwood, 73;
 Wantsford, 159
Eve, 8, 16, 21, 24, 36, 70, 77,
 80, 98, 99
Evelina, 54, 59, 81, 87, 90, 104,
 137, 139, 145, 147, 150, 151,
 152, 157, 163, 164
Even, 37
EVENS: James G., 77; Jesse,
 70
EVES: Elizabeth, 97
Evilisca, 142

Ewell, 164
EWELL: Alfred, 65; Capt.
 Thomas W., 22; Charlotte,
 95, 103; Dr. Solomon, 85;
 Edwin H., 95; James, 57;
 James B., 167; Jane, 65;
 Jesse, 47, 48, 57; Joseph F.,
 95; Lucy, 95; Sarah, 95;
 Sarah Ann, 95; Sarah B., 85;
 Solomon, 17, 57
EWELL Jr.: Charles, 95
Ezekiel, 94, 149, 150
F. Simpson, 145
F. Williams, 145
FAGANS: James, 58; Jenny,
 58; Margaret, 58
Fairfax: Bob, 163; Joan, 163;
 Robert, 157
FAIRFAX: Bendecter, 31;
 Elizabeth, 31; Henry, 83,
 142, 145; Letty, 142; Sarah,
 31; William, 31, 32, 142
FALKNER: Thomas, 11, 13
Fame, 49
Fan, 36, 70
Fancy, 102
Fanny, 12, 13, 21, 22, 24, 25,
 27, 29, 31, 32, 33, 34, 36, 37,
 39, 40, 41, 42, 43, 46, 47, 49,
 50, 52, 57, 59, 60, 61, 62, 63,
 64, 68, 69, 72, 73, 74, 77, 78,
 80, 82, 83, 84, 86, 87, 88, 89,
 90, 91, 92, 93, 95, 96, 98, 99,
 100, 101, 102, 103, 105, 106,
 109, 111, 112, 113, 114, 115,
 117, 122, 125, 129, 135, 138,
 140, 141, 143, 145, 147, 148,
 152, 154, 160, 161, 163, 167
Fanny Jr., 154
FANON: Mrs., 25
FARR: John, 141

FARROW: Abraham, 8, 9;
  Abram, 8; Elizabeth, 32;
  George, 13, 15; Isaac, 8, 46;
  John, 2, 32, 46; Joseph, 154;
  Sibell, 8
FARROWS: Issac, 62
FAULKNER: Thomas, 36, 62
Fauny, 75
FEAGAN: Edward, 8, 9;
  Francis, 78; Henry, 78;
  James, 64, 78; Margaret, 77;
  Raughly, 78; Sarah, 64;
  Susannah, 78
FEAGANS: Francis, 82; Gracy,
  82; Susanna, 82
Felding, 85
Fele, 129
Felicia, 118, 168
Fender, 47, 66
Fenix: Lance, 163; Laura, 164
Fenton, 60, 63
Ferdinand, 111
FERGUSON: James, 61; John,
  81
FERWELL: Sarah Ann, 161
FEWELL: Ann E., 158;
  Elizabeth, 79; James, 121;
  Peggy, 79; Thomas T., 158;
  William, 79; William S., 158
FIELDER: Janney, 15
Fielding, 79, 85, 94
Filice, 24
Fill, 105
FISHBACK: John, 1
Fisher: Ann, 145
Fitzhough: Sally, 163
Fitzhugh: Sally, 164
FITZHUGH: Caroline Matilda,
  109; Daniel McCarty, 109;
  Harriet Helen, 109; John T.,
  60; John Thornton, 55;
  Margaret, 14; Thomas, 109;
  William, 46
Flora, 33, 64, 78, 112, 114
FLORENCE: Ann, 165;
  George, 70, 89, 90; William,
  92, 97, 104, 109
Foley: William, 166
FOLEY: Cassin, 162; Enoch,
  166; Presley, 99
FOOTE: Catherine, 12;
  Elizabeth, 12; G. William,
  110; G.W., 122; Hayward,
  129; Haywood, 118; Helen,
  118, 129; Richard, 12, 14, 27,
  30, 125, 126, 129; Richard
  L., 118; Sarah L., 118;
  William, 117; William L.,
  118, 129
FORBES: David, 24; Dr.
  David, 31; Margaret, 24
FORLY: Betsy, 161
Fortune, 21, 106
FORTUNE: Gainer, 106;
  Garner, 58, 114; Lucy, 106;
  Nancy, 106; Polly, 106;
  Thomas, 106
FOSTER: Daniel, 95, 102, 137,
  142; Elizabeth, 130, 131;
  George, 12; Isaac, 130;
  James, 39, 41, 142; Margaret,
  142; Mary Mildred, 142;
  Redman, 142, 148;
  Redmond, 155; Susan
  Amelia, 143; Thomas, 107;
  William P., 142
FOUCHE: Temple, 114, 122
FOWKE: Mary, 34
Fox: Richard, 8
FOX: Emily, 123; Mildred, 122
Fran, 25
Frances, 54, 105, 114, 125, 129,
  138, 142, 148, 150, 154, 165

Francis, 12, 17, 20, 95, 99, 111, 112, 117, 134, 138, 151, 152, 155, 162
Frank, 4, 7, 13, 14, 15, 19, 23, 24, 25, 26, 29, 30, 34, 37, 39, 40, 41, 46, 47, 48, 49, 53, 54, 58, 60, 62, 67, 69, 77, 85, 97, 98, 104, 106, 109, 111, 113, 117, 128, 144, 152, 161, 168
Frankey, 87
Franklin, 54, 59, 61, 68, 69, 87, 147
Franky, 23, 59, 61, 77, 90, 119, 149, 156
Fred, 155
Frederick, 14, 15, 35, 47, 58, 60, 64, 81, 91, 103, 125, 129, 148, 149, 150, 161, 163, 164
Frederick Howard, 143
Fredonia, 113
Fredrick, 45, 96
FRENCH: Daniel, 2; Susan Ann, 140; William, 104, 113, 115
Friday, 80, 121, 125, 129, 148
FRYAR: Jabez, 47
G. Blackston, 61
Gabriel, 13, 25, 26, 30, 33, 34, 36, 41, 52, 62, 114
Gabriel Jr., 62
Gabriel Sr., 62
Gabril, 3
GAINES: Catherine, 31; Nancy, 80; Sarah, 80; Thomas A., 155; William, 46
GAINS: Augustin, 92; William, 47
Galba, 6, 65
GALLAGHER: Ann, 124; Bernard, 89, 91; Julis, 124; Margaret, 89, 124; Mary C., 114

GALLAGHER Jr.: Bernard, 148
GALLAHER: Brian, 161; Mrs., 161; Thomas H., 161
Ganderson, 132
Gandy, 122
GARNER: Nancy, 161; Richard, 50, 54
Garrard, 12
Garret, 134
GEBBS: Foushee, 26
Gene, 78
General, 145
Gengs, 118
Geofrey, 22
George, 3, 4, 6, 11, 12, 13, 15, 16, 18, 20, 24, 25, 29, 32, 33, 34, 35, 37, 38, 39, 40, 41, 46, 48, 50, 51, 52, 54, 57, 59, 60, 61, 63, 64, 65, 66, 67, 68, 69, 70, 72, 77, 78, 79, 80, 81, 83, 84, 85, 86, 87, 88, 89, 90, 91, 92, 93, 94, 95, 97, 98, 99, 101, 103, 104, 105, 106, 107, 109, 110, 111, 112, 113, 114, 116, 117, 118, 121, 123, 124, 125, 126, 127, 128, 131, 132, 134, 137, 138, 140, 141, 142, 143, 144, 145, 149, 150, 151, 152, 153, 154, 156, 157, 162, 163, 164, 166, 168
GEORGE: Benjamin, 54, 59, 61; Frances, 61; Hannah, 61
George A., 134
George Berkeley, 143
George Dallas, 143
George William, 151
Georgiana, 151, 152, 153, 154, 157, 165
Gerard, 32, 84, 90, 93, 104, 106, 111, 113, 121
German: Henry, 165

Gerrard, 50
GERRARD: Elizabeth, 13
Gerry, 111
GESHING: Simon, 9
GIBSON: Frances B., 125, 140, 143; John, 51, 52, 66, 82, 140, 143
GIBSON Jr.: John, 125
Gilbert, 40, 47, 140, 145, 168
GILBERT: Joseph R., 112, 117
Giles, 5
GILL: Ann S., 137, 138, 139; Presly, 59; Richard, 137
GILL, Jr.: John, 65
Gilson, 51
Ginny, 3, 30, 40, 109
GLASCOCK: R.C., 160
Glasgow, 21
Gloster, 35
Godfrey, 63, 66, 77, 134
GOING: Elixander, 4; Susannah, 4
GOSLING: John, 5; Simon, 5
GOSSOM: Ruth, 161
Gowen, 8, 9, 13
Gowin, 14, 41, 66, 103
Grace, 2, 8, 12, 15, 29, 31, 34, 38, 57, 62, 63, 64, 77, 80, 123, 124, 138, 141
GRADY: James, 83
GRAGHAM: Col., 86; William, 92
Graham: G., 20
GRAHAM, 167; Dr. George, 75; Dr. William, 99, 168; Elizabeth, 167; Francis S., 156; George, 34, 82; H.L., 161; Hannah, 98; James, 64, 79; Jane, 71; Jean, 168; Jenny, 167; John, 23, 34, 150, 151, 161, 168; Mrs., 71; Pane, 23; Reginald, 20; Richard, 34; Robert R., 156; Susannah F., 118; Thomas, 72, 99; Walls, 167; Walter, 167; William, 20, 23, 100
GRAHAM Sr.: John, 156
Granderson, 105, 165
Grandison, 102
Grant: Peter, 8
GRANT: John, 38, 55; Liby, 16; Mary Whitledge, 38; Posey D., 66
Grassy, 65
GRAVET: Ellis, 83
Gray: James, 163
GRAY: James, 41; Richard, 41, 42; William, 41
Grayson, 68, 70, 90
GRAYSON: Rev. Spencer, 38; William, 52
Greasten, 41
GREEN: Amy, 24; Elizabeth, 111, 131; Frances E., 111; George, 17, 24, 25, 26; George E., 105; James, 24, 51, 105, 111, 116, 123; Jesse, 24; Lucinda, 97; Margaret, 24; Mary, 24; Nancy, 24, 97; Patty, 24; Staunton, 97; Thomas, 22, 24, 98, 102; Thompson, 97, 98, 110, 116; Townshend _., 97; Wesley, 97; William, 77, 81, 82, 97
GREGG: John, 8; William, 2
GREGORY: Benjamin, 36, 37; Carolina, 65; Mary, 32, 36
Griffin, 41, 72, 128
GRIGSBY: A.L., 157, 162; Aaron, 54; Charlotte, 45; W., 121
Grimes: Henry, 149, 150
GRINSTEAD: Elizabeth, 50; James, 50, 51, 87; John, 50;

Leonard, 50; Lynna, 50;
William, 50
GRUBBS: Richard, 22
GUESS: Joseph, 5
Gula, 113
Guonby, 23
Gusta, 64, 107, 151
Gustavus, 55, 63, 78, 103, 106, 111
Gusty, 40, 96, 99, 152, 154
Guy, 11, 64
Guynette, 111
GWATHIN: Charles, 51; Elizabeth, 51; James, 121
GWATKIN: Edward, 102; Edwin, 102; James, 37, 51, 58; Margaret, 37; Mary S., 156, 157; Prudence, 78
GWYNN: Nancy, 86
HADDUX Sr.: John, 81
Haden, 46, 53, 62
Hagan, 3
Hagar, 5, 11, 13, 15, 20, 26, 45, 50, 51, 57, 58, 64, 102
HAISE: Sally E., 95
HAISLIP: Nathan, 110, 112, 114
HAM___: W., 138
HAMILTON: Maria, 96, 100; Robert, 128, 131; Thomas B., 98
HAMMETT: Ann, 47
HAMMILL: John, 39
HAMMITT: Ann, 46; John, 46, 47
Hampton, 82
HAMPTON: Henry, 12, 63; Thomas R., 109; William, 66
HANCOCK: Ann, 5; Catharine, 127; Catherine, 129; Catherine L., 125, 132; John,
5; Margaret, 50; Margaret L., 132; Moses, 150; Scarlet, 5, 6
Hanna, 21
Hannah, 5, 13, 14, 16, 18, 24, 25, 26, 31, 32, 33, 36, 40, 41, 42, 43, 45, 48, 49, 50, 51, 52, 54, 55, 57, 60, 62, 63, 64, 65, 71, 77, 78, 79, 80, 82, 83, 87, 88, 90, 96, 97, 98, 99, 103, 106, 107, 113, 116, 118, 127, 128, 131, 132, 134, 135, 137, 141, 144, 145,150, 152, 154, 157, 167, 168
Hannah Jr., 103
Hanner, 4, 30, 32, 49, 50, 51, 52, 68
Hanney, 38
Hannibal, 82, 95
Hanny, 57, 70
Hanson, 123
HARDEN: Edward, 79
HARDIN: Mark, 1; Mary, 1
HARDING: Edward, 162
Harper, 6
Harrie, 5
Harriet, 24, 41, 48, 50, 51, 57, 58, 63, 64, 65, 66, 68, 71, 72, 73, 78, 83, 88, 89, 93, 94, 95, 96, 97, 98, 99, 100, 101, 103, 105, 106, 111, 113, 116, 117, 121, 124, 125, 129, 132, 134, 137, 140, 141, 143, 145, 147, 148, 152, 153, 161, 162
Harriett, 124, 126, 157
Harrietta, 116
Harriette, 156
Harris: Henry, 125; Nathaniel, 143, 168
HARRIS: Mary, 13; Thomas, 2
Harrison, 51, 83, 92, 105, 107, 109, 115, 118, 134, 142, 144, 148, 149, 150, 161

HARRISON, 99; A., 121;
Allen, 118; Ann, 19; Ann C.,
118; Ann Catharine, 26; B.E.,
141; Burr, 26; Col. Burr, 30;
Cuthbert, 26; Cuthburt, 13,
14, 19; Frances Barn, 19;
Jane, 118; John L., 100; John
P., 118; John S., 110, 128;
M., 121; Mary Ann, 26;
Maryann, 45; Matthew, 26,
52, 111; Peyton, 39; Rev.
Thomas, 62, 85; Sarah, 61;
Seth, 13, 19; T.I., 159;
Thomas, 19, 26, 61, 62, 68,
77, 115; William, 99
Harry, 1, 2, 3, 4, 5, 7, 8, 9, 11,
13, 14, 15, 16, 17, 18, 19, 21,
22, 23, 25, 26, 29, 32, 34, 36,
37, 38, 39, 40, 41, 42, 45, 49,
51, 53, 54, 58, 59, 60, 61, 62,
64, 65, 66, 68, 69, 71, 72, 74,
77, 80, 81, 83, 86, 87, 88, 90,
91, 94, 96, 97, 98, 102, 106,
109,116, 118, 122, 123, 126,
127, 128, 129, 130, 131, 145,
147, 159, 167
Harry Sr., 26
Harshall, 41
HASKINS: John, 22
HASKINS Jr.: John, 22
HASLO_: Reason, 83
Hatty, 144
Haywood, 104
Heartly, 125
HEATH: Charles, 157; Ewell,
57; Fanny, 144; Isaac, 144,
157; Maryann Mariah, 57;
Sally, 144
Heathy, 37
Hector, 40
HEDGES: Robert, 33, 45
HEDGES Sr.: Robert, 45

Helen, 77, 138, 156, 157, 159,
168
HELM: Elizabeth, 25; George,
55; John, 55; Lina, 55;
Lynaugh, 25, 34
HENDERSON: Alexander, 73,
78, 99, 168; John G., 100
Hendly, 114
HENDON: Jeremiah, 33
Henna, 50, 57
Henney, 19
Hennie, 162
Henny, 24, 25, 52, 57, 64, 77,
83, 93, 117, 133, 141, 143,
157, 168
Henrietta, 81, 93, 151, 153
Henry, 6, 12, 16, 19, 21, 23, 31,
38, 39, 47, 50, 51, 53, 54, 58,
59, 60, 62, 63, 66, 67, 73, 74,
77, 78, 79, 82, 83, 84, 85, 87,
88, 91, 92, 93, 94, 96, 97, 99,
100, 102, 103, 104, 105, 106,
107, 111, 116, 117, 121, 122,
124, 125, 127, 129, 130, 131,
137, 138,139, 140, 141, 142,
147, 148, 149, 150, 152, 153,
154, 155, 156, 157, 160, 161,
163, 164, 165
HENRY: Mrs., 91
Henry Dade, 39
Hensey, 143
Henson, 55, 77, 79, 80, 81, 96,
104, 105, 109, 111, 115, 118,
124, 132, 159
Hepney, 38
Herbert, 142
HEREFORD: Alice Thornton,
109; Maryann, 45
HERNDON: Betty Taylor, 33;
Fanney, 33; Frances, 33;
George, 33; James White, 33;

John, 33; Peggy, 33; Rachael, 33; William, 33, 34, 42
Herrington, 92
Hester, 11, 27, 35, 36, 50, 52, 54, 58, 59, 61, 67, 70, 72, 88, 89, 104, 113, 121, 137, 138
Hester Ann, 159
Hethaliah, 29
Heuy, 144
Hey, 92
Hezekiah, 148
Heziah, 53
Hill, 40, 41; George, 143
Hincheloe, 34
HITH: Mrs., 121
HOFF: Moore, 107; Thomas, 112
Hoffman, 153, 154
HOGAN: Al_n, 12; Charlotte, 12; Elizabeth, 12; Sarah, 12; Thomas, 12, 13; William, 12, 160
HOLISFIELD: Mary, 11
HOLLIDAY: Ann, 65; James, 94, 97
Hom, 23
HOMES: Thomas, 83
HOMES Jr.: Thomas, 94
HOOE, 100; Alfred Luckett, 119; Ann, 135, 168; Ann Frances, 168; Ann Gailand, 118; Anna Maria, 118; Bernard, 103, 118, 168; Cecilia, 118; Dade, 34, 130; Edward, 123; Ellen, 118; Frances, 34; Francis, 95; Francis Townshend, 131; George James, 131; Henry D., 50, 55; Henry Dade, 50, 54; Houson, 123, 124; Howson, 34; James, 123, 133; James H., 101; Jane, 133; John, 34, 118, 168; Joseph Thompson, 119; Mary, 55, 131; Mary Elizabeth, 118; Mary Francis, 95; Mrs. Robert, 91; Richard, 123; Robert H., 121; Seymour, 95; Susanna, 95; Susanna Fooke, 168; Thomas B., 126; Thomas B.C., 118; Thomas B.P., 118; Thomas P., 130; Thomas Pratt, 54; Virginia, 118; William, 168; William Arthur, 118
HOOE Jr.: Bernard, 57; John, 131, 139, 142
HOOE Sr.: Bernard, 54
HOOE, Jr.: Capt. Bernard, 61; John, 119
HOOMES: Elizabeth, 39, 45
Horace, 78, 125, 152, 154
HORTON: Cossom, 83; Cravon, 67; Darcus, 67; Elizabeth, 89; James, 67; Meredith W., 159, 164; Nathaniel, 67; Roy W., 159, 164; Russell E., 159, 164; Snowden, 36, 67; William, 39, 42, 67
Howard, 48, 143
HOWISON: A., 100; Stephen, 72
Howson, 101
Hubbard, 152, 154
HUBER: G., 65; George F., 103, 125, 127; Joseph, 81, 83, 91; Verlinda, 103
HUDNALL: Thomas, 5, 6; William, 5; Winney, 5
Hugh, 1
HUIE: Helen G., 72, 73
Huk, 115
Hulda, 149, 150

Huly, 49
Humphrey, 16, 82, 132, 144, 145, 147
HUNNINGTON: Charles W.C., 150
HUNTER: Mrs., 81
Hunton, 149
HUNTON: Charles, 90, 99, 151; Maj. Charles, 118; Thomas, 79
Husley, 57
Hutcha, 98
HUTCHINSON: Gustavus A., 159; Henry B., 159; Jane, 54; John, 147
HUTCHISON: John, 138; L., 121
Hysom, 150
Iamus, 138
Immanuel, 57
Imy, 13
Indian, 89
Indy, 118
Ira, 118
Irail, 147
Iris, 38
Isaac, 37, 39, 48, 49, 64, 71, 72, 77, 78, 79, 80, 81, 86, 92, 95, 98, 100, 104, 105, 111, 113, 118, 124, 138, 153, 160
Isabel, 8, 72
Isabell, 51, 77
Isabella, 60, 90, 126
Isack, 144
ISMONGROVE: Anny Guy, 20; Lydia Musgrove, 20
Israel, 77, 78, 96, 99, 113, 147
Ivy, 2
Izabella, 116
Jack, 2, 3, 4, 5, 6, 7, 12, 13, 14, 18, 19, 20, 25, 26, 30, 31, 35, 36, 37, 40, 41, 47, 49, 53, 59, 60, 63, 65, 66, 67, 69, 72, 73, 78, 81, 82, 86, 88, 90, 92, 94, 96, 97, 99, 107, 114, 118, 126, 129, 144, 148, 167, 168
Jack F., 64
Jack H., 64
Jack M., 64
Jackson, 82, 105, 107, 109, 141, 145, 153; Andrew, 131; Harrison, 161; Henry, 161; Humphrey, 144; John, 142; Thomas, 139; William, 161; Winney, 133
JACKSON: Elizabeth, 70; Farrow, 70; Francis, 15, 21, 70; George, 21; George W., 84; George Washington, 70; Jane, 70; John, 21, 32; John Farrow, 46; Mary, 46, 70; Samuel, 21, 22, 70, 72, 84, 117
Jacob, 2, 6, 17, 21, 22, 23, 30, 42, 43, 46, 47, 48, 49, 53, 54, 55, 57, 60, 65, 69, 72, 73, 78, 87, 93, 103, 104, 111, 117, 127, 128, 144, 149, 150, 157, 166, 168
Jain, 147
Jake, 154
James, 2, 4, 8, 11, 12, 13, 14, 16, 19, 20, 21, 22, 23, 25, 26, 27, 29, 34, 35, 37, 38, 39, 40, 42, 45, 46, 47, 49, 50, 54, 55, 59, 61, 62, 63, 64, 67, 70, 72, 73, 77, 81, 82, 83, 87, 88, 90, 91, 92, 94, 96, 97, 98, 99, 101, 102, 104, 105, 106, 109, 112, 114, 115, 116, 117, 118, 121, 122, 124, 126, 127, 130, 131, 134, 135, 137, 138, 139, 140, 147, 148, 150, 151, 152,

153, 154, 157, 159, 163, 168;
Susan, 99
JAMES: Martha, 55, 84;
Westwood Wallace, 84
James Henry, 125, 140, 143, 147
James K.P., 138, 139
James Robert, 152
JAMESON: David, 32, 51, 59, 126; Patty, 32; Sarah, 32
Jamey, 4
Jamie, 4
Jamima, 57, 168
Jamina, 143
JAMISON: David, 130; Milley, 35
Jammy, 41
Jamson, 92
Jan, 18
Jane, 3, 14, 16, 17, 18, 20, 26, 29, 33, 34, 39, 45, 46, 47, 49, 54, 55, 58, 63, 69, 71, 75, 80, 81, 83, 86, 87, 89, 91, 92, 94, 95, 96, 97, 99, 102, 103, 104, 105, 106, 109, 111, 112, 114, 116, 118, 121, 122, 123, 124, 125, 130, 131, 134, 138, 139, 141, 142, 144, 147, 148, 149, 150, 151, 152, 157, 159, 160, 161, 162, 163, 164, 168
Janet, 154
Janey, 21, 35
Janinsa, 144
Janney, 41, 54, 62, 64, 126
JANNINGS: Elizabeth, 106
Jannis, 26
Janny, 41, 61, 92, 98
Jarard, 145
Jarrett, 50, 113
Jarrod, 162
JARVIS: Richard, 11
Jasper, 142, 148

Jeff, 150, 151, 159
Jefferson, 117
Jeffery, 45, 49, 58
Jeffrey, 100, 102, 134, 138, 139
JEFFRIES: Moses, 45; Rachael, 45
Jeffry, 60, 72, 85
Jeffy, 113
Jehnah, 121
Jem, 18, 27
Jemima, 24, 98, 150
Jemina, 149
Jemmima, 96
JEMMISON: Enoch, 54
Jemmy, 13, 49
Jenkins, 33
JENKINS: John, 6
Jenn, 25
Jenne, 14
Jennette, 82
Jennie, 152
JENNINGS: E., 110; James, 99, 110
Jennins, 83
Jenny, 2, 3, 6, 8, 11, 15, 19, 24, 26, 27, 34, 36, 37, 39, 40, 42, 45, 47, 48, 52, 53, 58, 60, 67, 68, 70, 77, 78, 80, 81, 83, 86, 87, 88, 92, 96, 99, 100, 101, 103, 104, 112, 118, 128, 129, 132, 142, 148, 152, 154, 160, 161
Jenoral, 57
Jered, 67
Jeremiah, 39, 47
Jerkey, 4
Jerret, 51
Jerry, 5, 18, 26, 59, 60, 63, 66, 70, 78, 80, 81, 92, 99, 107, 123, 124, 128, 130, 133

Jess, 19, 38, 45, 49, 51, 66, 67, 68, 69, 70, 73, 86, 103, 117, 155
Jesse, 11, 12, 14, 15, 18, 19, 20, 23, 24, 25, 27, 29, 31, 33, 34, 40, 41, 45, 46, 49, 50, 51, 55, 57, 62, 63, 64, 65, 66, 67, 68, 69, 71, 72, 73, 74, 75, 79, 80, 81, 82, 83, 84, 88, 91, 92, 93, 96, 97, 103, 104, 109, 115, 118, 121, 123, 124, 125, 126, 127, 129, 130, 137, 138, 143, 148, 150, 151, 155, 159, 165, 168
JETT: Ann, 95
Jeul, 147
Jiles, 60, 121
Jilly, 33
Jilson, 49
Jim, 11, 14, 15, 20, 33, 38, 48, 52, 60, 65, 69, 73, 74, 77, 78, 80, 82, 86, 88, 89, 94, 95, 99, 100, 102, 106, 113, 123, 144, 145, 151, 152, 153, 159, 162, 166, 167
Jimmy, 2, 9, 13
Jinna, 19
Jinney, 94, 113, 125
Jinnie, 159, 162
Jinny, 5, 67, 78, 129, 131
Joan, 25, 45, 52, 78, 111, 130, 163
Job, 2, 60, 69, 75, 81
Joe, 3, 4, 5, 6, 16, 17, 18, 23, 25, 32, 33, 34, 37, 38, 40, 41, 47, 49, 53, 57, 58, 63, 72, 73, 77, 80, 85, 86, 92, 93, 96, 102, 105, 106, 112, 118, 125, 126, 127, 129, 132, 138, 165, 168
John, 2, 3, 4, 5, 8, 14, 21, 22, 26, 27, 32, 34, 35, 38, 39, 41, 48, 49, 50, 51, 52, 54, 55, 58, 60, 63, 64, 65, 67, 68, 69, 70, 71, 72, 75, 77, 78, 79, 80, 81, 83, 85, 86, 88, 90, 91, 92, 93, 96, 97, 98, 99, 100, 101, 102, 103, 106, 109, 111, 112, 113, 115, 116, 117, 118, 121, 122, 123, 124, 125, 126, 127, 130, 131, 132, 135, 138, 139, 140, 142, 143, 144, 145, 147, 148, 150, 151, 152, 153, 154, 155, 156, 157, 159, 160, 161, 162, 163, 164, 168
John C., 138, 139
John Henry, 124, 142, 145, 160
John William, 95, 143
Johnathan, 121
Johnson, 73; Luke, 127
JOHNSON: Annie M., 156; Emily E., 156; French, 97; George W., 156; James, 37; John, 18; Joseph, 149, 156, 160; Joseph B., 156; Rutland, 98; Sarah E., 156
Johnston, 54, 59, 65, 87
JOHNSTON: Benjamin, 105; Francis, 54
Jona, 109
Jonah, 163
Jonas, 77
JONAS: Samuel, 11
Jonathan, 69, 81, 87, 104, 113
JONES: Joseph, 114; Sarah B., 141
Jonney, 12
JORDAN: Rachael, 22
JORDON: John, 30
Jose, 41
Joseph, 9, 17, 24, 32, 33, 40, 57, 63, 70, 74, 106, 116, 127, 132, 134, 145, 147

Joshua, 14, 15, 36, 48, 68, 69, 70, 71, 72, 77, 78, 95, 104, 109, 113, 117, 125, 127, 131, 135, 141, 150, 151, 161
Joy, 81
Joyce, 41
Juba, 12, 13, 82, 83, 99, 100
Juber, 52
Juda, 11, 12, 20, 60, 63, 121
Judah, 7, 11, 15, 29, 33, 39, 40, 62, 67, 89, 90, 103
Jude, 12, 14, 15, 20, 26, 30, 33, 35, 37, 45, 78, 104, 109
Judith, 17, 18, 25, 41, 80, 81, 82, 84, 123, 149, 150, 165
Judson, 112, 114
Judy, 2, 3, 4, 8, 11, 12, 23, 24, 31, 36, 38, 41, 49, 52, 57, 63, 72, 74, 82, 96, 97, 98, 103, 113, 132, 155, 162
Jules, 138
Julia, 2, 41, 84, 114, 133, 139, 142, 143, 148, 151
Julia Ann, 125, 134, 145
Julian, 82, 93, 123, 127, 140, 143
Juliana, 53, 124
Juliann, 81
Julianna, 78
Julianne, 113
Juliet, 58, 86, 128, 167
Julius, 77, 90
Julya, 72
June, 16, 151
Junius, 127
Junnie, 83
Juno, 67
Jupiter, 48
Jury, 30
Kate, 2, 6, 8, 20, 23, 29, 31, 33, 35, 41, 42, 52, 54, 65, 74, 77, 106, 111, 125, 148, 159

Katherine, 115, 122
Katy, 40, 41, 77
KEBBLE: Anderson, 66
KEECH: Sally, 64
KEES: Elizabeth, 50
Kegeah, 68, 69
KEICH: Sarah, 62
Kelley, 14
Kellis, 94
Kelly: David, 3
KELLY: James, 80
Kemp, 109, 115
Kempe, 40
Kent, 25, 66
KEOGH: Michael, 59
Kesiah, 32
Kessey, 34
KEYES: Harriet, 137
KEYS: John, 70
Kezia, 88
Keziah, 24, 54, 59, 61
Kezial, 87
KIEMOR: Winifred, 80
Kildare, 8
Kincheloe, 34
KINCHELOE, 36; John, 38; Mrs. Jon, 4
KINCHILOE: Caroline, 130
King: Billy, 127
KING: Daniel, 82, 123; Sarah, 123; Stephen, 70, 83; Stephen K., 68
Kissy, 121
KITCHEN: George, 53
Kitt, 40, 41, 168
Kitty, 57, 61, 63, 64, 67, 69, 73, 77, 78, 80, 82, 86, 92, 95, 96, 101, 106, 111, 113, 116, 117, 118, 123, 125, 137, 139, 140, 142, 144, 148, 152, 155, 161
Kiziah, 80
Kizzey, 40

Kizziah, 125, 129
Kizzy, 87
Kneal, 99
Kneel, 96
L__ Ann, 106
La_hny, 78
LACON: Francis, 9; Jane, 9
Lafayette, 156
Lamore, 72
Lance, 163
LANDMAN: Elizabeth, 24; Mary Ann, 24; William, 24
LANE: George, 43
LANGFIT: Susanna, 70
LANGYHER: Jacob, 134
Lannon, 145
LANPKINS: George, 25
Lanra, 138
LANSDOWN: John, 63, 64, 65
LANSDOWN Jr.: John, 62
LARKIN: Henry D., 165; Thomas, 88
LATHAM: John, 121; Lucy, 122, 127; Robert, 121, 122, 123, 124; Sarah, 121; Thomas, 122
LATIMER: G., 121; Samuel, 147
Latitia, 58
Laura, 121, 143, 145, 147, 149, 151, 156, 157, 162, 163
Laurence, 80
Laurinda, 139, 149
Lavender, 142
Lavina, 55, 57, 65, 124
Lavinah, 22
Lavinia, 63, 113, 123, 132, 149
Lawson, 46, 121, 132
LAWSON: Marmaduke, 8
Laxy, 86
Lea, 99

LEACH: William, 24; William Haney, 24
LEACHMAN: Ann P., 161; John, 105; John T., 161; Robert C., 161; Thomas, 65
Leah, 92, 126
Lean: Martha M., 164
Leanah, 118
Leanna, 49, 109, 151
Leannah, 121, 132
LEBERMAN: John, 149; William, 121
Lebey, 38
Lee, 14, 15
LEE: David, 54, 57; Elizabeth, 63; Emiline, 144; Henry, 23; John, 143, 144, 148, 168; Margaret, 54; Margaret Virginia, 144; Mary E., 143, 168; Matthew A., 143, 168; Thomas, 48
LEE Sr.: Thomas, 31, 47
LEGG: James, 105
Leige, 106
LEITCH: Andrew, 13
Lelah, 21
Lemo, 74, 80
Lemont, 49
Lemuel, 23, 40
Len, 63
Lena, 142
Leney, 60
Lenora, 127, 161
Leny, 52
Leoisa, 77
Leon: Martha M., 163
Leotha, 26
LESLEY: Maria, 79
Let, 12, 69
Leticia, 149
Letitia, 48, 64, 150
Lett, 13, 18, 21, 42, 49

Lettice, 8, 15, 67, 70, 88, 95, 104
Letty, 15, 19, 22, 33, 37, 45, 47, 49, 63, 67, 69, 77, 80, 93, 95, 102, 113, 121, 138, 139
Letty Felicia Corbin, 60, 63
Leumales, 143
Levi, 20, 41, 90, 138, 139
Levina, 70
Leviney, 59
Levinia, 133, 150
Lewis, 14, 15, 16, 19, 25, 26, 32, 39, 40, 46, 47, 50, 51, 52, 53, 55, 57, 58, 60, 61, 62, 64, 65, 67, 69, 70, 75, 78, 80, 84, 86, 92, 95, 96, 102, 106, 109, 110, 111, 113, 116, 117, 119, 121, 123, 124, 125, 126, 128, 132, 133, 135, 137, 142, 143, 145, 147, 148, 153, 155, 160, 162, 165, 168
LEWIS: Anna, 68; Catey, 67; Fanny, 150; Frances Tasker, 115; Francis M., 68; Francis Montgomery, 67; H.M., 107; Harriot, 68; Henry, 68; James, 67, 68; John, 150; Louisa, 68; Nancy, 67; Sally, 68; Searles, 67; Susanna, 67; William M., 68; Zacharia, 36; Zachariah, 37, 38
Liah, 96
Lias, 96
Lib, 50, 77
Libby, 30, 87
Lidda, 68
Liddy, 31, 41, 51, 72, 77, 86, 96
Lidia, 23, 101
Lige, 35, 49, 74
Ligge, 50
Lilah, 49
Lilera, 122

Lily, 130
Limbrick, 8
Lina, 109, 148
LINCOCKS: Thomas, 60
LINDEN: William, 2
LINDRUM: William, 16
LINDSAY: Martha, 142
Linney, 31, 57
Linnney, 70
Linny, 93
Linssy, 161
LINTEN: John, 106; Mary, 41
LINTON: Ann, 71; John, 71, 80, 86, 100, 106, 123; John T., 71; Sally, 127; Sarah, 131; Sarah E., 127; William, 8; William A., 71
Linus, 69
LIPSCOMB: Elizabeth, 142; P.D., 155
Lissy, 65
LITTLE: Elizabeth How, 82; William Henry, 82
Livy, 161
Liza, 67, 99
Lizett, 87
Lizy, 51, 60
Lizza, 21, 52, 60, 63
Lizzy, 18, 58, 67, 168
Lloyd: Daniel, 47
Loannah, 107
Lockart, 78
Lockman, 152
Lockrun, 154
Loisa, 95
Lolly, 138, 168
London, 2, 6, 33, 35, 70, 72, 73, 82, 90, 94, 96
Loney, 127
LONG: John, 111; William, 133
Lonon, 81

Lonora, 131
Lorenda, 92
Lorenzo, 125, 129, 138, 139
Lorinda, 104, 113
Lott, 14, 24, 63
Lotty, 58
Lou, 134
Loue, 83
Louis, 116
LOUIS: William, 7
Louisa, 71, 77, 96, 104, 105, 106, 107, 113, 118, 123, 128, 129, 132, 135, 138, 139, 144, 149, 150, 152, 156, 160, 163
Louisa Jr., 154
Louisa Maria, 160
Louisa Sr., 154
Louise, 78
Lousa, 140
LOVE: Augustine, 23; Charles, 29; John, 66; Samuel, 23
LOWDON: Ann, 107; John, 107
LOWE: John, 27, 29
Luan, 149
Luboy, 43
Luce, 1, 30, 39, 41, 42, 69, 70
Lucey, 40
Lucien, 155
Lucinda, 16, 22, 31, 37, 40, 51, 54, 59, 69, 78, 87, 89, 92, 104, 113, 140, 143, 145, 147, 148, 155, 162
Lucinda Clary, 113
Lucinda Sally, 96
Luck, 68
Lucreta, 163
Lucretia, 157, 164, 165
Lucy, 1, 2, 3, 4, 5, 6, 7, 12, 13, 14, 16, 21, 22, 26, 27, 33, 34, 36, 38, 39, 40, 46, 47, 48, 49, 50, 51, 52, 53, 57, 58, 60, 61,

62, 63, 64, 65, 67, 68, 77, 78, 83, 86, 88, 89, 90, 91, 92, 95, 97, 98, 99, 102, 103, 105, 106, 107, 110, 111, 112, 113, 121, 123, 124, 125, 127, 131, 132, 134, 138, 140, 142, 149, 151, 152, 154, 156, 157, 160, 167, 168
Lucy Ann, 125, 138, 139, 143
Lucy C., 64
Lucy Ellen, 134
Lucy Jr., 103
Lucy Locket, 143
Lud, 33
Ludd, 148
Ludwell, 144
Luend, 143, 168
Luisa, 41
Luke, 19, 40, 53, 90, 112, 116, 117, 143
Lundy, 83
Lunner Jr., 164
Lunner Sr., 164
Lunnon, 71, 151, 163
Lunnon Jr., 163
Lunnon Sr., 163
Lunnore, 164
LUNTON: William, 18
Lusey, 5
Luther, 152, 154, 156, 157
LUTTLE: James, 70; Strother, 31
LUTTRELL: Jane, 84; Nancy, 84; Peggy, 84; Robert, 12, 84, 101; Simon, 12, 38, 83, 84; Thomas, 84, 109
Luzan, 106
Lyah, 40
Lyda, 60
Lydda, 33
Lydia, 16, 26, 30, 65, 74, 77, 80, 83, 88, 89, 92, 115, 135,

138, 149, 150, 152, 154, 156, 167
Lyia Ann, 134
Lyna, 60
Lynda, 47, 129
LYNN: Benson, 59, 161; Eleanor P., 125; Eleanor R., 96; Elizabeth, 99; John, 51, 126; Joseph R., 99; Levi C., 161; Michael, 51; Moses, 51; Nehemiah, 96, 98; S., 121; William, 128; William M., 166
LYON: Maryary, 23
Lysha, 61
Macin: Peter Daniel, 23
Mack, 105, 107, 130
MACKEYS, 83
Macrae: Daniel, 168
MACRAE: Capt., 81; John, 64, 74, 80, 81; Mary Wallace, 55
MADDEN: Peggy, 19; Scarlet, 35
MADDOX: Allison, 117; Henly, 71; Ignatious, 117; John, 54; Matilda, 161; Noah, 117; Orela, 103; Peggy H., 89; Sarah, 117; Thomas, 117; William, 35
MADDUX: Martin, 90; William, 38
Madison, 69, 75
Maggy, 59
Magoo: Edward, 5
MAGUIRE: Elizabeth, 3
Mahala, 69, 78, 84, 91, 96, 99, 104, 109, 140, 141, 149, 150
Mahaley, 86
Mahalia, 115
Mahaly, 127, 135
MAHENNY: Thomas, 96
Malicia, 96

Malida, 148
Malinda, 61, 70, 75, 127, 135, 142, 147, 149
Mall, 16
Malvina, 113
Manda, 112
Manewell, 50
MANKIN: M.H. Math, 35
Mantier: Thomas, 2
Manuel, 16, 19, 23, 27, 31, 34, 37, 49, 54, 61, 106, 118, 124, 125, 129, 130, 138, 139, 149, 150, 155, 157, 162
MANUEL: Sarah Jane, 165
Maranda, 19
Margaret, 6, 53, 86, 95, 98, 116, 118, 123, 124, 141, 142, 144, 147, 148, 150, 151, 152, 155, 156, 157, 159, 163, 164
Margaret Jane, 141
Margery, 23, 47
Margret, 64
Maria, 9, 16, 17, 27, 36, 40, 41, 42, 43, 49, 53, 54, 58, 59, 61, 62, 63, 64, 66, 73, 77, 80, 81, 82, 83, 85, 86, 87, 89, 92, 93, 94, 95, 98, 99, 102, 105, 106, 110, 114, 115, 116, 118, 124, 130, 132, 134, 135, 137, 138, 139, 140, 143, 144, 145, 147, 148, 149, 150, 152, 153, 154, 155, 156, 157, 163, 164, 168
Maria Frances, 143
Mariah, 43, 49, 50, 51, 62, 78, 79, 80, 81, 87, 88, 97, 102, 104, 113, 126, 130, 139, 151
Mariah Jr., 129
Mariah Sr., 129
Marian, 96
Mariel, 52
Marinda, 16, 20
Mark, 60

MARLOW: Jane, 15
Marner, 147
MARR: Christopher, 8; Daniel, 8; Elizabeth, 8; John, 8, 9
Marshall, 92, 98, 118, 124, 149, 151; Alexander, 116
Marten, 139
Martha, 41, 50, 54, 55, 72, 87, 98, 99, 105, 109, 111, 115, 121, 122, 124, 125, 127, 129, 130, 131, 132, 134, 135, 137, 140, 143, 144, 145, 147, 148, 149, 150, 151, 152, 154, 155, 156, 157, 159, 163, 164
Martha Jane, 143
Martha M, 164
Martha M., 163
Marthy, 92
Martin, 41, 78, 96, 99, 113, 131, 139, 142, 148, 160
MARTIN: Betty, 14; Catherine, 33; Elias B., 116; Hezekiah, 110, 115; I.L., 122; Leanna, 115, 116
Mary, 1, 2, 13, 14, 17, 18, 20, 22, 25, 27, 29, 30, 31, 35, 36, 38, 40, 41, 42, 45, 46, 49, 50, 51, 52, 53, 54, 55, 57, 58, 59, 61, 62, 63, 65, 66, 67, 68, 69, 70, 71, 72, 73, 74, 77, 78, 80, 81, 83, 84, 86, 87, 88, 89, 90, 91, 92, 94, 95, 96, 97, 98, 101, 102, 103, 105, 106, 107, 109, 111, 112, 113, 114, 115, 116, 117, 118, 121, 123, 124, 125, 126, 127, 129, 131, 132, 134, 137, 138, 139, 140, 142, 143, 144, 145, 147, 148, 149, 150, 151, 152, 154, 155, 156, 157, 158, 160, 162, 163, 165
Mary Adalin, 135

Mary Ann, 64, 68, 80, 96, 103, 111, 118, 121, 125, 132, 163
Mary Anne, 167
Mary Ellen, 109, 159
Mary Evelena, 152
Mary Evelina, 154
Mary Frances, 154
Mary Francis, 152
Mary Jane, 116, 124, 137, 148, 157
Mary Sr., 89
Mary Virginia, 143
Maryann, 92
Maskill, 23
Mason, 40, 46, 67, 70, 72, 105, 107, 112, 114, 123, 124, 125, 133, 145, 161, 162; Evelina, 163, 164
MASON: Col. George, 7; George, 2, 6, 15; Gerard, 145; J. Seddon, 130; Sarah, 37; Sarah B., 74; Thomas, 47, 145
Massey, 168
MASSON: Mary, 14
Mathew, 60
Matilda, 51, 53, 57, 59, 60, 61, 62, 63, 64, 68, 69, 70, 72, 77, 78, 81, 83, 84, 85, 87, 89, 90, 94, 97, 98, 102, 105, 106, 107, 111, 113, 116, 117, 121, 125, 127, 129, 131, 133, 141, 143, 147, 151, 152, 160, 165, 168
Matilday, 142
Matile, 54
Matt, 2, 6, 33, 61, 63, 66, 147, 152
Matthe, 4
Matthew, 27, 53, 62, 68, 85
MATTHEW: Elias, 93; George W., 166; Henry, 144; Henry

P., 143, 168; Jane Matilda, 143, 168
MATTHEWS: William, 16
MATTOX: Jean, 32
Matty, 40, 80, 140
May, 30, 109
McClain: Martha, 157
McCLENACHAN: James, 79, 101; John, 79, 87, 88, 101
McCORMICK: Francis, 33
McMILLIAN: John, 84
McMILLIAN, Jr.: John, 62
McNAMARA: Mrs., 118
MEALON, 79
Meg, 78
Meggie, 163
Meggy, 151, 157, 163
Melinda, 49, 68, 69, 78, 117, 126, 156, 161
Melindy, 71
Mellory, 27
MELTON Jr.: William, 13
Melze, 139, 162
Mema, 74
Menos, 139
Mercer: Charles Fenton, 63; Fenton, 60, 63
MERCHANT: Catherine, 140; Robert, 155; Robert B., 150; William, 94
Meriah, 40, 59
Merideth, 40, 41
Michael, 32, 35, 77, 78, 95, 96, 99, 121, 138
Michael Jr., 63
Michael Sr., 63
Mildred, 37, 88, 111, 138, 139, 148, 157
Miles, 41
MILES: John, 165
Milia, 139
Mill, 25, 26, 49
Milla, 25, 109
Mille, 20
Milley, 16, 113
Millford, 132
MILLS: John, 105; Linissy, 161
Milly, 12, 19, 21, 23, 24, 26, 32, 34, 36, 38, 40, 47, 49, 50, 54, 58, 63, 64, 65, 66, 67, 68, 71, 77, 78, 81, 82, 83, 86, 88, 92, 94, 96, 98, 99, 100, 103, 105, 107, 111, 112, 114, 116, 122, 124, 126, 127, 130, 132, 134, 135, 138, 139, 142, 145, 147, 153, 154,162
MILSTEAD: Samuel, 135; Susan, 161
Milton, 148
Milze, 138
Mima, 16, 37, 64, 72, 78, 80, 82, 83, 86, 90, 94, 110, 112, 113, 128, 138, 139, 149, 150
Mimah, 22, 40, 41, 49, 57
Mime, 67
Mimey, 33
Mimy, 40, 74, 118
Mina, 151
Mingo, 2, 6, 31, 46, 49, 168
Minna, 147
Minnea, 38
Minny, 18, 51
Minor, 13
Minta, 37, 97, 155, 162
Minty, 121
Minum, 26
Missy, 160
Mitchell, 65; Betsy, 55; Charles, 55
MITCHELL: Carl, 84; Charlotte M., 151; Richard T., 151
Mo, 20

Moll, 8, 11, 14, 15, 16, 17, 23, 34, 35, 36, 63, 96, 117, 128
Molly, 12, 16, 38, 47, 48, 50, 54, 59, 64, 72, 73, 78, 87, 99, 132, 143
Mona, 16
Mongo, 63
Monmouth, 4, 5
Monroe: Milton, 148
MONTGOMERIE: Thomas, 29, 31, 38
MONTGOMERY: Frances, 67; Francis, 69
Montjoy: Sam, 47
Moor, 144
MOOR: Margaret, 20
MOORE: Jeremiah, 45; Silbina, 140
MOOREHEAD: Lewis, 36; Presley, 36
Moreah, 11
Morgan, 2
Moriah, 82, 114, 121
Morrice, 106
Morris, 106, 114
MORRISS: Ann, 97
Mortimer, 141
Mortin, 96
Mose, 1
MOSE: Lidie, 35
Moses, 13, 14, 15, 20, 23, 25, 26, 31, 34, 36, 39, 41, 45, 47, 51, 52, 54, 57, 58, 60, 62, 66, 67, 70, 72, 73, 74, 75, 77, 80, 81, 83, 84, 86, 88, 89, 91, 92, 93, 94, 98, 103, 104, 109, 113, 115, 117, 118, 121, 124, 126, 127, 133, 138, 139, 147, 149, 150, 151, 152, 156, 160, 168
Moses Jr., 103
Moten, 99, 103

MOUNT: Sarah E., 156; William, 78, 99, 100
MOUNTS: William, 96
MOXLEY: Gilbert J., 63, 98
MOXLY: Aminta Elizabeth, 107
MURPHEY: Hedgeman, 83; William C., 122
Murray, 111
MURRAY: Elizabeth, 17; Hugh, 17; John, 17, 18, 57
MUSCHETT: Alexander, 93; Charles H., 52; Edward, 52; Elizabeth H., 52; Frances, 50; Frances Ballendine, 31; James, 31, 50; James A.M., 106; James Montifix, 93; L.C., 163; Louisa C., 157; Luisa C., 93; S.C., 163
Na__ace, 40
Nace, 30, 38, 41, 50, 54, 64, 67, 69, 77, 80, 81
NAILER: Elizabeth, 42, 58
Nan, 1, 2, 3, 6, 8, 13, 14, 16, 21, 25, 30, 36, 39, 42, 47, 65, 67, 132, 168
Nan__, 157
Nana, 163
Nance, 14, 16, 34, 49
Nancy, 23, 25, 26, 27, 31, 32, 33, 34, 36, 38, 39, 41, 47, 49, 51, 52, 55, 57, 58, 62, 63, 64, 67, 69, 75, 77, 81, 82, 90, 92, 95, 100, 101, 105, 106, 107, 109, 111, 113, 116, 117, 121, 122, 123, 124, 125, 126, 127, 128, 129, 131, 138, 139, 142, 149, 150, 156, 163, 164, 167
Nanny, 17, 24, 33, 41, 43, 51, 53, 82
Nany, 149
Nanz, 50

Nat, 24, 49, 68, 69, 78, 79, 81, 87, 98, 104, 106, 113, 126, 127, 144, 149, 150
Nate, 13, 59
Nathan, 14, 15, 37, 38, 53, 134, 138, 141
Nathaniel, 115, 143, 168
Natt, 41, 81
NAWAL: Peyton, 105
Neabsco, 154
Nead, 148
Neal, 96, 99
Neale, 64, 78
NEALE: Christopher, 7; Jonathon, 4; Lidia, 7; Mary, 69; Mary Nelson, 69; Richard H., 69; Rodham, 7; William P.L., 69
NEALES: Mary, 75
Ned, 3, 6, 7, 14, 19, 22, 27, 29, 33, 36, 45, 49, 51, 57, 58, 64, 66, 77, 80, 83, 86, 88, 94, 101, 106, 109, 110, 111, 121, 133, 135, 143, 149, 150, 152, 155, 168
Nell, 12, 14, 15, 16, 17, 18, 25, 29, 35, 38, 39, 41, 42, 46, 47, 51, 52, 58, 72, 79, 86, 99
Nelly, 11, 20, 27, 29, 35, 46, 49, 51, 60, 71, 73, 77, 78, 82, 83, 84, 85, 88, 94, 95, 99, 103, 105, 111, 112, 114, 116, 118, 121, 123, 132, 134, 138, 139, 141, 147, 152, 154, 160
Nelson, 35, 37, 39, 47, 54, 60, 68, 69, 70, 95, 98, 105, 107, 111, 114, 117, 118, 125, 132, 147, 148, 152, 168
NELSON: Eliza J., 160; Elizabeth Stonestreet, 90; James, 135; Mary, 139; Mrs., 141; Thomas, 90

Nero, 6, 67
NESBETT: Ann Linton, 79; James, 80
NEUMAN: Emily H., 152; James T., 152; Sarah E., 152; T. Wallace, 152; Theron W., 152; William B., 152
Newman, 48
NEWMAN: Ann E., 158; Catherine N., 153, 154; Catherine Newton, 86; Eleanor, 86; Elias, 86; Fanny, 19; James, 103; James T., 141; Nancy Jett, 86; Peggy, 86; Phoebe, 141, 142; Richard, 113, 122; Theron W., 147, 152, 160; Thomas, 11, 86, 88; Thomas I., 112; Thomas Jett, 86; William J., 101; William Jett, 86
Newton, 8, 74, 80, 138; Bob, 64
Nichols, 41
NILSON: Archebald, 24
Nimrod, 7
NISBETT: Anne, 18; Dr. James, 18; George, 18; James, 18; Margaret, 18; Mary, 18; Susannah, 18
Noah, 68, 70, 102
NOEL: Nancy, 33
NOLON: Thomas P., 99
Norman, 85; Bob, 64
NORMAN: Charles E., 155; Elizabeth, 86; James, 86; Patsy, 86; Thomas, 34; William, 39
NORRIS: George H., 105; James, 39
NORTHEN: Elizabeth Conway, 109
NORVILLE: Peyton, 121, 148
NOWLAND: Phillip, 2

Nuly, 69
Nutty, 72, 77, 86, 118
O_endo, 19
O'LOCHLON: Catherine, 168; Cornelius, 168
O'NEIL: Charles, 71; Rev. Charles, 72
Oaradise, 78
Obannion, 78
OBANNON: Betsy, 67; Joseph, 67
OBERALL: John, 7, 8
OBRIAN: Daniel, 16
Olina, 123
Oliphant: John, 63
Oliver, 35, 96, 127, 132
OLIVER: Thomas, 33, 37
Olivia Douglas, 143
Ophelia, 155, 162
Orange, 104
ORGAN: Matthew, 3
Osborn, 137
OSBORN: Margaret, 5; Mary Ann, 5; Mrs., 4; Thomas, 3, 4
Osborne, 130
OSBORNE: Thomas, 4
Osburn, 65, 77; George, 113
Oscar, 143
Osmond, 60
Osten, 48
Otoway, 144
OVERALL: Elizabeth, 20; John, 53
Owens, 77
OWENS: Joshua, 12; Nancy, 13
Pack, 23
PADDERSON: Catherine, 4
Page, 35, 39, 47, 109, 115, 121
PAGE: Elizabeth, 9; Gonynn, 119; John, 9; Thomas T., 94
Paleshane, 138, 139
Palestine, 159

Pallas, 168
PALLIE: D.M., 161
PALVERT: John, 42
Pamela, 102
Paris, 139, 142
Parke, 125
Parker: Davy, 111; John, 118; Tom, 168
Parlow, 41
Parthany, 138, 139
Parton: John, 77
Pat, 3, 17, 18, 20, 23, 29, 41, 50, 54, 67
Patience, 14, 15, 26, 46, 49, 50, 57, 60, 62, 71, 78, 100, 103, 140
Patrick, 15
Patsy, 77, 92, 105
Patt, 34, 57, 86
PATTERSON: John, 48; John W., 131
Patty, 41, 48, 58, 68, 78, 82, 88, 137, 143
Paul, 41, 72, 73, 96, 99
PAYNE: Henry R., 71
Peach Blossom, 166
Peg, 7, 9, 13, 17, 19, 23, 59, 63, 78, 86, 93
Pegg, 60
Pegga, 137
Peggy, 20, 40, 41, 46, 49, 59, 60, 62, 82, 88, 113, 115, 127, 137
PEIDMORE: Mary, 145
PELL: Elizabeth, 31
Pendleton, 143, 144, 168
Penny, 23, 25, 41, 52, 86, 87, 111, 113, 114
PERCELL: George, 21; John, 49, 55; Sarah, 36; William, 21, 36, 38
Perry: William, 150

PERSELL: Frances, 16
Peter, 1, 5, 8, 14, 15, 16, 21, 23, 24, 26, 29, 32, 33, 34, 37, 39, 40, 41, 47, 50, 51, 52, 53, 54, 66, 69, 71, 73, 75, 77, 78, 82, 83, 86, 88, 92, 93, 96, 98, 99, 101, 105, 106, 113, 117, 121, 123, 124, 132, 134, 145, 155, 156, 157, 162, 167
Peterson: James, 105
PETTY: Joseph, 21, 23, 71
PEUGH: Sallie E., 166
Peyton, 161, 162
PEYTON: Burr, 39; Capt. Valentine, 22; Col. Henry, 48; Craven, 21; Eliza S., 89; Frances, 14; Henry, 14, 15; John, 14, 21, 35; Margaret, 14; Martha E., 98, 114; Mrs., 71; Prudence, 21; Robert, 21; Sibellah, 86; Sybilla, 71; Thomas, 14; Valentine, 21, 25, 39
Phalmore, 72
Phebe, 15, 41, 50, 67, 91, 147
Pheby, 36
Phil, 11, 14, 15, 24, 41, 48, 51, 54, 61, 63, 68, 69, 70, 74, 77, 80, 83, 87, 95, 97, 101, 102, 105, 106, 110, 111, 118, 123, 132, 138, 149, 163
Philander, 41
Philip, 45, 98, 105, 106, 121, 143, 151, 152, 154, 156, 165
PHILIPS: Richard H., 112, 113, 121, 125
Phill, 30, 63, 104, 110
Phillip, 8, 31, 37, 38, 70, 77, 132
Phillips: Mary, 2
PHILLIPS: C. Ann R., 121; R.H., 121

Phillis, 2, 3, 11, 12, 17, 18, 19, 23, 25, 30, 31, 33, 34, 35, 39, 40, 41, 45, 49, 73, 86, 96, 105, 112, 114, 143, 156
Phoebe, 14, 34, 39, 67, 125, 129, 152, 160
Phoeby, 33
Phyllis, 151
Pimbay: Alan, 101
Piney, 102
PLUMMER: Benjamin, 88; Margaret, 88; Sally, 88; Sally H., 88
Pocus, 2
Polk, 143, 144, 168; James, 151
Poll, 6, 25, 26, 29, 30, 35, 36, 47
Polly, 13, 27, 29, 31, 35, 36, 40, 41, 47, 49, 52, 59, 63, 64, 67, 69, 70, 71, 72, 75, 77, 78, 80, 81, 82, 84, 87, 93, 94, 100, 102, 104, 115, 125, 127, 129, 131, 149, 152, 154
Pompey, 2, 47, 52, 64, 78, 125, 129
Pomprey, 129
POMROY: Francis D., 110
Poor: Margaret, 6
Porus, 6
POSEY: Zaphemiah, 39
POTTS: John, 98, 99, 103; Maryann, 99
Powell: G.D., 163; Winney, 163; Winnie, 163
POWELL: Bailey, 46, 47; Francis, 52; H.B., 131; William, 32
Presley, 62, 103
Preston, 30, 31, 160
Price, 132
Pricilla, 77

PRIDMORE: Benjamin, 141, 147; Benjamin H., 147; Lydia, 144, 145; Martha Ann, 144; Mary D., 144; Sarah C., 144
PRIEST: Matthew, 139
Primus, 22
Princz, 23
Priscella, 139
Priscilla, 81, 87, 88, 92, 99, 102, 105, 106, 115, 135, 139, 153, 157
Priss, 19, 113, 154, 160
Prissey, 137
Privey, 104
PROSSER: Elizabeth, 69; William, 69
Pru, 63
Prue, 36, 48, 95
Prycey, 167
PRYOR: Fanny, 119
Pug, 105, 113
PURCELL: Samuel, 83, 85; William, 21
QUEEN: Jon, 4
Rachael, 69, 163
Rachel, 11, 13, 14, 15, 17, 23, 24, 26, 30, 31, 34, 35, 36, 37, 40, 49, 51, 52, 53, 61, 63, 64, 67, 77, 78, 80, 82, 86, 89, 93, 96, 98, 106, 109, 111, 114, 115, 121, 138, 143, 147, 152, 153, 157, 160, 163, 168
RAINIE: George, 69; Samuel Symour, 69
RALLS: Elizabeth, 32
Ralph, 14, 15, 26, 33, 39, 41, 65, 67, 73, 86, 105
RAMEY: George, 72
Ramos, 58
Ramsay: Molly, 64

Randall, 31, 34, 90, 124, 156, 157
Randle, 121
Rando, 41
Randolph, 46, 49, 143; Maria, 143
RANDOLPH: Ann, 26; Elizabeth, 97; Ellender, 29; John, 26, 27, 30; William, 29, 30, 31
Raphne, 168
RATCLIFF: Lucinda Helm, 109; Quinton, 83
Ratter, 143
Rawleigh, 15
Rawley, 14
RAWLINGS: William, 15
REACH: William, 160
Rebecah, 88
Rebecca, 90, 92, 102, 105, 132, 147, 152, 153, 160
Rebekah, 39
RECH: Nancy, 21
RECTOR: Lawson, 156; Margaret, 156; Samson, 140; Susan E., 156
Redman, 145
REDMAN: John, 32
Redmond, 147
REEVE: John, 16; Jonathan, 130
REID: James, 83, 91; John F., 142, 155; Peyton, 118; Richard J., 155
Reilly, 142
Remus, 99
RENNOW: David, 53
RENOE: Ann, 30; David, 53, 99; Dolley, 35; Elizabeth, 109; Enoch, 29, 35, 122; Francis, 39, 45; George, 45; George N.B., 109; Jane, 35,

97; Libby, 46; Mildred, 17; Nancy, 99; Strother, 134; Thomas, 12; William, 12, 46, 109, 115
RENOE, Sr.: Francis, 35
Rese, 24
Reuben, 38, 46, 58, 60, 74, 77, 86, 89, 90, 92, 96, 105, 109, 117, 125, 129, 139, 141, 142, 144, 145, 147, 153, 154, 157, 160
Reuben Jr., 129
Rhemus, 92
RHODES: Tolemiah, 83
Rhodum, 15
Richard, 5, 8, 26, 29, 35, 39, 41, 42, 55, 60, 63, 64, 74, 77, 83, 93, 94, 96, 98, 99, 105, 109, 118, 121, 123, 124, 129, 130, 131, 132, 137, 139, 151, 157, 160, 163, 164
Richards: Molly, 143
RICHMOND: B., 65
RIED: Peggy, 42
RIXEY: Elizabeth, 22; Richard, 22
Riz, 39
ROACH: Margaret, 158; William, 90, 133, 158
Roberson, 46
Robert, 41, 45, 46, 53, 58, 73, 77, 90, 96, 99, 101, 102, 112, 115, 125, 129, 134, 138, 140, 143, 147, 148, 149, 150, 153, 154, 155, 157, 159, 160, 163, 164
Roberta, 148, 152, 154
Robertson, 116, 124
ROBERTSON: Athaliah, 67; Elenor, 67; George, 135, 137; Lucy, 67

Robin, 2, 4, 5, 7, 16, 23, 25, 35, 36, 49, 61, 63, 70, 105
Robinson: James, 143
ROBINSON: Arthur L., 73; James, 143, 168; William, 64
Robison: James, 168
Rodger, 16, 62
RODGERS: William, 66
Rodham, 14
ROE: C.C., 124; Catherine C., 116; Henry F., 116, 124
Roger, 19, 35, 52, 57, 104, 113
ROGERS: Elizabeth, 114; H., 122; Martha, 114; William, 114, 116
Roley: Jenny, 47
ROLLINS: John P., 128; Nancy, 128
Rolly, 125, 126, 129, 130, 133, 142, 148
Rosa, 143
Rosanna, 46
Rose, 14, 15, 33, 34, 36, 57, 60, 62, 82, 95, 96, 101, 105, 112, 132, 150, 152, 154, 155, 156, 162, 168
ROSE: Mary, 134
Rose Ann, 122
ROSE Sr.: William, 134
Roses, 50
Rosetta, 48, 82, 104
ROSSEN: John, 132
ROSSOW: Frances, 131
ROUCH: Mrs., 137
Rozetta, 123, 128
RUBLEMAN: John G., 117
Rush, 113
RUSSELL: Albert, 118; Col. Albert, 118; James, 118; John, 118
Ruth, 25, 26, 30, 31, 52, 94, 111, 127

Ruth Ann, 154
Ruthe, 49
Sabrina, 51
Sal, 21, 27, 38, 39, 67, 70, 78, 163
Salina, 144
Sall, 15, 17, 18, 21, 25, 26, 30, 33, 35, 37, 39, 41, 42, 45, 48, 69, 98, 111
Sally, 19, 36, 39, 40, 41, 49, 50, 54, 59, 60, 65, 68, 69, 72, 74, 78, 85, 86, 87, 88, 90, 91, 94, 98, 100, 101, 105, 106, 109, 115, 117, 132, 138, 139, 142, 145, 149, 150, 153, 157, 160, 163, 164
Sam, 1, 3, 12, 13, 17, 18, 19, 24, 30, 34, 36, 38, 41, 47, 48, 49, 51, 52, 60, 63, 64, 66, 67, 71, 75, 78, 79, 80, 82, 87, 88, 94, 95, 97, 103, 106, 107, 111, 114, 116, 117, 126, 135, 140, 142, 143, 148, 149, 150, 151, 155, 159, 160, 162, 163, 168
Sambad, 11
Sambo, 1, 2, 15
Samboy, 14
Sammy, 41
Sampson, 52, 74, 80, 83, 85, 132
Samson, 72
Samuel, 14, 22, 23, 26, 31, 37, 46, 50, 51, 59, 62, 84, 89, 94, 103, 106, 138, 147, 149, 150, 157, 163, 164
Sanders, 81, 92, 93; Maria, 163, 164
SANDERS: Ann Eliza, 138; Leonard, 109; Mathew, 38; Matthew, 109; Nancy, 109
Sandie, 78

Sandy, 11, 26, 36, 39, 47, 48, 57, 59, 61, 63, 64, 66, 73, 77, 80, 86, 89, 91, 92, 94, 95, 98, 102, 103, 104, 105, 107, 110, 112, 116, 117, 126, 127, 128, 131, 132, 134, 135, 148, 150, 155, 156, 157, 158, 163, 164
Sanford, 67, 84, 117, 130
Sania, 163
Sara, 51, 105
Sarah, 2, 4, 5, 6, 7, 8, 12, 14, 15, 16, 19, 20, 21, 22, 24, 25, 26, 31, 32, 34, 35, 38, 39, 41, 42, 46, 47, 48, 49, 53, 54, 55, 59, 60, 63, 69, 70, 72, 73, 77, 78, 82, 83, 84, 87, 88, 89, 91, 92, 94, 98, 99, 101, 102, 105, 107, 111, 114, 116, 117, 121, 123, 124, 125, 129, 130, 135, 138, 139, 141, 147, 149, 150, 151, 152, 153, 155, 162, 165, 168
Sarah Ann, 53, 111, 152, 154
Sarah Anne, 113
Sarah Jane, 134, 157
Sarah Philips, 143
Saray, 21
Sarkin: Thomas, 164
Sary, 8
Saunders, 87
SAUNDERS: J.M., 121
Sauney, 26
Sawney, 32, 67, 111
Scilla, 127
Scintha, 157
Scipio, 91
Scott, 77; Frances, 154; John, 152, 154; Levi, 58; Louisa, 152; Polly, 154
SCOTT: Abraham M., 100; Ann, 58, 66; Charles, 83; Clarinda, 110, 114; Henrietta

Price, 58, 66; James, 16, 17, 19; James W., 103, 114, 117; Jesse, 103; Levi, 58, 66; Richard P., 133; Richard Price, 58, 66; Sarah, 20, 60; William, 33, 35; William L., 103, 110
Scye, 115
Scyntha, 113
SEAL: John, 24
Seale, 101
SEALE: Anne, 15; Anthony, 15, 23; John, 15; Timothy, 15
Seally, 72, 140
Seaman, 46
Sebra, 29
Segismend, 115
Seilla, 13
Selah, 39, 62
SELECMAN: John F., 143; William, 135
Selia, 84
Selina, 124
Senett, 152
Sephia, 40
Sepio, 7
Seppio, 17
Seqismond, 109
Serena, 53
Servant: Alex Grant, 8; Andrew Garner, 8; Ann, 139; Barny Dan, 21; Bryant Alliston, 6; Charles, 3, 38, 167; Charlotte, 139; David Kelly, 3; Edward, 5; Edward _oarzison, 8; Edward Magoo, 5; Eleanor, 103; Harry, 116; Henry German, 165; Jacob, 6; James, 2; James Cuthull, 8; John, 2, 3, 29, 139; Lucy, 125; Margaret, 6; Mariah, 139; Mary, 2, 139; Milly

Starks, 68; Nancy Buckner, 95; Peter Daniel Macin, 23; Peter Grant, 8; Prescilla, 139; Richard, 5; Richard Fox, 8; Somersett, 38; Willard, 5; William Smith, 8
Seth, 14, 16, 92
SETTLE: Francis, 81; James, 81
SEUR: James, 22
Seymor, 39
Seymore, 122
Seymour, 67
SHACKLET: Richard D., 153
Shaderack, 72
Shadrach, 27, 39, 47, 62, 67, 140
Shadrack, 21, 26, 53, 91, 113
Shadrick, 78
Sharlett, 26, 30, 149
Sharlot, 16, 39, 50, 53, 80, 81, 105, 114
Sharlott, 34, 61, 62
Sharlotte, 15, 31, 86, 92, 124
Sharper, 5, 16, 17, 18, 59
SHAW: Mary A.M., 160; William, 54, 63, 102, 105
SHIP: Mildred, 109
SHIRLEY: Richard O., 157
SHORT: Frances, 19
SHUMAN: John, 144
SHUTE: Fanny, 19; John, 29
Sib, 23, 35, 39, 71
Sibba, 31, 32
Sibyll, 22
Sidney, 46, 50, 54, 67, 129, 153
Sil, 39
Sila, 70
Silas, 89, 113, 130, 134, 148
Silby, 72
Siller, 58, 68, 69, 82
Silve, 30

Silvey, 79
Silvia, 11, 41
Silvy, 31, 68, 104
SIMAN: Charles, 131
Simms, 77
SIMMS: B., 129
Simon, 16, 19, 25, 29, 35, 39, 41, 49, 63, 72, 77, 78, 79, 81, 84, 85, 91, 99, 100, 104, 105, 109, 113, 123, 125, 153, 164
SIMPSON: James H., 156; John W., 145, 147; Joseph, 83; M__, 162; Matilda, 144
Sims: Isabel, 8; James, 8
SIMSON: Thomas, 1, 2
Sina, 141, 162
Sinah, 14, 15, 23, 24, 32, 34, 51, 60, 79, 84, 93, 106, 111, 131, 132, 141, 150, 161, 168
Sinar, 161
SINCLAIR: Margaret, 144; Mary F., 144; Thomas B., 79, 99
Siner, 23, 81, 104
SINGER: John, 33; William, 50
Sipeo, 69
Sipyou, 17
SKINNER: Cornelius, 128, 131, 133
SLADE: Charles, 89
SLAUGHTER: Jane A., 69; Jane Alexander, 67
SLYE: Gwynnella P., 137; Marian G., 137; Roberta, 137
SMALLWOOD: G., 122; George, 110
Smith: Jim, 153; William, 8
SMITH: Agatha, 11; Elizabeth, 30, 46; George, 92, 138; Hugh, 41; Jane, 32; John, 46, 98; John L., 98; John S., 90; Lewis M., 69; Margaret, 41;
Nancy, 41; Peter, 30, 41, 53, 98, 162; William, 54, 133
SMOOT: George Mattox, 18; Henry, 18; James, 18; Thomas, 18; William, 97
Snass, 143
Sol, 21, 23
Solomon, 23, 29, 33, 49, 54, 80, 87, 88, 94, 116, 121, 122, 124, 127, 131, 132, 168
Somersett, 38
Sook, 47, 69
Sooky, 73, 123
Sophia, 47, 48, 50, 54, 59, 61, 64, 68, 69, 70, 80, 87, 88, 92, 101, 105, 106, 112, 122, 137, 138, 140, 147, 150
Sophy, 82, 84, 87, 111, 125
Spence, 134
SPENCE: Dr. John, 113; John, 83
Spencer, 19, 24, 32, 52, 79, 107, 121, 152, 154
SPENCER: Sarah S., 134
SPILLER: Diana, 141; Dianer, 86, 91; Dianna, 148; Philip, 86; Phillip, 91; Rachael, 3; Rachel, 9; William, 3
SPILLER, Jr.: William, 9
SPILMAN: Susanna, 50
SPINDLE: James A., 144; Mary, 86
SPINKS: Ann, 72, 89, 90; Gerard, 72, 74, 80; Susannah, 72
SPRAGGINS: Samuel, 83
Sprigg, 118
SPRIGG: Richard, 15
St. HENLY: Notly, 18; Thomas, 18; William Mattox, 18
Stafford, 19, 40, 62

STANGLE: Ann Eliza, 103; John, 103
Stanton, 138, 139
STARK: Euphan, 137
STARKE: Mrs., 68; William, 59
Starks: Mary Ann, 68; Milly, 68; Patty, 68; Sally, 68
Stefany, 49
Stephany, 100
Stephen, 2, 6, 14, 16, 17, 23, 25, 34, 37, 41, 58, 62, 64, 66, 72, 83, 85, 102, 109, 154
Stephney, 83, 86
Stepney, 51, 103, 130
Steven, 57
STEWART: John, 55
Stith, 111
STITH: Griffin, 106
STOCKE: B.W., 87
STONE: Charles, 115; Fanny, 115; John, 115; Josiah, 115; Josias, 89; Miss, 115; Richard, 156
STONEL: Mary, 97
STONNEL: Richard, 129, 156, 157; William, 129
STORK: Baily, 61; Eliza, 61; Mrs., 139; Mrs. Euphan, 140
Storke, 88
STORKE, 87; John, 95; Seymour Hooe, 95; William Jett, 95
Strother, 50
STROTHER: Elizabeth Battaile, 65
Strout: James, 106
Stue, 3
STUMP: John, 85
Suck, 16, 19, 22, 25, 26, 27, 30, 34, 40, 58, 69, 106

Suckey, 24, 31, 40, 59, 60, 64, 65, 67, 73, 87, 92, 98, 112, 113, 121, 125
Sucky, 20, 51, 54, 77, 83, 102, 123, 134, 143
Sue, 2, 3, 5, 7, 8, 16, 18, 21, 35, 99
Suke, 29, 96
Sukey, 34, 40, 41, 48, 49, 67, 81, 109, 113, 115, 118, 140, 167, 168
Suky, 80, 97
Sully, 139
Sumesette, 94
Susan, 8, 25, 37, 42, 50, 53, 59, 73, 78, 88, 93, 94, 99, 105, 106, 117, 125, 129, 130, 132, 137, 138, 140, 143, 144, 145, 147, 149, 150, 151, 152, 154, 156, 157, 161, 163, 164
Susan Jr., 106
Susanna, 23, 57, 92
Susannah, 29, 75, 113
SUTO: Edward, 4; Elizabeth, 4; Margaret, 4; Mary, 4
Sutte, 50
SUTTLE: Henry Hampton, 30; Strother, 30; William, 30
Swam, 103
SWEENY: George, 119; Hugh, 119; John Eugene, 118; John H., 118; Sarah B., 119; Sarah Burdett, 168; Susan Hooe, 118
Sydney, 78, 125
Syl, 31
Sylla, 78, 126, 133
Syller, 48, 168
Sylva, 49
Sylvanus, 74, 77
Sylvester, 8

Sylvia, 21, 26, 27, 70, 74, 80, 81
Syphuse, 78
Syrus, 81, 82
TA_TE: Peter, 24
Tab, 25
Tabby, 49
Tabithy, 60
Tacey, 52
TACKETT: Fanny, 35; Lewis, 17; William, 17, 19
Talbot, 41
Talitha, 14
Talliaferro, 68
Tammy, 103
TANSILL: Fanny, 137; Samuel, 133; Thomas, 137
Tapley, 13
Tapsalow, 7
Tasco, 74, 111, 144
Tascoe, 114
TASKE: Sarah, 139
Tasker, 41, 72
Tate, 14, 16
TAYLOE: Benjamin Ogle, 165
Taylor, 111; George, 150; Mary, 126; Nancy, 55
TAYLOR: Elizabeth, 128; Maryann, 45
TEBB: Frances, 55
TEBBS: Betsey, 26; Betsy, 167; Charlote, 7; Daniel, 7; Foushee, 20; George, 7; James, 7, 23; Mary Anne, 49; William, 7; William H., 65; Willoughby, 45, 127, 131; Willoughby W., 128
Temple, 149, 153
Tenar, 121
Tender, 9
Tener, 88

TENNELL: Benjamin, 13; Francis, 13, 14; Jemima, 13; John, 13; Joseph, 13; Margaret, 13; Mary, 13
TENNILL: Francis, 58; George, 58
TENNILLE: Alexander, 134; George, 134; James D., 134; Sarah, 143
Tennison, 41
TENNISON: William, 19
Teny, 61
Tepson, 7
Terry, 77, 104
Thaddeus, 64
THARP: Mark, 57, 93; Susanna, 55
Theoderick, 144
THERMAN: Elizabeth, 104; Robert, 104; Thomas, 104
Thom, 13
Thomas, 2, 19, 27, 31, 35, 38, 46, 57, 59, 62, 64, 81, 84, 87, 89, 96, 104, 112, 113, 114, 115, 121, 124, 125, 126, 129, 137, 139, 141, 144, 147, 151, 156, 157, 158, 159, 163, 164
THOMAS: Benjamin, 31, 34, 39; George, 14; Mary, 134; Samuel, 100
Thomas Henry, 143
Thomley, 13
THOMOY: John, 39
Thompson, 53, 87, 117
THOMPSON: Mrs., 58
Thomson, 69
THORNBERRY: Daniel, 116
Thornton, 37, 39, 58, 77, 80, 86, 87, 104, 113, 121, 123, 124, 125, 138, 139, 150, 153, 154, 155, 156, 157, 167

THORNTON: Caroline M., 112; Charles, 11; Dr. Thomas, 85; James B.C., 129; Jane Carr, 34; L.G., 90; Mary Frances Adeline, 112; Maryann, 64; Sarah L., 129; Stuart, 99; Stuart G., 112; Thomas, 34
THROGMORTON: John, 168; Mary Ann, 168
THURMAN: Franny A., 158; John, 140; Robert, 39, 79, 81, 83, 93; Sandford, 111; Sanford, 158, 160; Thomas, 83; Thomas L., 117
Tibe, 135
Tiberius, 121
TILDER: Samuel, 27
TILLETT: John, 1
Tim, 26, 85
Tippet, 143
Tipyon, 17
Titus, 5, 6, 16, 47, 109
Tobias, 154
Toby, 1, 48
Toliver, 104, 114
Tolly, 41
TOLSON: Amia N., 153; Ann, 164; James W., 153, 164; John N., 149, 153; Maj., 86; Margaret, 153; Margaret E., 153; Margarey E., 164; Mary T., 153; Mrs., 164; William, 156
Tom, 2, 5, 7, 8, 9, 11, 12, 14, 15, 18, 19, 23, 24, 25, 26, 30, 31, 32, 33, 34, 35, 36, 37, 38, 40, 41, 42, 46, 47, 48, 49, 50, 54, 58, 59, 60, 61, 62, 64, 66, 68, 69, 70, 71, 72, 74, 77, 78, 79, 80, 81, 83, 86, 87, 88, 93, 94, 95, 98, 101, 103, 106, 107, 109, 113, 114, 116, 117, 123, 124, 126, 127, 129, 130, 131, 134, 135, 138, 144, 147, 149, 152, 156, 162, 163, 164, 168
Tomas, 77
TOMLIN: Richard, 68, 72; William, 110, 112, 127
Tommy, 168
Toney, 4, 5
Tony, 17, 18, 103, 112, 149
TOTSON: Nelson, 97
Towerhill, 78
Townshend, 54, 87, 131
TOWNSHEND: T., 100; Turman, 130
Trashor: William, 6
Travers, 98
Travis, 68, 69, 118, 145
TRAVIS: Francis M., 145
TRENIS: Bertrand E., 95
TRIPLETT: James, 24; Margaret, 32; Nathaniel, 54; Thomas, 3
Tro_lous, 96
TRONE: James, 126, 162; John, 126; John L., 162; Lucinda, 126; Peter, 116, 126; Sarah A., 126, 162; William A., 126
Troy, 145
Trunion, 27
TURLEY: James, 83; John, 8
Turner, 138, 139; Jack, 148; Lucinda, 148
TURNER: Thomas, 130
Turney: Lucinda, 155; Sandy, 155
Turtle: George, 68, 87
Tyler, 81
TYLER: Benjamin, 27; Charles, 77, 81; Elizabeth,

27; Gustavus B., 118, 124; H.B., 141; J.W., 100; James M., 138, 141; John M., 90; John W., 127; Joseph, 21, 26, 27; Nancy, 27; R.B., 90; Richard B., 151; William, 32, 94; William B., 90
TYLER, Sr.: William, 77
Tyll, 49
TYLOR: Elizabeth, 68; John, 29
UNDERWOOD: Capt. John, 134; John, 134
Unis, 41
Urania, 85
Utterback: Beck Harmon, 20; Jerry, 20
Valmore, 71, 147
Vanessa, 23
VANPELT: Polly, 149; Richard, 149
Vaububau, 144
Venus, 34, 92, 96
Vergin, 37
Verlinda, 57, 60
Victoria, 148
Vina, 104, 117, 118
Vincent, 40, 41, 83, 114, 116, 147, 152
Vine, 37
Viney, 134, 167
Vinia, 122
Violet, 26, 35, 39, 50, 90, 110, 115
Virgin, 60, 118, 168
Virginia, 105, 107, 111, 142, 149, 156
Volmore, 145
W__is: Charles, 167
Wabler, 110
WAGENER: Beverly R., 74
WALKER: John, 2

Wall: Billy, 49; John, 49; Mary, 49, 58
Wallace, 96, 111, 121, 134, 148, 155
WALLACE: John R., 140; Mary, 55
Wallas, 147
Wallis, 98, 161, 162
Walter, 102
WALTON: John, 142
Wamer, 152
Ward: Winney, 157
WARD: Ann, 125, 148; Anna, 92; Anna Maria, 150; Enoch, 50; Zachariah, 92, 152
WARDEN: Jesse, 129; John, 129; Richard, 129; Walter, 129
WARDER: Ann, 31; Elizabeth, 97; Jesse, 97, 99; Jr., 97; Milfoard, 97; Walter, 97; William, 97
Warner, 62
Washington, 39, 61, 64, 69, 75, 77, 102, 104, 111, 113, 116, 117, 121, 122, 124, 125, 127, 129, 131, 132, 138, 149, 150, 155; Baily, 152; Charles, 139; General, 145; George, 59, 87, 123
WASHINGTON: Col. John M., 152, 154; H.W. Macrae, 154; James W., 140; John H., 59, 61, 87; M., 87; M. Euphan, 55; Mrs., 154; Mrs. George, 140; Needham L., 106; Verlinda I., 53; W., 77; Washington J., 79; William, 140; William T., 154
Wat, 111
WATKINS: William, 14
Wats, 131

Watson, 125, 129
Watt, 67, 72, 78, 111, 167
Weaver, 142
WEAVER: Jane, 141; William A., 141
Web, 74, 153
Webb: John, 2
Webster, 152, 154; Daniel, 74; James, 74; Lucy, 74
WEBSTER: Philip, 83; Philip G., 144, 152; William B., 144
WEEDEN: Ferdinand A., 124
WEEDON: Augustine, 126; Austin B., 162; Ferdinand A., 116; George, 116, 124, 126, 162; John C., 126, 162; Sarah, 96
WEEMS: F.M., 103; M.L., 103; Marianne, 57; Mrs., 85
WEIR: Alexander, 132; Charity, 132; Louisa, 150; Lucy C., 153; Robert, 138; Robert M., 160; Robert N., 153; Sarah E., 153; William I., 150; William J., 165
Wellington, 138, 139, 157, 164
Werden, 157
Wesley, 125, 129, 141
West, 104, 113
WEST: Hugh, 5
Westley, 116, 124
Westwood, 69, 75, 117
WHALEY: Elizabeth, 15
WHEELER: Ignatius M., 57; Mary E.M., 149; Nancy, 79; William, 104, 123, 128; William L.B., 155
White: George, 113
WHITE: James, 54; John, 79; Sally, 128; William, 53
WHITE Jr.: James, 65
WHITE, Sr.: James, 65

Whitehaven, 3
WHITFELL: Constantin, 94
WHITING: Cecelia Beverly, 60; Elizabeth, 60, 63, 66, 82; Elizabeth Braxton, 82; Francis Henry, 82; George B., 82; Henry, 35; I.F., 166; Lewis B., 60; Maria, 60; Matthew, 59, 63
WHITLEDGE: John, 29; Nancy, 35; William, 16, 18
Whitley, 41
Whitney, 134
WIATT: Elizabeth Mary, 167; James, 66; Mahala, 100; Malissa, 100; William, 100, 132, 167
WICKLIFF: Aaron, 46; Nathaniel, 26
WICKLIFFE: Moses, 38
WIGGINTON: Elizabeth, 11; Russell, 83
WILCOXIN: Josiah, 163
WILKENSON: John, 98
WILKINS: James W., 162; Thomas, 155, 162
Will, 2, 3, 4, 5, 8, 14, 16, 18, 20, 26, 27, 29, 30, 32, 33, 34, 35, 39, 40, 47, 51, 53, 60, 61, 67, 73, 74, 75, 81, 83, 88, 97, 118, 121, 125
Willaby, 148
Willard, 93; Richard, 5
WILLCOXEN: Josiah, 159
William, 6, 8, 19, 31, 32, 35, 40, 47, 50, 51, 58, 59, 63, 67, 68, 69, 70, 71, 72, 78, 80, 81, 82, 83, 84, 85, 87, 88, 92, 94, 95, 96, 97, 98, 99, 101, 103, 105, 106, 107, 109, 111, 112, 113, 114, 115, 117, 121, 125, 126, 127, 129, 130, 131, 132,

133, 135, 138, 139, 141, 142, 144, 147, 148, 149, 150, 155, 156, 157, 160, 161, 164, 166, 167
WILLIAM: Capt. John M., 64; Mary, 100
William (Pierce), 113
William Henry, 125, 143, 159
William Jr., 138, 141
William R., 64
William Sr., 138, 141
William W., 64
Williams: Nancy, 63
WILLIAMS: Emma J., 149; Even, 18; Flora, 150, 151; George, 106; Jesse, 106; John, 66; John W., 106; Lucy A., 162; Lucy Ann, 149; Margaret R., 149, 162; Sarah M., 149, 162
WILLIAMS, Jr.: Jons, 9
Williamson, 37, 57, 95, 111
WILLIAMSON: William, 83
Willie, 149, 150
Willis, 36, 37, 38, 39, 50, 60, 63, 81, 87, 116, 126, 132, 134, 153, 164
Willoughby, 49, 51, 65, 83, 109
Willy, 154
Wilson, 6, 49, 81, 86, 97, 148; Ann, 2; Jacob, 6; James, 55
WILSON: Henry, 12; Jeremiah, 11; Rupert, 11; Sarah, 11
WILSON Sr.: Henry, 11
Windsor, 2, 6, 66
WINDSOR: Alfred, 122; Christopher, 159; James

Thomas, 159; John Richard, 159; Sampson, 122; Sarah, 137
Winifred, 105
Winn, 25
Winna, 52, 81, 83, 109, 139
Winne, 138
Winney, 5, 6, 12, 13, 16, 19, 20, 21, 22, 23, 25, 26, 27, 29, 33, 35, 36, 37, 38, 41, 47, 49, 50, 54, 59, 60, 61, 62, 65, 66, 67, 69, 71, 72, 78, 86, 87, 88, 89, 92, 93, 99, 102, 103, 107, 113, 116, 118, 130, 131, 133, 134, 152, 157, 163, 168
Winnie, 82, 163
Winson, 51
Wood: Ann, 145
WOOD: James, 33; John, 29
WOODARD: Clement, 45
Worden, 145, 163
WORK: Frances, 133
WRIGHT: Ann, 7; Francis, 7; John, 8, 89; John Lee, 29; John R., 66; Thomas, 45; Thomas S., 144
WROE: Andrew D., 149, 151
WYATT: James, 79; William, 71
York, 38, 41, 88, 101, 137, 148, 160
YOUNG: John, 29; Robert, 26
Zach, 25, 26
Zachariah, 63
Zachary, 60, 63

www.ingramcontent.com/pod-product-compliance
Lightning Source LLC
Chambersburg PA
CBHW070942230426
43666CB00011B/2528